THE VOICE
OF BLOOD

THE VOICE OF BLOOD

FIVE CHRISTIAN MARTYRS OF OUR TIME

by WILLIAM J. O'MALLEY, S.J.

Yahweh asked Cain, "What have you done to your brother, Abel?" "I do not know where he is." he answered. "Am I my brother's keeper?" "Listen! The voice of the blood of your brother is crying out to Me from the earth!"

Genesis 4/9-10

ORBIS BOOKS

Maryknoll, New York 10545

The Catholic Foreign Mission Society of America (Maryknoll) recruits and trains people for overseas missionary service. Through Orbis Books Maryknoll aims to foster the international dialogue that is essential to mission. The books published, however, reflect the opinions of their authors and are not meant to represent the official position of the society.

Library of Congress Cataloging in Publication Data

O'Malley, William J.
  The voice of blood

  1. Christian martyrs—Salvador—Biography.
2. Christian martyrs—Rhodesia, Southern—Biography.
3. Christian martyrs—Brazil—Biography. I. Title.
BX4655.2.04   272   79-90055
ISBN 0-88344-539-5

First published 1980 by Orbis Books, Maryknoll, NY 10545, under special arrangement with Skyline Books, Box 122, Ringwood, NJ 07456

Manufactured in the United States of America

For Bill Jenks
and for Judy O'Malley
who have made me understand
what being truly human means.

Imprimatur: Joseph L. Hogan, D.D.
                       Bishop of Rochester
                       November 20, 1978

Imprimi Potest: Vincent Cooke, S.J.
                       June 11, 1979

Acknowledgements

Very few people read acknowledgements; publishers, one assumes, consider them wasteful of ink and space. But to the author they are most important; they keep him humble, because they are public admission that he could not have done the work by himself. Therefore, I declare my indebtedness for help in translation to Francis Dineen, S.J. and his Georgetown students, Robert Bolanos, S.J., Vito Marcello, and Alexander Wyse, O.F.M. Edward Babinski, S.J., typed the manuscript with patient and relentless accuracy, and Edmund Nagle, S.J. and Simon Smith, S.J., scrupulously proofread it for me. The financial support of Daniel Fitzpatrick, S.J., and James Connor, S.J., freed me of teaching summer school or some such travail in order to write. Richard Todd, C.M.F., Donald Campion, S.J., and Henry Wardale, S.J., were most helpful in gathering depositions. I owe a special debt of gratitude to the eyewitnesses, Bishop Pedro Casaldàliga, C.M.F., and especially Dunstan Myerscough, S.J. Also I must thank the necessarily anonymous Salvadorean author of the life of Rutilio Grande. Finally, two men worked as tirelessly doing research on my behalf as if they were writing the book themselves; it would never have been written without the generosity of Thomas Cullen, S.J., and that grand man, Gerald Finnieston, S.J. "A brother helped by a brother is like a strong city."

Preface

This is a book about five ordinary men who knew where they stood, and who held their places even under the threat of death. And these stories are not ancient history. They all occurred within the last three months of 1976 and the first three months of 1977, well within the lifetime even of the very youngest of us.

The five men were unlikely heroes. Rutilio Grande was ravaged for years with groundless doubts about his own worth. Christopher Shepherd-Smith was a not particularly talented young man. Martin Thomas often seemed distant. John Conway talked so much that one had to "subtract eleven and divide by two." John-Bosco Burnier was more or less a disaster as vice-provincial and as master of novices.

The word "hero" itself is misleading when one speaks of martyrs. Martyrdom has nothing to do with heroic stature or heroic struggle or heroic image. It is a remarkably sober and undramatic way to die, unlike the heroism which is really a misnomer for foolhardiness. Leave that for race car drivers and tightrope walkers. Martyrdom is located in precisely the opposite direction. It is not the urge to surpass all the others but the urge to serve all the others, at whatever cost.

Martyrdom cannot be improvised. Either a whole lifetime prepares one for it, or it will never occur. If the word has fallen into disuse, the reality has not. And perhaps these stories may help to make both the word and the reality honorable once more.

William J. O'Malley
Rochester, New York

EL SALVADOR

RUTILIO GRANDE, S.J.

Time: 5:55 p.m., 12 March 1977

Place: The road between Aguilares and El Paisnal,
26 miles north of the capital of El Salvador,
Central America

*The whole assembly then rose, and
they brought him before Pilate. They
began their accusation by saying, "We
found this man inciting our people to
revolt."*

—Luke 23, 1-2

It was nearly six in the evening. The air of upcountry El Salvador in March was smoldering and still. A few lay helpers and two of the Jesuits of the pastoral team of the parish of Aguilares-El Paisnal had finished eating dinner on the crusty little walkway outside the old parish house. They had hoped in vain to catch at least a hint of breeze from the muggy closeness. The rains would not come for months.

Father Rutilio Grande, the Jesuit pastor, rose from the table and blessed himself, silent for a moment. He was not tall, but he was a tall man for that place. Like his parishioners he was a *mestizo* of mixed dark Indian and white Spanish blood; as he said, "completely mixed up, like coffee with milk." Ironically, this priest who triggered such seething anger among the local landowners was a gentle man—quiet, simple, elegant, with just a twinkle of ironic humor in nearly everything he said. He had the look of a man who had wrestled with weakness in the very depth of himself. And he had won peace.

He nodded to old Don Manuel and to the boy, Rutilio Lemus. "We had better be going, my friends. It's quarter to six. The Mass in El Paisnal begins at seven."

The boy stood, ready for the trip back home to El Paisnal, where of all the boys he held the very formidable post of bell ringer for the church. But one of the other laymen protested. "Now wait, Father Tilo. An old man and a boy are not enough protection. You've seen that car that's been circling around here all day, snooping. They're watching you."

Rutilio smiled. "So? Aren't they always watching me?"

"Things are getting too tense. Think! Those volunteer boys from the university were taken away and tortured. The landowners aren't just grumbling any more about this learning of the Gospel and this . . . this courage you've given the peasants." He said nothing of the priests who had already been exiled. He said nothing of the disappearances, the beatings, the tortures, the rapes of peasants at the hands of the National Guard. He said nothing of the maimings, the murders, the beheadings. All of them knew that. They lived with it as they lived with the stifling heat of the March evening. "Father Tilo, there are warnings enough, surely. They're telling you: watch your step, priest! Something could happen."

3

Yes. The Mass in El Paisnal will happen. And the novena to St. Joseph.

"I will come with you instead of the old man. It's my job. I can distribute those Bibles some other time."

Old Don Manuel stood there stiffly, his eyes cast down, proudly hurt and silent. At 72 he was lean and tough as a rake, tightened to rawhide by three generations of peon work in the canefields. But he could still do odd jobs. He was always "around," more than the others could be. He was a Delegate for one of the sub-communities of the parish, wasn't he? He could protect Father Tilo.

Rutilio smiled his tight, kindly little smile. "Don't worry. Don Manuel will come. Let's go, my old friend. Come along, Tilo."

The two men and the boy moved along the walkway under the overhang, toward the shed where the jeep Safari was parked. Behind them the conversation buzzed up again; there were plates to clear; there were half-looks at the departing threesome: the white-haired priest, the stiff-backed old man, and the proud boy. For a moment, it looked like some primitive painting of the Last Supper, gauzy in the heat, caught too late by the artist.

Rutilio crossed to the driver's side, past the cross-shaped slash marks someone had cut in the back canvas of the Safari the day before. Almost like a threat. Or a target. Father Chamba had patched it back together with tape that afternoon. Oh, well. The work goes on.

The men climbed in on either side of the car, Manuel in the middle, the boy on the right squeezed into the single seat. The doors slammed. Rutilio gunned the engine and backed out in a V, shifted, and started forward down the yard past the men cleaning the table. There were a couple of waves, and the Safari went through the gate and turned right into the street to the corner. Then it turned left along the sunburned plaza between the church and the town hall of Aguilares and headed out toward the railroad crossing. They didn't say much. They were three quiet men.

And they were watching.

* * * * * * * *

Rutilio knew the road well. In four months it would be fifty years since he had been born in the village of El Paisnal, about five miles ahead of them down this road. In such a small place, his father,

4

Salvador, had been an important man. He sold things from his oxcart to the villagers of the area and knew everyone for miles around. He had been the mayor of El Paisnal for many years and many times. Now, including all the little *cantones* of huts clustered within walking distance, Aguilares was becoming a job-market beehive, the busy focus of all the desperate workers searching for any kind of employment in the canefields and in the three large sugar refineries. It was that or starve. The land the rich allowed them for wages was as barren as brick.

Rutilio's mother, Cristina Garcìa, had died when he was four, and for the next ten years he had lived with his grandmother, who he believed truly rooted in his soul the movement of his vocation. Then, when he was still just a boy, he had met Monsignor Luis Chàvez, Archbishop of the capital city of San Salvador, when the priest had come north for his pastoral visit to El Paisnal. Surely even they could not have said what this young prelate had seen in this pudgy little boy from the country, but from the beginning the two became fast friends, and the archbishop treated him like the son he had never had. They began a lifelong correspondence, letters and cards that Rutilio still kept in a briefcase, with the picture of the young archbishop taped to the inside of the lid.

In May of 1940, when he was twelve, Rutilio had first written to the archbishop telling him that he wanted to be a priest. The archbishop wrote back telling him to be patient and to keep writing to him but also to put special care into his school work. In the following year, despite his father's waning health, Rutilio had entered the diocesan minor seminary which, though training parish priests, was run by the Jesuits. And at the end of his high school studies, at the age of seventeen and with the blessing of the archbishop, he had followed the call to become a Jesuit.

There had been only one problem with Rutilio Grande's vocation, right from the beginning: he was very, very good. But no one ever seemed to have taken the time to tell him about it, straight out, so anxious were they that he become even better. What's more, he was trying so eagerly to improve that he could not allow himself the liberating humility of acknowledging his own worth or even any progress at all. He was too humble for the truth that—however imperfect—he was a good man.

An eagerly generous boy of seventeen can become terribly confused expecting heroic perfection in the next moment, if he just strains hard enough. Without the perspective and balance of experience and wisdom, rising to the challenges of Jesus can be a tormented journey.

5

One wants so desperately to be like him: perfect. And yet there is only One who is perfect, and at times he can remain infuriatingly silent. Man is not perfectible; he is only improvable. But a boy of seventeen doesn't know that.

C.S. Lewis never tired of reminding us that the Enemy doesn't need to make us vicious; an over-awareness of one's shortcomings will do quite as nicely. As long as the Enemy can keep our attention on ourselves, virtues unattained will work just as well as vices indulged. With Rutilio Grande—and so many others of us—it worked very well indeed for nearly twenty years.

One can see the progression of the disease in his pictures over those years: first, the chubby-cheeked little boy, grinning shyly among his classmates in the minor seminary; and later, thinning out with adolescence, the crew-cut hair, the broadly beaming face of the new novice, the eyes squinting and gleeful; but then during philosophy in Spain, in 1953, twenty-five now, unsmiling, the brows beginning to knit together, almost wary; and finally seven years after that at the end of his theology, heavy-faced, dour, brows seemingly locked with pain, only the faintest hint of a smile that failed. Even the pictures of his ordination show no peace or joy, only apprehension.

After two years of novitiate in Los Chorros, Venezuela, Rutilio had taken his first private perpetual vows as a Jesuit and then moved on for two years of studies in humanities and science in Quito, Ecuador. But the pressure of those two rigorous years of study was too much for him, and it was impossible for him to go directly to three more intensive years of philosophy. He wanted nothing but his unalloyed best and could not settle for "almost." As a result, he was constantly tense, depressed, anxious over the quality of his work, his prayer, his dealings with others—so much so that people found it a burden to talk with him.

Because of all this, his superiors had decided to interrupt his studies and send him to work as a teacher for a year at Xavier High School in Panama. Even there, he was hospitalized for a short time because of yet another nervous crisis. At the end of that year, he had still not been ready to face the isolation and intellectual struggles of further study, so he had been sent for two more years to his old minor seminary in San Salvador, teaching Latin, Spanish, Geography, and History.

Here he seems to have tasted some hint of happiness and just a touch of inner peace. His superiors found he was a hard worker, as so many perfectionists are, and faithful to a fault to his responsibilities.

He had a good judgment and a remarkable talent for working with little boys and young men. With them, he didn't have to prove himself despite himself. What's more, adolescents have a way of short-circuiting both one's perfectionism and one's self-centeredness. They are so relentlessly imperfectible that one has, at least for a time, to settle for less than an angelic world. And they are so candidly and constantly in need of help that one simply has no time to think of himself or lock himself into a cocoon of his own shortcomings. Teaching had been the tonic of the apostolate, and just what Rutilio Grande had needed to ready him to face the rest of his own seminary studies for the priesthood.

In October, 1953, he had been moved to Oña, in Spain, and in three years had received his degree in philosophy. Three months later, too little time, he was thrust into a nightmare of four more years of studying theology. He was not a speculative thinker. And yet how could anyone be a good Jesuit and not be a speculative thinker? Each day brought more evidence of his ineptitude. The airy theses eluded him like so many metaphysical wraiths. But he ground onward, with the dull loyalty and persistence of a wounded bulldog. What kept him going, at least in part, was the request from the people of Oña for a young seminarian to take charge of the sixteen-year-old boys of the Kostka Society. At least for a few hours every week, he did not have to pretend to be what he was not: Thomas Aquinas, Robert Bellarmine, Teilhard de Chardin. He could feel free of pressure and the need to wrestle with fog. He could be what he was: a good, kind man. It had been a case of his need meeting their need.

But it had not been enough.

———————

12 March 1977,
5:48 p.m.

———————

The Safari grumbled over the railroad tracks at the town limits. The sun was going down, and it would be cool soon. Or at least less hot. The sugar factory hunched there, silent, dark, empty. It was still the growing season, the cane not yet waist-high along the road. In July, the temperature inside the mill would hit 110° on a cool day. The workers, shellacked with sweat, would be skimming the hot syrup of bees and bugs. But the sheds were quiet and abandoned now. The fires were cold. The bugs sped busily hither and fro in their last foragings for provisions before dark. A few batted themselves witlessly into tiny splotches on the windscreen.

Young Rutilio Lemus looked back into the gathering dusk at Aguilares. They were not being followed.

* * * * * * * *

In July of 1959, just before the three days when he would be ordained successively subdeacon, deacon and priest, Rutilio finally crawled to the depths of the greatest personal crisis of his life. He was a raw tangle of nerves. Doubts racked his mind about whether he had received even his minor orders worthily. And if minor orders, what of major orders? He *knew* he was called to be a priest, and yet . . . ? That could also be his own arrogance, his own refusal after all of the years he had invested in preparation to admit that it had been a self-delusion from the start, the wish to please his grandmother and the archbishop, to be looked up to and praised even though he was a nobody from a nowhere village in a small, overcrowded, impoverished little pocket of Central America.

Who was he—this stumbler, this simpleton—to be a priest of God? "Another Christ?" Surely it would be a sin—the worst of sins—for such a man to hold out his hands for such a gift. If he were to be ordained, it would be a sin engrafted into him for the rest of his life, with no hope of escape or forgiveness. And the closer he plodded toward the day of his ordination to the subdiaconate, the more he was wrenched, this way and that, by nightmarish doubts, until he was at the point of physical exhaustion. Finally, nearly at the brink of commitment, his nerves were so ravaged that he asked that his ordination be postponed.

His provincial, and the rector of the seminary, and his spiritual confidant, Marcelino Zalba, S.J., all agreed that he should be ordained, that this fretful confusion could not come from the Spirit of God but must be a temptation that could be survived only by manfully facing it down.

It is difficult for a sophisticate even to understand this state of mind, much less to feel much honest compassion for it. Self-doubt lurks inside each of us, but we palliate it with placebos: "It's only human. Everybody makes mistakes. Let's have another drink." But for the man who faces his own soul—his self—alone on the bare plain of a reality he shares with an unspeakably holy God, it can be a surrealist nightmare. It is the dark night of the soul.

There is in such a man a true conviction at the very depths of his being that, despite his incompetence, he is called into the mysterious plan of God. Didn't God use a spindly shepherd boy to conquer Goliath, an unlettered peasant girl to be the Queen of all mankind, a crucified Felon to redeem us all from meaninglessness? But like Peter called out onto the water, one forgets the power of Him who calls and instead focuses fearfully on the clumsiness of the one called. Those others were great, heroic, made of sterner stuff, sure of themselves and their missions, while I . . . ? One craves so deeply to serve well—no, perfectly. But I can do nothing except ineptly, halfway, uncertainly, wretchedly. And yet . . . ? And so the soul lacerates itself in solitude.

To face the matter squarely, Rutilio resolved to compose a formula in which he set down in writing his absolute and unchangeable intention to accept his priesthood, no matter what. He had no faith in himself. He had no faith in what seemed like a delusive call from God. He could only lock his jaws and put his faith in his provincial, in his rector and, above all, in Zalba. Version after version he scribbled, crossed out, revised, tore up, began again. And again. Unendingly. He had self-doubts even about his ability to express his *doubts* with perfect clarity and exactitude.

Finally, he wrote: "I manifest before God, freely and consciously, that I wish to receive the major orders of subdiaconate, diaconate, and priesthood, without any kind of condition or reservation, even under the supposition that, in receiving them, I would commit any kind of sin, *including formal sin*." His friend Zalba suggested to him, after they'd discussed it, that he substitute for the words he had underlined: "including any sin that could occur from receiving them *illicitly*." He was trying, poor man, to force the question into the legal realm instead of the realm of culpable moral guilt. That afternoon, Rutilio left Zalba's room more or less satisfied.

And then it had all begun again. During the night he was seized again with doubt. Hadn't Zalba suggested earlier that he omit those words entirely? Zalba was a very good and wise man, but he couldn't see Rutilio as Rutilio saw him, from inside. Why not? Because Rutilio the stumbler could not find the words to show what an excrescence he was! And yet . . . ? Wouldn't it be still another sin to say he'd be ordained even if ordination itself was a sin for him? Round and round the leaden labyrinth, hour after hour. It was too late to see Zalba that night. He'd see him first thing in the morning before the ceremony.

9

When Rutilio got up very early on the morning of subdiaconate, he had gone searching for Zalba. He couldn't find him. He would just have to . . . he would just have to go through with it, trusting in vain that Zalba had been right. As he was walking to the church for his ordination as a subdeacon, with the formula he had written in the breast pocket of his cassock, he was assaulted by doubts again. On the one hand, it seemed that his difficulties were the result of witless scrupulosity. And yet at the very same time they seemed to be perfectly reasonable doubts. For the sake of getting some peace, he made an act of contrition during the ordination Mass, but instead of reaching peace, he became even more distraught. After all, wasn't that act of contrition an open admission that he was indeed committing a sin by being ordained? Could you apologize for a sin and then go ahead and commit it? How could he honestly and truly intend to be ordained when that intention was an intention to commit a sin?—If, indeed, it was a sin.

In a tormented daze, he walked numbly through the rite of subdiaconate. And the next day the rite of diaconate. And the third day the rite of priesthood. He was so paralyzed by the absolute foolishness—by the absolute seriousness—of what he was doing that he couldn't even bring himself to speak to Zalba again. He had seen him so often. Zalba always said the same thing: you're wrong, be at peace. But there was no peace. The very priesthood for which he had prepared and yearned since he had been a boy in El Paisnal had become a swamp of despair.

For days, he went through the ritual of his first Mass, the little party given for him by a family of the town, the blessings and the kissing of his unworthy hands. He pretended, held back, delayed without revealing his preoccupations to anyone. Finally, he decided to speak to Zalba. Once again, perhaps a bit more harshly now, Zalba told him to stop this foolish agonizing and humble himself to accept the gift he had been given. From that time on, he had tried to abide by Zalba's judgment, but it did not exorcise from his soul "those wrenching doubts which sometimes bothered me with pounding insistence."

The year after his ordination, the completion of his theological studies, was slated to take place in the United States, but his shattered health seemed to make that unwise. So he had doggedly finished out the year at Oña, and returned to El Salvador to teach for two more years in the seminary. Once again, it was a bit better there: "a life filled with work and responsibilities that helped me in every sense." So much did those two years help him that he returned to Spain in August

1962 to complete his training with tertianship: the year in which all ordained Jesuits return to repeat the novitiate as priests and to make for the second time the thirty-day Spiritual Exercises of St. Ignatius Loyola. He left El Salvador for Spain more than a little fearful of the dangers involved in reassuming a life too cloistered, too secluded and, above all, too reflective. He was not looking forward to the test.

His fears proved to have been justified. All the old devils which had been shunted aside during the bustle of active work began to emerge once again from the dark backrooms of his mind. During his Long Retreat, he resolved to put in writing to Zalba his situation from the time of his ordination. But he did not do it. By the end of his tertianship, his doubts still unresolved, he was sent to *Lumen Vitae*, the international institute of catechetics in Brussels. That was to be the time of the first true conversion of his life.

In the first place, the studies themselves were far more liberal and pastoral than the more suffocating theologizing of the seminary. One was encouraged to think for himself, to search out the loving Father of the Prodigal Son rather than the wrathful caricature of a vengeful Deity. Far more important, the Church itself in Vatican II had courageously faced up to what many considered centuries of blindness, sanctimoniousness, formalism. And the Church's conversion become Rutilio Grande's conversion. Slowly, ever so slowly, he began to see that he was not called to be a perfect plaster saint unceasingly rapt in adoration; he was called to be a pastor, an outcast and imperfect Samaritan helping his fellow imperfect outcasts who lay battered along his road. He had begun to see that there is not merely a vertical dimension to his priesthood—reaching upward only to God—but also a horizontal dimension—reaching the love of God outward to his brothers and sisters in Christ.

Rutilio had endured five years of incessant inner upheaval to the point that he thought he would either go insane or kill himself. He had even been on the point of leaving the religious life and the priestly ministry in order to find the internal peace to which every man has a right. He had felt that the essence of what was deepest in him was disintegrating. Now he had begun to realize that it was not he, by his incessant efforts, who must scrabble to heal his own wounds. Rather, he had only to accept, humbly and gratefully, the healing freely given to him by the One whose wounds healed all our wounds.

Before leaving Brussels for El Salvador in the late summer of 1964, he took the formula he had carried in his cassock pocket on the day of ordination and tore it to shreds. It would never torment him again. As he wrote to Zalba, "What an incredibly heroic feat for me to have torn that up!"

The following year, back in the seminary in San Salvador, he wrote during his yearly retreat: "When God, for one reason or other, brings it about that one lives a hidden life, and one fails humanly—even if he fails entirely!—it is not necessarily a failure for the glory of God. *Always—but especially in these times of the unknown future—confidence in God my Father who directs everything for my good!* It is an attitude which, even humanly, carries one forth to that which *is*—without foolish fears. How much I need to forget about myself! I promise not to be a perfectionist again. I will learn to swim by swimming! I put all my trust in Jesus; he is the only thing that remains."

Rutilio Grande, that good man, had been set free.

---

12 March 1977,

Up ahead of them, in a tiny, solemn procession, three tattered little boys were walking by the side of the road at the edge of the cane. When they heard the sound of the car, they turned. Tense. Fearful. As they recognized the car, their dark brown eyes disappeared into squinty grins, and they waved.

Rutilio pulled up next to them and stopped. With grave good manners, the boys doffed their splintery straw hats and held them to their skinny chests. "Good afternoon, Father Tilo."

"Come, get in. We're going to El Paisnal, too. We'll get you home before your mamas get worried, all right?"

"Oh, yes, Father Tilo!" And they scrambled in, elbowing one another, wide-eyed. To be driven in a car, and by this famous and holy man! They settled in a silent huddle on the bare floor at the back of the Safari, staring up in awe at Father Tilo sitting tall at the wheel.

Rutilio downshifted, and the jeep moved forward again. In the sideview mirror he saw a cloud of dust back along the road behind them. The old man and the boy did not notice. Dust in the air. Someone else was going to El Paisnal. Or they were being followed.

* * * * * * * *

In 1965, Rutilio had returned once again to the seminary in San Salvador as professor of pastoral theology and director of the social action projects of the seminarians. In the nine years he spent off and on teaching there, he was to have a very great effect on the future of the Church in El Salvador—because his life touched the lives of all the young clergy of the country. And now he was not only a man set free; he was a man set on fire. At the seminary he ignited that fire in the future Salvadorean priests, and they in their turn carried it out to the people. Christianity could no longer be used as an opiate for the people. It was a challenge to hope.

Until he had returned to San Salvador, most of the theology had been as vertical and hierarchical as the institutional Church had been before Vatican II: from the top down, teacher-centered, the ingestion of indigestible iron truths, indomitable and inflexible certitudes. Now, however, while Rutilio Grande was teaching future priests, there would be no more "Here's the thesis; memorize it; repeat it back to me." Most of the men in his classes were not going to be future seminary professors and scholars, spinning out more nets to capture the inscrutable; they were going to be priests, fishers of men. Nor were they going to be priests merely for the priesthood's sake; they were to be priests for the Salvadorean people, rich and poor. Theses were not going to rouse a peasant from his dull resignation to slavery nor an aristocrat from his arrogant insensitivity to his workers' mindless drudgery. So Rutilio Grande sent his students out to dirty their hands among the poor, to temper their laudable idealism with an equally laudable splash of cold reality.

They went out into the barrios and shantytowns—sometimes 80 at a time—lived in the squalor, worked beside the exploited and dispossessed, listened to them, shared the burden of their despair. Then they returned exhausted and exalted to the seminary to wrestle for answers to that despair—in the scriptures, in books, in prayer, in discussions. There were no lectures. These young men were not ferreting out plastic answers for an exam; they were conceiving living answers for the minds and hearts of human beings.

For many of those seminarians, it was a wrenching experience. It was not at all the life they had been prepared to live. Many of them had come from wealthy families. Many had thought of a priest as the contented cleric strolling the patio of his rectory with his breviary, or sharing tea and biscuits and soothing pieties with the ladies of the parish. But this ordained peasant from El Paisnal, for all his natural sensitivity, was not going to allow them such comfortably confining illusions. If they were going to follow the call of the priesthood, then let it be the call to Calvary, not the call to aloof and subsidized privilege. They were going to feel down to their marrow how the other half—the other 98%—of their people lived. If it could be called living. They were, after all, in the footsteps of the Son of God, who himself had surrendered privilege in order to share the indignities of Galilean peasants.

El Salvador is the smallest country of Central America, sixty miles wide and one hundred sixty miles long, about the size of Massachusetts. You can get from the capital to any other point in about two or three hours by car. Nestled halfway under the isthmus, it slopes down from under the craggy Sierra Madre cordillera to the Pacific, pocketed between Guatemala to the West and Honduras to the North and East. But unlike its neighbors which have a great deal of unused land and relatively few people, El Salvador has the highest population density in the Western Hemisphere, with the possible exception of Trinidad. While the other countries of Central America average 78 people per square mile and the U.S. has 60 people per square mile, El Salvador averages 403 people per square mile. More important, half of the people are under sixteen, with a rate of population growth already so high that by 1985 the population will swell from four million to six million people crowded together into that tiny "republic."

There is no coal or iron, very little gold or minerals to be mined. There is no heavy industry. All that there is is the land. That is their gold. And every inch of usable land is owned. And there lies the tragedy. El Salvador is like an over-crowded and understocked lifeboat.

An oligarchy—the so-called "Fourteen Families" who are all related to one another by marriage, god-parentage, and joint investments— owns whatever land that can sustain even a weed. Rather than growing food crops for home consumption, that land is used for the far more lucrative cash-export crops: sugar, coffee, cotton. About 20% of the land is too mountainous to farm; 60% is owned by 2% of the people; and the other 20% must be parceled out among 92% of the people. That is merely one more dithering statistic. Picture El Salvador as a single cow which God gives to ten people to be divided into ten parts. Some of the cow, as we have seen, is unusable; say, two parts. That leaves eight usable parts for ten people. Now in El Salvador two people have pushed in and grabbed the six best parts—which leaves only two parts to be divided among the other eight people. "That is not fair!" That is true.

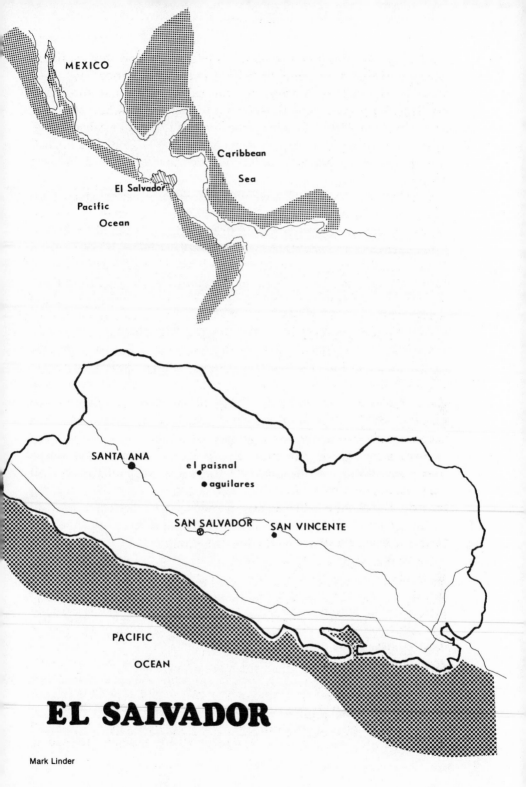

MEXICO

Caribbean

Sea

El Salvador

Pacific

Ocean

SANTA ANA

el paisnal

aguilares

SAN SALVADOR

SAN VINCENTE

PACIFIC

OCEAN

EL SALVADOR

Mark Linder

Put it another way: six wealthy families in El Salvador own as much land as 270,000 campesino (peasant) families. Or put it still another way: there are four million people in El Salvador. About 100,000 are very well fed indeed; the other 3,900,000 are in various stages of starvation. And for the past five hundred years, that 100,000 and their ancestors have been doing their damnedest to make sure things stay that way.

Therefore, there are almost ludicrous extremes of wealth and poverty, with very little in between (a small but growing middle class which is not going to do anything whatsoever to rock the lifeboat). In the capital city of San Salvador, the wealthy live in graceful estates on the eastern slopes of the sleeping volcano, where the manicured lawns in the patios are watered-green all year round, and the young people come laughing home from tennis at the club. From their stuccoed windows they can look down somewhat apprehensively on the squatter population tussling for space at the foot of the hill, huddled in packing cases and shanties gerryrigged from pilfered boards and flattened tin cans. Foul water carrying human waste floats from under privies and runs in black rivulets down the paths of the barrio. Big-bellied children play in them. And every day the shantytown grows, like a dirty swarm of maggots slowly creeping up the hills.

The experienced foreign traveler makes it a point not to eat in open-air restaurants in San Salvador, or if he does, to sit well back to the rear, because the child beggars will stand and stare hungrily at the food while he is eating. And when the visitor shows signs of having finished, the children will come up and ask politely for the remains of the meal. The meal is even less pleasant if the audience is a gauntly pregnant woman and her hollow-eyed children.

The same stark contrast spreads out beyond the capital into the farm country, where the absentee landlord's great villa generally sits unused except for a weekend in the country or a benevolent yearly fiesta for the peasants. But there is a minor difference in the country. The *patròn's* hacienda is in the valleys, which are rich volcanic soil and lush with green cane or red coffee berries. The peasants live in the thatched shanties in the hills, which are gravel.

Indulge a few more statistics. There are too many people for the land, and even when they can get a patch of dirt it will not feed their children. Therefore, because the peasants are hungry and willing to do any job for any pay, the *patròn* can name whatever salary he chooses

16

and the campesino will snatch at it—and be grateful, even if he ultimately receives less than he was promised, since the alternative is watching his children starve.

In early 1974, the president raised the minimum wage to U.S. $1.10 per day. Not per hour; per day. It is a 48-hour work week, although exceptions are made for children under ten. During the hectic months of harvest, there is no pay for overtime. Even that, however, is misleading. In the first place, most campesinos work for the *patròn* only during the planting and harvesting seasons. Other times, the coffee and cane pretty much take care of themselves. Therefore, over the course of a year, the $1.10 per day averages out to about forty cents a day—for a family of four, six, eight, ten. Secondly, a *patròn* may not pay in cash but, in exchange for a season's work, will allow a campesino to cultivate an acre or two of unyielding ground in the hills. It is useless to the landowner for a cash crop, but it pays for cheap labor.

Some peasants go into some marginal business during the off-seasons, making tin water jugs or wicker baskets. It profits a man, then, to have many children who will grow up to be workers by the time they are four or five. By that age, small boys are out tending their father's two or three ropy, diseased pigs, throwing rocks at them to get them moving. It is nothing to see tiny children who can't see the fire over the lip of the forge, standing for an hour cranking the bellows and staring at the brick. There is no shouting, no forcing them to work. They simply wander in, work until they are tired, and wander out without any verbal instruction. It is good training in futility.

50% of the population is illiterate, and though elementary school is free and absolutely compulsory by law, few rural schools can afford to offer more than two grades. Even if they could, the children have to work. The peasants face this denial philosophically: it would be fine to have an educated son, but we are hungry—now. And the peasant doctor or lawyer rarely wants to return to his people once he has tasted the fine life.

73% of the children of El Salvador are severely undernourished, some to the point of permanent mental retardation or even death. Fewer than 25% of the rural peasants have running water, and fewer than 1% have sewage disposal. They live in one-room huts, frames woven from sticks and crammed with clay, thatched with straw and infested with vermin. Of every thousand babies born, 63 will die before they are one year old. There are three doctors for every 10,000 people. But, even if one were available, a farm worker could not afford to take his child to a doctor more than once every two years. The Salvadorean Ministry of Planning itself admits that the average peasant cannot afford to spend more than one *colon* (40¢) a day.

8% of the people get one-half of the national income; 92% share the other half. Despite the fact that coffee prices have tripled for the land-owners since 1974, the minimum wage for farm workers (on days they can get work) is now $2.40 per day. Inflation ranges from 20% to 50% or higher. The campesinos receive the absolute minimum wage necessary to sustain life and to continue producing profit for the owners. The comparison is inevitable—to the notices in the glass display cases at Dachau, which show the probable length of time a prisoner can be kept in useful working shape on fifty cents worth of food a day. Then, the Gestapo's calculations of the value of his dental fillings and his eyeglasses. But few of the Salvadoreans have those.

These campesinos work land that they can never own and produce food their children can never eat. Why don't they leave? Why don't they revolt? They've tried both.

In the late 60's, there was just not even enough starvation work or enough patches of land to sustain the great number of campesinos. Many of them trudged to the cities where there was some money, only to be swallowed up in the indescribably foul shanty towns. Others— perhaps 300,000—slipped across the ill-defined borders into Honduras, where there were endless square miles of uncultivated land. But the Catholic Honduran farmers resented this encroachment, even though the land lay fallow, and after a series of border clashes, open war broke out between the two countries in July of 1969. Although El Salvador had the best of the little war, the Organization of American States prevented it from annexing any territory. And so hundreds of thousands of dispossessed campesinos came crowding back to a land which could not feed their children.

Periodically, the peasants' desperation has also driven them to a united revolt, the most dramatic of which took place in 1932. It was futile. At least 10,000 peasants were liquidated within a few days; some put the number as high as 20,000; no one knows for certain since they were peasants. It lasted four days; they called it *La Matanza*, "The Slaughter." Since that outbreak, to avoid another so disruptive occurrence, the government has been placed securely in the hands of the army, and all unions of farm workers have been absolutely forbidden by law. Every time rebellion or even united protest is whispered even in secret, the reply is always, "Quiet! We don't want another

'32!" And so for the most part, the peasants continue trying numbly to wring food out of their dead little plots, and the secret police and the bully boys from the haciendas make sure there is no expression of discontent. If anyone talks back, he simply "disappears." This is not the Soviet Union. It is a Western democracy whose leaders attend Mass every Sunday.

But for all the years of exploitation and defeat, the Salvadorean peasant is not a broken man. Though the values are slowly changing, the ideal Latin man, for both rich and poor and especially for the young, is still the dominant, macho, courteous and reckless male, who has lots of children to prove he possesses all those virtues. The ideal woman is still deferential, modest, uncomplaining. Her purpose is to have children, make her husband comfortable, and go to church. And the macho man goes nowhere without his machete. He uses it to harvest corn and cane, clear for planting, kill chickens, mow the patròn's lawn, and settle disputes at Saturday night dances. For many the three-to-four-dollar machete is their most expensive possession. Without it, a man is useless to the patròn; and yet with it, he is also dangerous to the patròn. Five hundred workers with machetes, seething with rage, can eventually outlast a handful of hired guns.

To counter this ever-present danger and to preserve "National Security," the elite families and the military government have spun an iron web of laws and enforcers which has effectively assured that the peasants will remain in their place. One would be tempted to compare modern El Salvador to "Gone With the Wind" if it were not even more like "The Godfather."

As with many other countries in Latin America, El Salvador does have elections, but it is a wastefully expensive lip-service to the democratic process. The invariable charges of election fraud are just as invariably true. Nonetheless, every five years the moderates and the only-slightly-left-of-center parties (all others are outlawed) put up a candidate for president—who is inevitably defeated and almost as inevitably sent into exile for his efforts. In some cases, weeks before the election, ballot boxes have been found already filled with votes pre-marked in favor of the government party. In other cases, the army conducts house-to-house searches "for concealed weapons" and incidentally warns the owners to vote correctly. In some rural towns, as soon as the polls have closed, the lights have been shut off, the polling place surrounded, the officials hustled out while soldiers went in and stuffed the ballot boxes.

During the week after the rigged election of 1977, the defeated presidential candidate and his supporters staged a massive protest rally in the central plaza of downtown San Salvador (called, ironically, Liberty Square). Attendance at the demonstrations fluctuated from between 2,000 and 5,000 people camped out in the square at night to some 10,000 to 15,000 during the day. Taking courage from this display of unified frustration, more and more workers in factories and on plantations came out on strike to protest the election, and by the weekend the capital was almost completely paralyzed. On Sunday the crowd had become 50,000 people, though by midnight it had dwindled again to about 6,000 people.

Suddenly the Plaza was surrounded by ORDEN vigilantes and soldiers with tanks and armored cars. They opened fire. Many escaped, but about two thousand people ran for sanctuary to the church of El Rosario and jammed into it. The soldiers threw tear gas in the windows. The demonstrators quickly surrendered and dispersed. At least 100 had been slaughtered. Eyewitnesses told of bodies dumped into ravines and sewers. The government declared a state of siege, suspending all constitutional rights of expression and assembly, and blamed the violence on "agents of communist subversion."

Not surprisingly, then, of the ten presidents since 1938, nine have been generals. (The one civilian was replaced after four months.) In the elections of 1972, the military party "captured" not only the presidency but every seat in congress and every one of the 250-odd mayorships.

The wealthy and the army of El Salvador have a coalition of convenience. For fifty years the oligarchy has delegated government to the military and has managed to control it. Any time a slightly more liberal president or congress makes motions in the direction of land reform, the oligarchy has always been able to quash them. After repressing the 1932 peasant rebellion, the government bought up great private estates to turn them into National Farms to placate the peasants, and these lands were duly subdivided and distributed to the landless campesinos. But inadequate financial and technical know-how left the peasants easy prey to trickery and loans, so that one by one they surrendered their plots back to the original owners in payment of debts. By 1950 the 72,000 acres were safely back in the hands of the oligarchy.

A modest redistribution of land was attempted again in 1950, and in the 60's, and in 1976, but through intimidation, exemplary torture, invoking legal technicalities, and especially through propaganda in the newspapers which they own or keep in business with their advertising, the wealthy few have always been able to rescue the status quo.

For the campesino, the only victory is survival.

As one citizen put it, "El Salvador is a country full of spies. In a tiny country where you have no work, that is one way to feed your children." One is tempted to describe the situation simply as Fascism, Brown Shirts rousting Jews and Reds, neighbors disappearing in the night. But there is no single lifetime Führer, no controlling ideology except the need to keep the peasants in their divinely ordained place and the wealthy in theirs. Rather, it is a kind of simplistic anti-leftism which unifies most of the military regimes of Latin America. They fear reform, revolution and Castro—which are all exact synonyms. To speak of giving land to the campesinos, to speak of justice and the peasant's human right to work, food, shelter, health care, literacy—all of this is, *ipso facto*, to propose Marxist communism. Any violence whatsoever in the country is automatically blamed on an international communist conspiracy. Communism and peasant organization mean one and the same thing. Therefore, the country lives in a more or less permanent state of siege, on guard against even the slightest non-conformity. Blind to any nuance or qualification or distinction, the government judges each citizen either a patriot (that is, unthinkingly loyal to the military regime) or a communist agitator. There is no alternative in between. It sounds preposterously simple-minded, but it is true.

Ironically, the government's very paranoia about communism is what actually gave rise to left-wing guerrilla activity. According to a U.S. Government source, there was no indication of communist guerrilla activity from 1932 to 1972. Even now, it is estimated that there are probably no more than 100 leftist guerrillas in El Salvador. On the other side, however, the army numbers 4,500, not including the national guard, the national police, or the treasury police. ORDEN ("Order"), a civic society which is also a pistol-packing vigilante force numbers 65,000 members. They receive permission to carry arms from the government and money to spy on those who go to Mass or listen to the broadcast of the archbishop's Mass from the cathedral. No one knows how many men belong to the secret White Warriors Union, a right-wing anti-communist terrorist group of ex-military men in service to the government.

One thing is sure. On the evening of 12 March 1977, around six o'clock, several men of that side were on the road between Aguilares and El Paisnal.

21

The Safari rattled over the dusty ruts, past a *canton* of three or four huts clustered down a path off to their left, Los Mangos. Far ahead of them the children could see a group of men standing at the edge of the canefields, two or three on either side of the dirt road. Perhaps they were also walking to El Paisnal. Or to Aguilares. But they were just standing there. They had not been working in the fields. It was nearly six o'clock on a Sunday evening.

The children watched the old man and the boy turn toward the priest, their faces stiffened and tense. The boy braced his back against the seat and his hand against the car door, as if there were going to be an accident. The children looked at one another in puzzlement. What were they afraid of? He had no uniform on, but even at this distance you could see that one of the men was a policeman from El Paisnal.

And the pickup truck behind them was much closer now.

Without turning his head, Father Grande said softly, "we must do what God asks of us."

* * * * * * *

By 1970 Rutilio had made himself a reputation not only in the seminary and the archdiocese but in the other four dioceses of the country as well, and the opinions of more than a few priests and bishops were not favorable. His "doctrine" was a reflection on themselves, they felt. What's more, it was angering their wealthier parishioners who saw it as crypto-socialism if not out-and-out communism. He was a truly dangerous man. Nonetheless, his lifelong friendship with the archbishop was still very real and very strong, and the archbishop asked him to work on the preparatory committee for the annual Bishops' Conference. It was to be a week of hard study of the actual social and economic reality of the Salvadorean Church, the majority of whom were peasants. It was also to be the beginning of the second great liberating conversion of Rutilio's life.

The working papers prepared by the committee for the bishops' discussions could not avoid the truth; over the course of centuries, the Church had allied itself with the wealthy minority of the Salvadorean church and by that very fact had connived at least implicitly in the oppression of the peasant majority. Rutilio wrote that the bishops had a grave duty to respond to the hope that the campesinos still had in the Church. He begged them not to disillusion these people, but rather to recognize the structural injustice and institutionalized violence in the country, to acknowledge that even within the church the transcendent vertical dimension between God and the individual had nearly eliminated the imminent horizontal dimension of brother to brother. He begged them to realize that, at least in their published decrees, many of them had acted as if Vatican II had never occurred.

To echo Queen Victoria, many of the bishops and auxiliary bishops were "not amused." Three of them took the papers very seriously; the others acted nearly as if the episcopal conference itself had also never taken place. They called it "radicalization motivated by a juvenile fever." Like the rest of us, bishops are imperfect, and they are no more comfortable than we when they are reminded that their mistakes and compromises might have had unsuspected or even sinful consequences.

Three months later, in November 1970, Rutilio still refused to be daunted in his uphill struggle to save the Church from the church. At a monthly meeting of the clergy he insisted that the major problem was rooted in the formation of future priests. Theology study had become essentialistic, dehumanized, scarcely biblical or existential or in touch with the worldly realities which moaned outside the seminary walls. Rather, future priests were led to seek uniform legalistic lives, based on fear and pharisaism rather than on personal responsibility to one's God and one's brothers. Look at the indifference to the church of the young, he said, the lack of confidence in the church on the part of the downtrodden, the exaggerated distance of the priest from the majority of the people. Both the government of the state and the government of the church are run by decrees based on calcified doctrine rather than on a search, with the poor, for life.

"We must break open a breech in our Wailing Wall in order to thrust into life the drama of faith as a story of liberation . . . From sterile immobility—which gives us a false sense of security—let us leap out and run the risk and the adventure of living a life of fidelity, in movement, in existential and dramatic tension! In crisis!"

The definitive moment of Rutilio's personal unshackling had come even before that, in August, when his friend the archbishop had asked him to preach the homily in the cathedral of San Salvador on the nation's patronal feast of the Transfiguration. In the church that day were the bishops of the nation, the highest government officials, the diplomatic corps and, more importantly, the people of El Salvador. He rose to tell them that Jesus was the foremost revolutionary of all time (*el revolucionario número uno de la historia*) because he had forever transformed the path of human life. Jesus was not a revolutionary of hatred and lies and confusion. He had come to destroy those. His revolutionary message was to announce the salvific liberation of the poor, the oppressed, the afflicted. He called for a conversion, a transformation of all human expectations.

"But are the people of El Salvador transfigured? Has the overwhelming majority of our people—the campesinos—been transfigured? Has the wealthy minority—who hold in their hands the economy, the power of decision, the control of the press and all the media—been transfigured? There are many baptized in our country who have not completely ingested the demands of the gospel: a total transfiguration. Their minds and hearts have not been transfigured. They have changed the message of *Jesús Salvador* into a message of selfishness, because the majority of our brother Christians, the campesinos, have found misery and not mercy.

"Why is personal and social transfiguration necessary? Because baptism is a sacred and demanding promise. The slogan of Jesus is: change your attitudes and your values! Purify your lives of everything abusive, demeaning, exclusive. The Christian revolution is based on a love which excludes no single human being. Jesus, after all, enfleshed himself as one of our peasants to share their miseries. Can we call ourselves his followers and not do the same?

"Jesus loved rich men, too, men like Zaccheus, Nicodemus, Joseph of Arimathea, and Lazarus, who recognized their mistakes, their swindling, their abuses of power and promised to make reparations for their sins. And it is this transfiguration and resurrection to new life which sum up the whole of the Christian gospel. It is not merely a personal transfiguration. It must burst out into a new aliveness in the heart of the family. It must leap out into the public squares, into the board rooms and hiring halls, into the chambers of congress, into every encounter we have with other human beings.

"Because we are all of us both baptized and citizens, the Church and the government must collaborate efficaciously, audaciously, urgently

24

to work out just, honest, decent laws to transfigure the Salvadorean people. Only then can we call *Cristo Salvador Transfigurado* our *Patròn*. Only then can we truly sing our national anthem: 'Liberty—full, complete, certain—for all the sons of God, the Salvadoreans!'"

This, we must remember, is the man who had savaged himself with self-doubts ten years before.

Surprisingly, almost as if he had not heard it, the president came forward after the Mass to congratulate Rutilio on his fine sermon and, in gratitude, to give him an autographed copy of the Constitution of the Republic. Rutilio kept that copy and later often took it out to use in his sermons when he denounced violations of that same Constitution. At those times, visibly infuriated, he would say that this primary and basic law of the republic was a "dead letter."

Not surprisingly, on the other hand, some of the bishops were far less than pleased with that sermon. The insults of the Episcopal Conference, now this sermon, and then the priests' meeting—it was all too much. In a word, they had lost confidence in him as a trustworthy teacher of their future priests—much less (as they had hinted earlier) as the next rector of the major seminary.

Rutilio had always said that his mission was to serve the church, but it was always a love that cost suffering. From that moment, he asked his vice-provincial to find him another job. Years later, reflecting on those times, he wrote, "Blessed be the Lord, and God grant that I can lift myself up from this gauntlet of tests which keep me humble and never self-sufficient. I ambition only the service of God and nothing else."

He left the seminary without rancor, with no doubt about the honor of his intentions nor his love of the church, but humanly he was a deeply broken man. He had been pilloried for speaking the truth without fear. As the first Christian had been. But this was also a death that would lead to far greater life.

Rutilio, the ex-seminary professor, had now to seek a second vocation. After a rather unhappy year as principal of a wealthy boys' high school, he finally settled on a course at the Latin American Pastoral Institute in Ecuador. Like his last year at *Lumen Vitae*, it was a providential opportunity to reflect, to consolidate, to focus his experience and his commitment toward the task he was destined to begin: the transformation of his country at the roots. He would form a pastoral team to work in a rural area or a ghetto and begin to raise the workers' awareness of their dignity and rights as human beings and as children of God. The team would begin small, as the gospel had, but it would spread: the liberation of mankind from meaninglessness.

The goal: a church made up of living communities of new men and women, alive to their human and divine vocations. The seed: a team of four Jesuits who were themselves dynamic, prophetic, fearless in the face of criticism even from fellow Catholics, no matter what their rank. They must stand side by side with the oppressed and avoid the traps and flatteries of the powerful who try to tame and monopolize the clergy.

This was the time Rutilio needed to assure himself that, although he had been dismissed by some of the very bishops he wanted to serve, he was not a failure. His struggle over his worthiness for the priesthood had prepared him for that. What's more, he became even more certain that he was in reality supported in this instance by the gospel, by Vatican II, by the Latin American bishops' reflections on that Council in Medellin, and by the whole purpose of the Society of Jesus.

The Gospel was clear:

"(The Father) has sent me to bring the good news to the poor, to proclaim liberty to captives and give sight to the blind, to set the oppressed free." (Lk 4/18)

You cannot love God whom you do not see, if you do not love human beings whom you do see. (I Jn 4/20)

Vatican II was equally clear:

If a person is in extreme necessity, he has the right to take from the riches of others what he himself needs. (Church Today 69)

"Feed the man dying of hunger, because if you have not fed him, you have murdered him." (CT 69)

The bishops of Latin America, meeting in 1968 at Medellin, were no less clear:

(The Church) must encourage and favor the efforts of the people to create and develop their grass-roots organizations in order to restore and consolidate their rights and their search for true justice. (Peace 27)

Rutilio's own Jesuit order had insisted on precisely the same mission for every one of its members:

The very survival of the human race depends on men caring for and sharing with one another. (Jesuits Today 7)

But if the call of the Christian is all so obvious, why have so many powerful Catholics—in the clergy as well as in government and business—managed to ignore it, or deny it outright, or even condemn it?

It is far too easy to say that the wealthy are, by definition, heartless pagan brutes, dogs-in-the-manger, monsters of profit, who sneer at the poor as lazy, immoral, irresponsible—but necessary—slaves. Such talk is naive rhetoric, and one must remember that many communist revolutionary movements can manipulate persons as unfeelingly as capitalism does.

Moreover, one has heard the deification of the Economy so often in the U.S. that it would seem that a well-to-do Salvadorean could just as easily appropriate the same arguments to himself: I work for my money, why can't they? I pay taxes; do we want a welfare state without the slightest bit of ambition? Look what happened to the National Farms in '32; I'm as humane as the next man, but how can you help someone who can't (or won't) help himself?—It has a familiar ring.

And in El Salvador there lurks the very real fear of communism which is just a stone's skip away across the Caribbean in Cuba. It is easy for us to condemn or rail at blind self-interest when we live in a land where the free exchange of any kind of idea becomes almost bewildering. In America both Nazis and anarchists can give speeches in Chicago parks without fear of arrest. But it is not so easy to forge a reasoned and freely chosen conscience in a country where thought-control is the rule, where the government commands ninety minutes of prime time for propaganda on all radio stations every evening.

The taproot of evil is not money or pride but the combination in one creature of (a) freedom and (b) an inadequate ability to apprehend the truth. One can suppose that very many of the wealthy in El Salvador love their families, pray sincerely, give to charities, refrain from beating their dogs or their children or their peasants. But if someone else does it, like the government, "Well, they've thought it all out more than I have time to do." And so napalming children or keeping peasants in their place must be "good for all of us in the long run."

Moreover, if the government (no matter how objectively perverse) hangs on for many years, it offers an illusion of continuity in a world of furious and infuriating change and that illusion begins to look temptingly like an eternal and trustworthy truth.

Who can say what causes this double-mindedness? In the first place, for both the rich and the poor, "it has always been that way." Whether in the ante-bellum American South or in the Thirty Years' War in Vietnam, if a set of circumstances continues insolubly for one's entire lifetime it begins to look like God's will, one of "the things that cannot be changed." The Georgia slave or the Khe San peasant adapts his values and expectations of life to what he finds. So, too, with the Salvadorean campesino and *patròn*.

In part, too, the situation is surely due to inertia: "Many men would rather die than think; most of them do." But there is also some mental circuit which is half-purposely left disconnected, some repressive mechanism which allows one to forget what is true, to separate sex or profit or even faith in God from justice to one's fellow human beings. They are isolated spheres of reality which never touch or overlap. Tolstoy showed it in *War and Peace*, where the wealthy wept in their warm opera boxes for the dying courtesan while the serfs guarding their carriages outside froze to death in the Moscow winter night. It is a self-defensive ignorance which will not allow two sections of one's brain to communicate with one another.

Some men are prisoners of war; others are prisoners of peace.

It is a combination of denial ("This is too necessary to be evil.") and then rationalization ("This is in fact the greater good, and those who try to prevent it are evil.") In short, because of that circuit too-long-left open, "morality" is sincerely judged by whether a given action helps or hinders me and mine.

But when does legitimate self-interest become injustice?

What is more shameful is that, for all sorts of good and bad reasons, the Church pandered to those comfortable self-deceptions, or at least became guilty by collusive silence. Like most American Catholics, the Salvadorean elite (and surely the illiterate peasants) have not read the documents of Vatican II or Medellin. They depend on simplistic popularizations in the press (if even that) and the homilies of their priests. "My bishop says nothing about this. He comes to my home for dinner and says nothing even unguardedly about this. Does this priest know more than a bishop?" Unfortunately most of the faithful the world over (including even some bishops) believe that episcopal consecration confers more powers than it actually does.

28

Even assuming a *patròn* of enlightened conscience, he would feel his hands automatically tied from the start. "Supposing I sell my hacienda or divide it among the poor, will that change the life of the peasants or the police state of El Salvador? Can one conscientious person convince enough others to join him, to sacrifice the trips to Majorca and our wives' Paris clothes in order to put food into the peasant babies' bellies? Would any American do that? It is futile. It is the cage into which we are all born, campesino and *patròn*."

At the root of this problem is a misapprehension of the true nature and mission of the members of the church, a misapprehension which Vatican II struggled strong-mindedly to correct. One view of the church is a bishop surrounded by a group of people who listen to him; the other view sees the church as a group of people surrounding a bishop who listens to them and to the Spirit and then focuses that discernment into a plan of action. Considering the history, politics, and social values of El Salvador it is obvious that the prevailing view of the church's nature there, even among the peasants, is paternalistic, from-the-top-down. Unwilling to sacrifice the very real advantages to the church of being on Caesar's good side, many of the Salvadorean bishops have preached caution, preservation of influence and remaining in the sanctuary of the church building. Most of the governments of Latin America would like nothing better than to see the Catholic Church retreat to the "spiritual realm" and leave sociology and economics to them. In their eyes, the church must deal solely with God and the Kingdom of Heaven—novenas, the altar and rosary society, the weekly Mass. Period. Within the State, the church's function is to offer solace, to convince the peon to accept his misery as a guarantee which will be paid off on that Great Come-and-Get-It Day. The Beatitudes, after all, are couched in the future tense. The Kingdom of Earth must be run on completely other—even contradictory—principles of utility, compromise, suspicion, and, if necessary, duplicity.

Have these people no compassion? The law of averages says that at least some of them must. But they see the campesino just standing there before the *patròn*, so obsequious, showing neither grief nor anger nor fear. His burned-out eyes seem indifferent, as if he too were equally willing to admit that exploitation is as natural and unchangeable as a hurricane. Americans would have done something: shaken their fists, raged, cursed, run away. But Americans have not been peasants for a long time. Perhaps the men and women of Harlem and Appalachia would understand. It is easy to be principled and righteously indignant when you sleep in a peaceful bed.

And the campesino, for his part, leaves the humiliating audience with the *patròn*, takes the few pennies he has hoarded for his family to the cantina and gets drunk. Perhaps this is as evil in the eyes of the righteous as the landowner's exploitation is evil, but it is better than going home to smell the failure as thick in the hut as the smell from the privy, to see his children's hungrily expectant eyes, to feel the silent keening of his wife's despair. Each new indignity grows tighter and tighter inside him until he is sure it must break. But it doesn't break. It becomes a permanent knot in his guts which the cantina can help him forget. It helps him find a compromise somewhere between shame and despair.

Because of the legal suppression of all but the most loyal opposition in Latin America, the church remains the only institution still free to be an adversary to totalitarianism. And the conclusions of Medellin show that at least in the anonymity of general assembly the bishops have bravely challenged the contradictions between the gospel which the rulers claim and the injustice which they practice.

Therefore, as church-going Catholics, reluctant to risk excommunication and thus loss of credibility, the rulers cannot challenge the church directly. Instead, they must resort to civil repression and to vigilantes with no provable connection to the government. They rely especially on newspaper articles and ads questioning the Catholic orthodoxy of progressive priests and bishops, "proving" that the church was founded to settle questions of the soul and not questions of sociology and economics, and constantly raising the bogey threat of communism. Such paid advertisements are always signed by hitherto unheard-of authorities, such as "Professora Aminta Amaya" and fictitious groups, such as "Patriot Women" and "Mothers Against Communism."

Although one wants to be just even to the perpetrators of that injustice, it would be less than truthful to deny the infamy that many Latin American leaders not only tolerate but set into motion. There follows the so-called Banzer Plan, named for the former president of Bolivia and, as we shall see, it is a bible in the struggle of the Salvadorean mandarins to maintain their position.

THE BANZER PLAN

1. Never attack the church as an institution and even less the bishops as a group. Rather attack the part of the church which is the most "progressive."

2. Attack, above all, the foreign clergy. Insist continuously that they are preaching armed warfare, that they are connected with international communism and have been sent to this country with the exclusive goal of moving the church toward communism.

3. Control certain religious orders.

4. The CIA has decided to intervene directly in this affair. It has promised to give us information about certain priests (personal documents, studies, friends, addresses, publications, foreign contacts.)

5. Control certain religious houses.

6. For the present, do not repress religious houses since this will stir up too much controversy.

7. Confront the hierarchy with deeds already done.

8. Arrests should be made in the countryside, on deserted streets or late at night. Once a priest has been arrested, the Minister should plant subversive material in his briefcase and, if possible, in his room or home, and a weapon, preferably a high caliber pistol. Have a story prepared disgracing him before his bishop and the public.

9. By any means of public communication, publish loose, daring, compromising material in order to discredit priests and religious who represent the tip of the progressive element in the church. Demand an official signature for any communique so that we can control where they come from and who writes them.

10. Maintain a friendly relationship with some bishops, with certain members of the church, and with some native priests. In

such a way we will assure that public opinion does not believe that there is a systematic persecution of the church, but only of a few of its dissident members. Insist on the authenticity of the national church (as opposed to the church in other countries).

11. Reward the agents who best work at enforcing this plan of action by giving them the belongings confiscated from the homes of priests and religious.

This is not a decree written in the age of Nero and the catacombs, nor in the age of Elizabeth I and the Tower. It is written in the present day in the Western hemisphere. Castro is not our only threat.

* * * * * * * *

And so in September 1972, because silence was more shameful than shame, Rutilio Grande came to Aguilares and his unsuspected rendezvous with greatness.

Because it was so near his birthplace, Rutilio would rather have chosen another area. There would be danger to his relatives and friends. But Aguilares was too ideal to pass by. It stood at the confluence of vital highways and commerce, a growing labor market for field workers, the site of a large new dam project which would involve construction workers as well. The parish was empty, and Archbishop Chavez wanted him there.

Aguilares was also a unique town in which all the contradictions and injustices of the country converged. There were about 30,000 people in the parish—10,000 in Aguilares, 2,000 in El Paisnal, and 18,000 scattered over the 170 square kilometers of the parish. The town itself was merely a nucleus of little businesses and artisans offering the basic services and coiled to spring their bills on the day the harvesting was done. The main business of the valley was the cultivation and processing of sugar-cane grown on the great haciendas and refined in the three family sugar works: La Cabaña, San Francisco, and Colima. Infant mortality in the parish was high, and so were broken marriages. The frustration of the workers was becoming critical, and the people of the area are particularly contentious. On 24 May 1973, less than a year after Rutilio's arrival, there was a strike at La Cabaña; the workers refused their pay because it was not what they had been promised. The place was like a volcano beginning to tremble.

Until quite recently, the religion of many peasants was very primitive and unenlightened. Since many of them were illiterate, they had not had any real study of the gospels except the readings at Mass when the priest could get to them. As a result, many pictured God as a capricious *patròn* to be placated. The priest was a man of learning and semi-magical powers who knew how to tranquilize God's anger and manipulate him. The peasants' Christianity was therefore often semi-magical and without much scriptural content beyond the figures in the Christmas crib and the crucifix. Since many of them are unschooled, they had been merely baptized and in no real sense "evangelized."

Though he might have been quietly enraged at his position in the world, the peasant was still as servile to God as he was to the military police, the security guards of the hacienda, the local patrols, and ORDEN—since that was his lot in life. He had little or no awareness of history or of the outside world, little comprehension of time and, therefore, little ability to be objective about his situation. The life of the peasant was just that way. Some are born crippled, some are born blind, some are born peasant.

Therefore, the task before Rutilio's team was threefold: first, to immerse themselves in the lives of the peasants, gaining their trust and learning their needs and susceptibilities by first-hand experience; second, to raise their level of awareness not merely of what the life of the campesino is but what it should and could be; and, third, to help them see their lives in relationship to the liberating message of the Gospel.

The team divided the parish into twenty-five segments, ten in the two towns and fifteen in the countryside. One by one each segment was visited by a member of the team; two members were always on the road, two always remained to cover the regular parish duties, one in each town. The mission men would go to one of the sub-communities and stay for two weeks, sharing the people's lives, homes, food. Every evening of the priest's stay everyone in that area was invited to a meeting: a reading and explanation of a passage from scripture, small-group discussion on the meaning of the passage in their situation—to see human history fusing into salvation history, and at the end a general sharing of insights. In the final days of the two weeks, the people elected men and women as leaders or "Delegates of the Word" to continue the process when the team had moved on to the next community. There was no condescending paternalism from the priest; *the church is not fossilized in the clergy.*

The purpose of these missions was an intelligent understanding, after all those years, that the gospel speaks to today. The peasants did not need to be told that their lives were miserable; what they needed to discover in the gospels was that resignation to misery was not God's plan for them at all. Rather, the Christian vocation was a challenge to struggle for the dignity which was indeed God's plan. As Rutilio often said, "God is not somewhere up in the clouds, lying in a hammock! God is here with us, building a Kingdom here on earth!"

Once all of the communities had been visited and delegates elected, the team was ready for the second stage: the formation of the delegates, training them to help people interpret the scriptures, catechetics, methods of group dynamics, formation of activities for the young. Others began to be attracted to help the team: seminary students, university students, diocesan priests from the capital.

But the tension had already begun. The strike at La Cabaña had not been the purpose of the evangelization of the communities, but it surely resulted from the campesinos' new awareness that they were created as human, by God, as their reluctant paymasters. In June 1973 when President Molina came to Aguilares to dedicate a school and the mayor asked Rutilio to give the invocation, Rutilio politely declined. Later, he wrote to the president explaining the climate of tension in Aguilares and the serious results he feared. Under the circumstances, especially the cloud of doubt under which Molina's election had occurred, he felt it would be wrong even to seem to align himself with any political party, whether with the government or with the outlawed peasants' unions.

Further, he begged the president to use the army as an organization for teaching and working with the people rather than as an instrument of fear. He had told the military police commandant of Aguilares, who had publicly called him a communist, that the army's job was to protect the poor who were exploited on the haciendas. He had told the soldiers that they were at the service of the majority; the Constitution of the Republic says, "The duty of a soldier is to love his country," but the country is the people. It also says, "Every man is free in the republic," but the country is filled with all kinds of prisons. Priests and soldiers have a common task: their covenant with the people.

He confessed to the president that he had had to denounce the commandant from the pulpit after the team had repeatedly and uselessly begged him to stop the spread of prostitution in Aguilares. For many families, however, it was their only hope for food. This antagonism with the police slowly escalated. In January 1974 the team visited the commandant to ask him to stop the talk that his soldiers were spreading in the parish that the priests were communist agitators. The Banzer Plan was beginning to be put in force. But it was only the beginning.

* * * * * * * *

29 Nov. 1974: More than 60 soldiers and members of ORDEN armed with automatic weapons, mortars, hand grenades and tear gas entered the hamlet of La Cayetana in San Vicente province. The villagers had been involved for some time in a dispute with the owner of a nearby hacienda. The soldiers ransacked the houses and terrorized the villagers on the pretext of searching for concealed weapons. As the detachment was leaving with thirteen prisoners, they met a group of peasants returning from the fields. The soldiers fired into the group, and six of the workers were killed. An attempt to have the matter investigated was blocked from higher up. The thirteen prisoners have "disappeared."

5 Feb. 1975: Rutilio met with President Colonel Arturo Molina in an attempt to defend his pastoral work from frequent charges in the press of subversion of the peasants. He attempted to be a lightning rod to the authorities to avoid complete suppression of the team and the parish.

21 Jun. 1975: At one in the morning, a detachment of soldiers and members of ORDEN entered the village of Tres Calles in Usulatán province. They broke into the home of Josè Ostorga, supposedly searching for weapons. They shot and killed him and his three sons. His fourth son, thirteen years old, was severely beaten. Another group attacked the nearby house of Santos Morales, and he, too was executed on the spot. There was no official inquiry.

17 Jul. 1975: Father Rutilio Grande was publicly accused of being subversive by the conservative Religious Preservation Front. In the article, the group suggested Father Grande remember the two subversive priests who had recently been assassinated in Honduras. Father Grande replied that if his accusers would read the gospel they would find that Jesus Christ was also a "subversive."

30 Jul. 1975: A peaceful student demonstration in the town of Santa Ana against military intervention found its route and all sidestreets blocked by tanks and troops. Security forces opened fire at point blank range. Amnesty International has a list of more than twenty students who were taken away and have never been seen since.

7 Aug. 1975: President Colonel Molina wrote criticizing "liberationist priests."Also, the first publication of FALANGE (Armed

Liberation Forces in the Anti-communist War of Elimination), who say that the country will never fall into the hands of communist journalists, deputies and priests. Since the beginning of 1975, sixteen union leaders have already been imprisoned, murdered, or disappeared.

* * * * * * * *

There was not only a tension between the growing sense of dignity in the peasants and the consequent growing anger of the landowners and the police; there was also a tension growing within Rutilio himself.

The team had formed 37 communities altogether, with 300 delegates serving in rotation. For the campesinos, the gospel was like light and air to men trapped all their lives in a mine shaft, and slowly they began to emerge from their magical ideas of religion. Little by little, they were rejecting their dull fatalism. Gradually, they began to understand that their humiliation was due not to the will of God but to the greed of some of their countrymen and to their own lifelong passivity. And they saw that the will of God was not that things go on as they had always been, that much of their misery was rooted in their own disunion. The parish team had treated with respect men and women who were fed up with being manipulated, and that respect was infectious. The campesinos were beginning to respect and trust one another and, what's more, they began to respect and trust themselves, conscious for the first time in their lives of their dignity as sons of God.

Then, naturally and inevitably, the movement of the gospel spirit of communion moved beyond the liturgy and the scripture seminars out into a new arena, a new phase of growth. Since they were sons of God, they began to expect to be treated as sons of God by their Catholic employers. As Rutilio tried to make clear in a letter to the president, "By virtue of their conversion and growth in faith, they naturally are becoming agents of change—as the very gospel asks them to be."

The church's evangelization was the first stage. Sooner or later the situation of the peasants—of its nature—had to become political. They had to cooperate and organize. But since the rebellion of 1932, peasant organization had been unconditionally outlawed, and for forty years any hint of it had been savagely crushed. However, the forbidden Federation of Christian Farm Workers (FECCAS—which the church had encouraged, despite government objection) had had a small powerless cell in Aguilares long before Rutilio Grande had arrived on the scene. Now, though, the newly awakened peasants began to be less fearful of it. Like the gospel, political organization seemed perfectly natural now, even essential. Drawn by news of this new spirit in the peasants, more organizers began coming north from the capital. Thus, the labor for political union reaped the fruits of the evangelistic labor for Christian union.

But this put Rutilio Grande between the sword and the wall. He began to wonder if things were not moving too fast. To the slave, freedom is a heady wine indeed.

Hacienda overseers began denying work to the organizers and reported them to the authorities. The peasants began to learn that the road they had chosen was going to be long and difficult. Rutilio saw that the truths he had set free could lead his people to harassment or physical punishment or worse.

Also, the younger members of the team were becoming reckless. One priest, for instance, had been invited by the peasants of the San Francisco plantation to say Mass at a fiesta their *patròn* was throwing for his workers on the feast of St. Francis. Although the owner was a graduate of the Jesuit high school in the capital, had made many eight-day retreats and visited the shrines of St. Ignatius in Spain, his major reason for the fiesta was not to reward his workers but to play the liege lord for many dignitaries, among them the country's candidate for the upcoming Miss Universe Contest to be held in San Salvador.

The owner approached the young priest and said, man-to-man, "Look, Father, say us a short Mass, eh? There's a big dinner, and many of the people from abroad are . . . well, you understand, right?" It was all the priest needed. It had, after all, been the peasants who had invited him. So he began the Mass and preached on the life of the ranch's patron, St. Francis, the rich man who had given up everything to be like the poor Christ. He preached about the wretched lives of the people of the San Francisco Hacienda—the children and their mothers aged before their time, the fathers refused work if they tried to demand basic human justice.

As he preached, he saw Miss El Salvador sitting in the front row, feverishly writing down every word. And the young priest said to himself, "Okay, lady, you just take notes. I bet I can tire you out." So he preached. And he preached. The Mass lasted two hours.

The next day, copies of the homily were spread all over the country among the wealthy; this is what these subversive priests are preaching: rebellion, subversion, communism! Copies were sent to President Molina and to Archbishop Chavez.

The *patròn* of the hacienda came in a fury to see Rutilio. "This priest is an agitator! A communist! He's trying to raise my peasants to revolt!" Rutilio laughed. "Why are you like this? Look, why don't we talk quietly about this?" Still fuming, the landowner appealed to Rutilio, "I was trained by the Jesuits! I can't count how many times I've made the Spiritual Exercises! I was at all the Ignatian shrines in Spain; I saw his room and his books and the daggers he used as a soldier!" Rutilio smiled softly. "It seems to me you spent too much time looking at the daggers." With one sentence he had cornered him. The *patròn* stormed out.

But Rutilio was troubled. He knew that at every Mass he himself said there were spies from ORDEN. He knew that among the university students who came to help the team on weekends there were government plants. Because he had become so influential, the anti-government guerrillas had tried to make contact with him, and even though he had definitively refused, who would believe that? Archbishop Chavez had summoned him to warn him, "Take care. You're moving too fast." Rutilio had tried to calm the archbishop's fears, but when he came back to Aguilares, he told his team, "Take care, guys, because I had a lot of problems down there in the city today."

One of the Jesuits, a Panamanian named Marcelino, was a heroically generous man, working with the peasants day and night, sleeping up in the mountains, in the woods, anywhere. Rutilio had preached often that if one were a Christian he had to take the risk of dying, as Jesus had. But what would happen if they killed Marcelino? He became preoccupied about the safety of the team. He was counting on his notoriety to keep himself safe. He never thought about himself being killed. Not until much later.

Thus, the inner tension. Rutilio saw clearly that his task was evangelization, not political organizing. But at the same time he knew that the realization of Christian dignity was inextricably connected with the realization of human injustice and oppression. On the one hand, he was a religious leader in the midst of his people, a man who should not get involved in the activities of the farm workers' unions. He believed that purely political activism would not only be unfitting to his priesthood, but it would certainly make the authorities see the communities and the unions as identical, even though they were not. He was afraid that the police would break up the seminars, despite the fact that they themselves were in no way political. And yet it was unavoidable that to be against dehumanization was *ipso facto* to be against a dehumanizing government and a dehumanizing economic structure.

On the other hand, he still had to share the lives of his people, who were indeed getting involved in situations which were political in the full sense of that word. Although he insisted that the Kingdom of God transcends any specific project and he adamantly refused to be used by any political group, nonetheless, when the conflicts broke out, he defended his people's right to organize and often took his stand bodily with them. What other alternative did he have?

"The ambiguity of the priesthood!" he wrote. "Some want him to be a kind of non-temporal abstraction. Others want him to be an agitator. He can be neither one nor the other. There is a difference of charisms in the Body of Christ. The priest is the animator of the community toward eternal values, but at the same time toward historical values. It is the members of the community who must now take the eternal values and make them practical with concrete projects and programs."

He begged his people to avoid individuals or groups who tried to manipulate them just the way the authorities had, to avoid fanaticism which could change into blind sectarianism and dogmatism. He prayed in the prayers of the faithful at Mass that the peasants' organizations would bring about just reforms and live the truth without fear.

Rutilio was becoming a very highly visible symbol. When he moved among the people, they looked at him in awe, as a savior. Therefore, he took exquisite care to separate the proclamation of the gospel from every kind of political organization—no matter how praiseworthy and legitimate. At times, painful times, he was accused by people whose ideas he inwardly shared of being insufficiently committed. But he was a man of peace, determined to unite the proclamation of faith with the promotion of justice, committed to be a voice for the voiceless.

Just before Christmas 1975, members of FECCAS, many of whom were also delegates, asked Rutilio for a Mass to start off an organization campaign. The team refused, lest it be misjudged by the authorities. Instead, they would have a "Farmworkers' Christmas," and the organizers could then leave the church and have their demonstration, but there could be no placards or outcries in the church itself. In his homily he said "We can't unite with political groups of any kind, but we cannot remain indifferent before politics which point to the common good of the great majority, the people. We cannot be disinterested, here and now." President Molina promptly accused Rutilio and the team before the archbishop.

The landowners and their newspapers kept insisting that the campesinos were by their very nature utterly incapable of organizing themselves. Therefore, it necessarily had to be the "bad priests" who were the brains behind the farm workers' movement. The workers who were demanding that land rents be lowered and wages be increased were creating chaos all over the country. The priests were revenge-seekers sowing hatred. If the peasants were organizing, they were being manipulated. The Jesuits imperiously ruled over them and plotted their every move. And nothing Rutilio did or said could change their minds.

What infuriated the elite most, perhaps, was facing the impossible: that the peasants were finally standing up and saying, "Enough! It is neither Christian nor human to treat us as you treat your cattle!"

Rutilio was a follower of the God of Exodus. He was never absolutely sure, never able to say, "I have it now. My path is unquestionable." Instead he said to his provincial, César Jerez, "The vow of poverty means permanent instability."

But like St. Thomas More before him, although he kept political silence, his country knew where he stood.

And like Christ before him, Rutilio Grande came to realize that standing for the truth was beginning to look like a flirtation with death.

* * * * * * * *

30 Jun. 76:   President Molina attempted a policy of land transforma-
tion. Essentially, it meant that the government (assisted largely by the U.S. Agency for International Development) would purchase lands from the oligarchy and resell it to 12,000 campesino families. The policy had a two-edged advantage: it pacified the growing demands of the peasants, and it offered great tax incentives to the wealthy to re-invest their earnings in industry. The plan would take decades to effect but, as the government said, it is "an insurance policy for your grandchildren." Nonetheless, the landowners began a furious campaign in the newspapers against this plan.

30 Jul. 76:   Members of the National Guard arrested 17 peasants in
Arcatao. Among them were four women, two of whom were pregnant. They were tied up, beaten, and tortured with electric shocks. They were eventually released.

20 Oct. 76:   The government gave in to the pressure of the campaign
of landowners and financiers. The land reform bill remains in force, but it has been gutted by revisions and will not be acted upon.

40

Fall 76:   Sometime, somewhere, it was decided that Colonel Carlos Humberto Romero would become the next president of El Salvador. He would not have the opportunity to be elected until 20 Feb. 1977, and he would not assume office until 1 Jul. 1977. But he would surely be president.—Colonel Romero promised to regain control over the situation of the peasant uprisings. He promised to "put the national clergy in order" and to "clean the country of foreign revolutionary priests."—Future-President Romero had served as Minister of Defense for the last four years. As such, he had been in charge of all police activities in the country as well. It is he who is supposed to have founded the vigilante society ORDEN. He had built up a law-and-order reputation based on the massacre of peasants at La Cayetana in 1974. As the Latin American Bureau in London has written, his denial of responsibility for the slaughter of students on 30 July 75 "must be treated with scepticism."—Colonel Romero has been quoted as saying there will not be a single Jesuit left in El Salvador within three months after his election.

3 Dec. 76:   The White Warriors Union claimed responsibility for the bombing of the Jesuit Central American University in San Salvador. It was the sixth bombing of the year at the university.

5 Dec. 76:   A hydroelectric dam project begun by President Molina on the Rio Lempa, in the parish of Aguilares, began to fill and flood the land behind it, especially in the Hacienda Colima, whose owners had sold the land to the government. Some of the peasant families who had lived on the plantation for fifty years were forced to move; the owners felt no obligation to help them relocate. On this date, a group of 250 peasants came to see Francisco Orellana, one of the owners. Shots were fired, and the owner's brother, Eduardo, was killed. Versions differ, but according to the peasants, Francisco panicked and began shooting, accidentally shooting his own brother. This version seems to be confirmed by the fact that the rural police arrested no peasants.

10 Dec. 76:   Landowners' and businessmen's organizations began a new campaign in the press. They spoke of "killer hordes" of peasants. They accused Father Rutilio Grande, S.J., by name of leading FECCAS: "Among those there stand out: the parish priests of Aguilares, Rutilio Grande . . ." (*Prensa Gràfica*) They continued to describe such priests as "communists" and "preachers of hate."

11 Dec. 76:   The following day, at the behest of the local landowners, the army occupied El Paisnal under the guise of a military exercise. As the local pastor, Father Rutilio Grande went out to El Paisnal to welcome them. He noticed that, for the sake of public relations, the soldiers had brought medical equipment with them. The priest was quoted as saying, "Ah! You have at last come to help the peasants! How are you? Welcome! We hope that this will not be the only time you come to make the peasants' lives more human!" It is said that, for all their guns, the soldiers looked confused.

41

25 Dec. 76: There continued to be a lack of harmony among the bishops of the country. In communiques the bishop of San Vicente diocese affirmed the autonomy of each diocese and stated that any priest allied with FECCAS in any way should be turned over to the civil law, since he has placed himself not only outside the law but outside his priestly ministry; the bishop of Santa Ana declared that there are indeed groups of "radicalized" priests and religious who are fomenting class struggle among the campesinos.

* * * * * * * *

The list goes on. And on. With the election approaching in February, the pace of the campaign of repression was stepped up. Two Jesuit scholastics who had worked in Aguilares and were in process of leaving the order were expelled from the country. Juan Ramirez, a former Jesuit priest, was arrested and tortured for ten days with electric shocks.

The persecution was focusing closer on Aguilares. Two students from the Catholic University who had been working with the team on weekends were abducted by National Guard members and tortured with electric cattle prods to the face, the body, the testicles. Over and over they were asked, "Are those people guerrillas? Where do they have their training camps?" Finally, they were subjected to *La Capucha*, sacks soaked with insecticide were forced over their heads and faces, searing their eyes and faces. Overwhelmed with terror and shock, they said yes to everything. When they were finally released and returned to the church, they were torn with shame at what they had done. A priest visiting the parish at the time told them, "Don't worry. If they came and tortured me, I'd say yes to everything, too."

At the same time, Rutilio took his provincial aside and said, "Look, if something should happen to me, because that's a strong possibility now—I have arranged with _____* to call you at your office because they have a phone. If you're not there, they'll call the high school and the cathedral, and they can pass the word on to you. And if they cut off the phone, the _____* family will come to San Salvador in their car and tell you what happened."

On 25 January 1977, Father Mario Bernal, whose radio program reached thousands of rural peasants, was arrested and deported without any charges or due process. On the 13th of February, to pro-

*For the safety of the men and women involved, their names cannot be used here.

test Bernal's expulsion, the people of his parish in Apopa held an outdoor concelebration, and at that Mass Rutilio Grande preached the greatest sermon of his life.

"We come to share at this table which is a symbol of our brotherhood, a table with a stool and a big napkin for each human being. We have a common Father, and therefore all of us are brothers. But there are groups of Cains in our family, here in this country. And Cain is an abortion of the plan of God. God in his plan gave us a material world without frontiers—that is not just what I say; it is what Genesis says. But these Cains cry out, 'I bought half of El Salvador with my money, and that gives me certain rights! You cannot argue with that! My word is law because I paid for the right!'

"That cry is a denial of God, who gave us a material world without property boundaries, a table to be shared by all of us as the Eucharist is. The code of the Kingdom of God is love, the key word which sums up all the ethical codes of humanity: love, without boundary lines, exalted and offered in Jesus. It is the love of brothers, which breaks down every sort of barrier and boundary and which must overcome hatred itself. We do not hate anyone; we love even these Cains. The Christian has no enemies, even these Cains. Even they are our brothers. But their contradiction of love creates moral violence which violates us and violates society. And yet the very violence they create unites us and brings us together even though they beat us down, because we bring love against their anti-love, against sin, injustice, the enslavement of mankind and the destruction of our brotherhood by our brother Cains.

"The enslaved masses of our people, those by the side of our road, live in a feudal system six centuries old. They own neither their land nor their own lives. They have to climb up into the trees, and even the trees don't belong to them! Mouths are full of the word 'Democracy,' but let us not fool ourselves. There is no democracy when the power of the people is the power of a wealthy minority, not of the people. You are Cains, and you crucify the Lord in the person of Manuel, of Luis, of Chavela, of the humble campesino.

"I'm quite aware that very soon the Bible and the Gospel won't be allowed to cross our borders. We'll get only the bindings, because all the pages are subversive. And I think that if Jesus himself came across the border at Chalatenango, they wouldn't let him in. They would accuse the Man-God, the prototype of man, of being a rabble-rouser, a foreign Jew, one who confused the people with exotic and foreign ideas, ideas against democracy—that is, against the wealthy minority, that clan of Cains! Brothers, without any doubt, they would crucify him again. And God forbid that I be one of the crucifiers!

"There are those in our brotherhood who would prefer a buried Christ, a dummy to carry through the streets in processions, a Christ with a muzzle in his mouth, a Christ made to the specifications of our whims and according to our own petty interests. They do not want a God who will question us and trouble our consciences, a God who cries out, 'Cain! What have you done to your brother Abel?' Some would rather have a God in the clouds, not Jesus of Nazareth who asks for lives lived in service to establishing a just order, the uplifting of the wretched, the values of the Gospel.

"It is dangerous to be a Christian in our world. It is almost illegal to be a Catholic in our world, where the very preaching of the gospel is subversive and where priests are exiled for preaching it!"

It was a very moving homily. And it did not go unnoticed.

Emboldened by the fact that there had been no other significant criticism of the persecutions from either the church or the public press, the government put on even more pressure. One day after the fraudulent election of General Romero, Fr. Rafael Barahona was kidnapped by the police and tortured. It was the one step too many. Since the beginning of the persecution, the Church had been silent. Now the bishops finally realized that the conflict had reached the point of no return. In the face of his inability to communicate with the authorities, Archbishop Chavez, 75, retired in favor of a younger man, Bishop Oscar Romero (no relation to the president).

The change of bishops was, at first, a disappointing choice in the eyes of the progressives, since Bishop Romero was known to be a meek and reticent man and quite conservative in his views. But it is surprising how quickly persecution can radicalize the true believer. The day after Fr. Barahona's apprehension, Bishop Romero was installed as archbishop with no public ceremony in the chapel of the seminary. That same day he met with President-Elect Romero to demand the release of Fr. Barahona, who then had to be hospitalized with a fractured skull from his torture. At that same meeting, the president-elect handed the new archbishop a list of subversive priests who had been given prior warning of their expulsion. Among them was Rutilio Grande. The president-elect was wasting no time in taking charge. And neither was the archbishop.

As soon as he left Romero's office, the new archbishop issued a communique condemning the new administration's attempt to intimidate

44

the church and interfere with its policy, including the expulsion of foreign priests whose only crime was helping the poor. He also drafted a pastoral letter to the entire archdiocese enumerating in terse, straightforward language the repressions, killings, tortures, disappearances, campaigns by landowners and businessmen against the Church and Archbishop Chavez, and the deportation of priests without consulting the hierarchy.

Completed March 5th, the letter stated that, even at the risk of being misunderstood, the church has to raise its voice and expose sin wherever it is, "in the Pharisees, priests, the wealthy, in Herod or Pilate. All or called by God, rich and poor, but the church must take its stand with the dispossessed."

One week after the new archbishop's meeting with the president-elect, 28 February, the protest against the election was held in Liberty Plaza and hundreds were killed. On March 4th, the National Guard and ORDEN tried to arrest Father Rutilio Sánchez, but they were foiled when he locked his church and began ringing the bells. A crowd gathered outside and prevented his arrest. The soldiers contented themselves with ransacking and plundering the home of four seminarians who lived in the parish.

It was Saturday, March 12, one month after the election of the man who had vowed to sweep El Salvador clean of all Jesuits within three months of his election. With a copy of the archbishop's letter condemning the persecution in his pocket, to read to the people of El Paisnal, Father Rutilio Grande was driving through the canefields toward El Paisnal with an old man, a boy, and three little children.

12 Mar. 1977,
5:55 p.m.

They were almost up to the men now. Father Tilo gripped the wheel with both hands, looking straight ahead, tight-lipped. The truck behind them had picked up speed and was close behind them. There were two men standing behind the cab, leaning on the roof, watching. The men by the road ahead seemed to be holding something at their sides, like hoes or machetes. The leader, the man who was a policeman from El Paisnal, took a drag on his cigarette, nodded, then dropped the cigarette and stepped on it. It was a signal like the one Judas gave: Yes, this is the communist who preached at Apopa.

It happened in an instant. The moment before the jeep came abreast of the men, the automatic rifles whipped up from their sides and flashed fire. Bullets ripped through Rutilio's throat and directly through his left ear, shattering his skull. Don Manuel, mouth agape and stupefied, saw the blood pouring out over this man he was to protect. Instinctively, while the car careened out of control, he clapped his hands to the priest's throat as if to stop the dead man bleeding. The next volley from the left and right shattered the old man's arm and chest. From the rear, nine-millimeter dum-dum bullets scythed through the canvas over the little boys' heads, riveting through the priest's buttocks and splintering his pelvis. The car veered across the road, hit the rusty barbed wire fence and capsized into the ditch, leaning over on its left side.

Two large holes had been torn in the patched back canvas by the bullets, perfectly triangulated onto the driver's seat. It had been expert shooting. And the children were screaming, screaming.

The pickup truck stopped. The men came up on either side of the jeep, angled into the ditch. The old man and the priest huddled, bloody and dead and staring, down against the left door. The boy, Rutilio Lemus, also sat staring, frozen with fear, at the men as they came slowly up to the window. They pulled open the door. Later when he was found, he had only one bullet wound. In his forehead. And the children were screaming.

The one in charge, the policeman with no uniform, looked at the three panic-stricken little boys and snarled, "You! Get the fuck out of here!" They climbed over the scarlet-smeared corpses, without looking, and ran through the canefields, their minds in a delirium of terror and shock, their legs getting heavier, running as if in a dream of relentless pursuit and helpless flight. Behind them they heard one more shot.

The men looked around quickly, leaped into the truck. The driver gunned the engine and they were gone.

The engine of the jeep was still running idly. The wheels still revolved in slow silent circles. The shredded strips of upholstery behind the motionless tangle of corpses rustled indifferently in the freshening evening breeze.

* * * * * * * *

Forty kilometers south of Aguilares, in the capital, Fr. César Jerez, provincial of the Central American Jesuits, was finishing up a four-hour session with one of the small communities of the university faculty. They had talked over and over about their jobs, about the situation of the community, about the growing unrest in the country. As Jerez was about to leave for the community of scholastics where he was staying, the phone rang. The call was for the provincial, from one of the scholastics. Jerez picked up the receiver.

"Gordo!" The voice was tense and shaking. "Gordo, something horrible has happened in Aguilares. Rutilio has been shot. We don't know whether he's alive or not."

Jerez felt a clench in his guts. What they had all known would happen and what they had prayed wouldn't happen had happened.

"All right, stay there. I have my car. I'll come and pick you up, and we'll go right up to Aguilares. I'll be as fast as I can."

On the short ride to the house of the scholastics, Gordo's mind chased itself in circles, from rage to panic to horror to heartache to fear of what reprisals this would trigger. "Oh, God, don't let it be true! Don't let it be true!" But before he could even arrive at the house, the scholastics and a few priests met Jerez on the street, running to meet him, breathless.

"The parish priest of the cathedral called the other university house, and couldn't find you, so I said I'd give a try, too. When we called back to tell them we'd found you, the housekeeper said he was already on his way to Aguilares."

"All right then, let's get to Aguilares ourselves."

One of the scholastics who was a very good driver said, "Gordo, you're too nervous. If you like, let me drive." And Jerez moved over.

One of the fathers said he'd like to come along, but Jerez said, "Look, Ricardo, you're here on a tourist visa. If the police stop us and ask for our papers it'll be be 'how' and 'why' and 'why don't you go back where you came from?' Let Paco come. He's the former provincial, and he was born in El Salvador, and I need a Salvadorean."

So they raced up the highway north to Aguilares, very fast, passing several other cars filled with Jesuits along the way. As they went, Gordo

Jerez kept saying, "Oh, my God, I wish this were just a dream. But it's real. Maybe they've only machine-gunned the house." But when they arrived in Aguilares and saw so many people crowded around the plaza, around the Church, around the house, he knew that something very, very bad had happened. They had come from the communities of the hills and valleys, merely to stand and wait. As he pushed through the weeping crowd, he heard them staying, "Father Provincial is coming; let Father Provincial through. Let him go into the house."

As he opened the gate and closed it on the noisy crowd, he found the yard between the church and the house strangely quiet. And then he saw them. Laid out on the tables where they had eaten their last supper a couple of hours before were the three bloodied bodies. For a minute Jerez was dizzy with it. After all the uncertainty and wondering and hoping for the best, the reality was like a blow in the stomach. Somebody had already changed Rutilio's shirt, but the back of his head was a sodden mass. His arms were folded over his chest, and blood was soaking through the new shirt.

More Jesuits began hesitantly to come through the gate. Jerez took a deep breath and turned to them. "Let's have Mass. Let's bring the bodies into the church so that the people will not keep suspecting maybe yes, maybe no. They should know that they have been killed. And we will have a liturgy and try to give them some hope, so that they won't hate."

At that moment, the provincial was a very powerful man. The feeling in that plaza was so incendiary that a mere word from him could have ignited a riot. Later, when the new president accused the Jesuits of being inciters to violence, Jerez could say to him, "Look. That night. What we *could* have done! We could have destroyed the whole town that night. With one word!" But like his old friend whose body the men were lifting to their shoulders and carrying behind him through the crowds to the church, César Jerez did not live by politicians' rules.

The three bodies were laid on rough tables in front of the altar. A dozen priests were getting vested, and the crowds were packing into the pews and along the aisles and in the windows and outside in the square. As they were about to begin, the new archbishop arrived and agreed to preside. His jaws working and his emotions held tightly in check, Jerez preached the homily. He preached on the fourth decree of the last Jesuit Congregation, on "the faith that must do justice." Rutilio had been trying to teach precisely that, and for so doing he was dead. He had been slaughtered with an old peasant who had borne the injustice his whole lifetime and with a young peasant who he hoped would never have to accustom himself to the same lifelong degradation. All three of them had died because their faith in the transforming Savior had called them to work for the transformation of their country. They had been killed on their way to offer Mass, and here they were at last.

At the very moment Jerez was preaching, however, units of the army were taking up positions all around the town. All roads in and out had been blocked. For some reason, all of the telephones in the town went temporarily out of service.

The first thing to be done after the Mass was to have an autopsy. The auxiliary bishop, who was an expert in canon law, and several other priests went to the judge to demand that the bodies be examined. But everything in town had simply "stopped." There was no time; it was too late. No one is capable. We haven't the right instruments. The final official documents state: "the deaths occurred as a result of lesions produced by firearms;" nothing more.

Finally, Jerez found a doctor who had had experience in forensic medicine who agreed to examine the bodies. His findings show that the bullets were 9 mm. armor-plated "dum-dum" bullets from Mantzer automatic rifles, the kind issued to the police. The soft bullets make a small opening and then when they press into the flesh expand to many times their original thickness. Rutilio had taken twelve shots, which were fired from a distance of about ten yards, all of them deadly except for one in his foot. Jerez stayed at the doctor's side for the whole bloody ritual.

Then the father of Rutilio Lemus came and, humbly, asked for the body of his boy. His wife was at home, waiting, to wash the body and sit watch with it through the night. Jerez took the man by the arm, "You are right. But the archbishop would like to have a big Mass in the cathedral, with all three together, so that no one will ever forget these deaths, so that it may help keep this from happening to other men's sons."

The man looked at the priest, his face impassive and his eyes full of tears. "All right." And Jerez knew that the man had approved not for the country, nor for his fellow peasants, but because he had loved Rutilio, and so had this priest. That was enough.

The provincial had decided that there would be no special coffin for the priest, but that all three would be buried in exactly the same kind of coffin. The archbishop said, "When I left my house, I didn't know what had happened, so I grabbed whatever money I could find. If you need this, please take it."

"No, Monsignor," Jerez answered, "We have the money."

"Please?"

"Fine."

The bodies were washed and dressed, the priest in white vestments with a large wooden cross in his hands, the two peasants in bleached white collarless peasant shirts, and they were carried in their open coffins back to the main aisle of the church. All night long the towns-people came filing by—tear-washed faces, angry faces, deadened faces—to look down at the peaceful faces of the white-haired priest, the stiff-backed old man, and the proud boy.

The first Mass that Sunday morning was said by Marcelino, but Jerez had to warn him before he began, "Be careful of what you preach. I don't want another Rutilio murdered." Again at 9:00 the Mass was packed with people, weeping and singing, in resolutely joyful mourning.

Probably the only Americans who can understand the feeling of the country that weekend are those who lived through the three numbing days after the assassination of John Kennedy. It was still too great and awesome to comprehend. Here was a man of hope, crushed. And for precisely that reason, Jerez and the archbishop had to be extremely cautious. On the one hand, there was no way in the world they could allow this tragedy to go unnoticed; on the other hand, they had to be scrupulously careful that whatever they said or did would not provoke either rioting by the peasants or even further reprisals by the army.

At mid-morning, red-eyed with fatigue, César Jerez drove south to San Salvador, spoke with the General of the Society of Jesus in Rome by transatlantic phone, and slept for about one hour. He had been up for over thirty hours without sleep, and was to direct a meeting of all the available Jesuits and then to attend a meeting of all the priests in the capital to plan a united response to the tragedy. "Please, Gordo," they begged him, "be very clear-headed. Think before whatever you say."

At the meeting with the archbishop, the priests realized that the confrontation time for the united church had come. It was proposed that the following Sunday there would be only one Mass celebrated in the entire archdiocese. All other churches would be closed. All the Catholic schools in the archdiocese would be closed for a week. Any free assembly had been prohibited by martial law. But, despite the opposition of the government, the archbishop agreed. He also issued a bulletin announcing the *ipso facto* excommunication for anyone who has murdered a priest. He described Rutilio as a priest who made the peasants "conscious of their dignity as persons, of the fundamental rights that belong to every person as a human being. That kind of work disturbs many; and so to end it, its promotor had to be liquidated." Like the prophets of the Old Testament, Rutilio had refused to leave their consciences limply at peace.

Monday morning the cathedral was packed to the walls and to the ceiling, and thousands upon thousands jammed the plaza outside. Over a hundred thousand people gathered with two hundred priests, four bishops, and the papal nuncio for the funeral Mass. Thousands more were turned back by the National Guard troops. Massive participation by the peasants and poor—on a work day and despite a law expressly forbidding such a gathering—began to signal the strengthening of an alliance between the reawakened peasants and the reawakened church which the government found particularly unsettling.

When the Mass was over, the three coffins were carried through the overwhelming crowds first by vested priests and then passed from hand to hand by the people into the waiting hearses. "To travel with Rutilio on the way to El Paisnal," they said, "is to travel with Christ on his way to the cross." The bodies were driven north to their home parish and, at three in the afternoon, they were buried. The people returned with their guitars to sing, to share their food—and to applaud! The prophet of peace and of the poor was finally laid to rest among his own—he who had once thought himself unworthy to be a priest.

* * * * * * * *

But that was not the end, not by any means. If the forces of repression believed that exterminating one priest was sufficient warning to end further opposition, they were severely mistaken. It was, in fact, the critical catalyst which galvanized many of the previously disparate elements of the Salvadorean church. There had been many, even bishops, who had sided with the oligarchy, deploring Rutilio's methods if not, perhaps, his message. But when old friends are killed, many of our old self-delusions are killed along with them.

Rutilio's death brought about a radical change of perspective in many Salvadorean Christians. What's more, his blood was seed—like dragon's teeth—which grew quietly into a peaceful army of men and women who finally realized that they couldn't take it any more. But the government did not knuckle under to this upsurge of hope, nor did its bullyboys. The struggle to establish the Kingdom of Heaven was very clearly not going to be waged in the clouds but in the backstreets and prisons of El Salvador.

* * * * * * * *

5 Mar. 77: At 8 p.m. on the Saturday before Fr. Grande's death, Felipe Salinas had been apprehended in his house in the village of La Finquita by agents of the National Guard. They dragged him from his house in his underwear and interrogated him about the religious services he had organized and about his meetings with the parish priest. When they did not get the answers they wanted, they beat him up and put on him a long red cape and a crown. They put a make-shift cross on his shoulders and hauled him along the road from Coma-sagua to Shila. After three miles the Guards tired of the game and left him battered by the side of the road.—Ten days later, Salinas was again dragged from his house by the same soldiers, interrogated about his religious work and told that he was going to be cut to pieces if he did not answer. They made surface cuts on both his arms and packed his mouth with mud made from urine. They dragged him along the ground, stamped on his chest with their boots, and left him with the promise that the next time they would kill him.

Holy Week: FECCAS, the peasant organization, occupied unused land overgrown with weeds owned by Señora Faustina Tejada with the hope of buying or renting the land. As one campesino put it: "There are hundreds of rural workers in this area who have more than eight children and nowhere to get work. Where are they going to work? Everyone should answer that question. Is it a crime to work land that this woman is not working at all and was just producing weeds? Is that a crime? Is it a crime to eat? Is it a crime to work in order to raise a family?" Señora Tejada refused to negotiate. Landowners accused the archbishop of being connected with these land seizures.

19 Apr. 77: Mauricio Borgonovo, the Salvadorean Foreign Minister, was kidnapped by the Popular Forces of Liberation, one of the two left-wing guerrilla groups in the country, who previously had claimed also to have killed the Minister of Tourism and a former president. Borgonovo belonged to one of the country's richest families, but was known to have fairly progressive ideas, even to supporting Land Reform in the face of almost unanimous opposition from the Establishment. The family offered to pay a ransom, but the kidnappers demanded the release of 37 political prisoners. The Government at first denied holding any prisoners at all, and then admitted it held only six of them.

It refused to negotiate, in spite of the pleas of the family and the archbishop's offer to mediate. Several observers suggested at the time that the Government could not negotiate because most of the 37 had already been eliminated. The kidnappers remained just as adamant, resisting even a plea from Pope Paul VI.

21 Apr. 77:   The clandestine White Warriors Union accused the Jesuits of responsibility for the Borgonovo kidnapping and publicly vowed vengeance on all subversive priests if the Minister was killed.

1 May 77:   In the midst of the mounting tension over the Borgonovo kidnapping, government troops broke up a Labor Day rally, killing at least eight people. The government claimed that the eight had been guerrillas who had opened fire on the armed forces; their corpses were displayed in Cuscatlan Park. Eyewitnesses claimed that the demonstration had been peaceful and that the number of dead was actually between 20 and 30.

That same evening, Jorge Sarsandas, a young Panamanian Jesuit, who had worked with Rutilio Grande in Aguilares, returned by bus to San Salvador after spending the night and saying Mass in a rural parish some distance away from the capital. Police arrested him shortly after his return and accused him of organizing that morning's demonstration, even though he had been miles away. He was also accused of "a long record of subversive activities." Five days later he was deported back to Panama. The newspaper *El Mundo* headlined the story **"Priest Expelled for Subversive Activities."** Despite the fact that there had been no trial, the paper did not use the word "alleged."

11 May 77:   The corpse of Foreign Minister Borgonovo was finally found dumped by the side of a road ten miles south of San Salvador. He had been shot twice in the head. That evening, men armed with machine guns burst into a youth meeting in the Church of Fr. Alfonso Navarro, whose church and car had been bombed eight months before. The intruders gunned down Navarro and Fr. Navarro said, "I know I die for preaching the gospel and teaching the truth. I know who are guilty of my death. I want them to know I forgive them." In a quite different tone, the White Warriors Union telephoned a newspaper three hours later: "This is only the beginning of our vengeance for Minister Borgonovo."

12 May 77:   The day after the retaliatory murder of Fr. Navarro, the Cattlemen's Association took out a full-page ad in the newspapers accusing the Jesuits of being a vast subversive group ready to take over the country and establish a communist state. Smaller ads had been appearing all along, signed by phantom groups calling themselves Followers of Christ the King, Association for Catholic Improvement, Salvadorean Christian Society. All of them proclaimed messages like: "**Communism threatens your children. Don't let it be enthroned in our nation!**" Or, "**Mothers! Terrorism threatens your children. Unite to defend them!**"

The most chilling of all was a printed flyer which appeared tacked up in the residential areas of the capital: **BE A PATRIOT! KILL A PRIEST!**

18 May 77: Government troops moved into El Paisnal to evict 150 peasant families who had begun to squat on unused land in the San Francisco Hacienda. The land had traditionally been rented out to peasants but this year, for some reason, the estate owner had refused. Transported by helicopters and armored trucks, hundreds of troops and National Guards forced the squatters off the land at gunpoint and sealed off the town. They conducted house-to-house searches; property deeds were stolen; occupants were beaten and tortured at random; people were shot and hundreds were arrested and taken away. El Paisnal was held incommunicado.

19 May 77: Moving south to Aguilares at dawn the following day, 45 truckloads of soldiers and police surrounded the town, blocked any entrance or exit, and effectively rendered the entire area incommunicado. On the grounds that the church was turning the death of Rutilio Grande into an excuse for violent uprisings and seizure of land by the peasants, the parish was turned into an armed camp. The army code name for the raid was "Operation Rutilio."

Soldiers and policemen surrounded the church with tanks and broke down the door. They grabbed the three Jesuits and the three laymen with them, knocked them down, stripped them and blindfolded them. Then they began to tear the church apart. First they pulled down and destroyed the large picture of Grande that had been set up over the altar. They smashed windows and overturned the pews. Then they blasted open the tabernacle with bullets, threw the hosts all over the floor and trampled on them. The police chaplain, Fr. José Vides, tried to intervene to save the Blessed Sacrament and was himself arrested. The church was turned into a barracks.

The troops then moved out into the town to conduct a house-to-house search "for concealed weapons and subversive literature." If anyone had a picture of Rutilio in his home, he or she was tortured, arrested, and—capriciously—either taken away in trucks or released or shot. By 2:30 in the afternoon, one army squad was detailed exclusively to dig graves and another just to bring bodies and bury them. The official government bulletin said that only seven were killed in the "police action." Four priests and two nuns who were there said that hundreds were slaughtered.

One victim, Mario Cardena, was handcuffed so tightly for ten hours to another prisoner that his hands turned purple. The two men were bent over in such a way that their own excrement and urine ran into their mouths.

54

One priest who was imprisoned and tortured during the eight days Aguilares was under siege was Fr. Victor Guevara Siguenza. He and about fifty others had their thumbs bounds together with wire. Soldiers forced Guevara to spread out face down on the floor and they stomped on his back. When he rolled over in agony, they kicked him in the stomach. They laughed at him: "all priests should lick the ground the way you do!"

Homes were searched and looted; women were raped. Several foreign correspondents had come to the perimeter to witness the so-called "army maneuvers." But the sergeant gave them a complete body search and told them, "You have two minutes to get out of here, or I'll handcuff you and take you with me."

One eyewitness asked the question: "Is it a crime to have a photo of Father Grande? Is it a crime to have the Gospel in your house? Is it a crime to study the Bible with your family and your neighbors?"

20 May 77:   The Minister of Defense and the Minister of Interior issued bulletins implicating the Jesuit Fathers of Aguilares in subversion.

21 May 77:   Archbishop Romero himself was refused permission to enter Aguilares and recover the Eucharist.

22 May 77:   President Molina gave a speech on national television assuring his people that there was no persecution of the church. There was positive proof that many priests have actively participated in subversive activities, and he had never made any promises to leave these traitorous men to the disposal of their archbishop.

25 May 77:   FARO, the landowners' organization, published a paid advertisement linking Archbishop Romero with Marxist infiltration. "The church is not being persecuted by the government; rather, it is the other way around. To persecute Jesuits is not to persecute the church."

On that same day, the government stepped up its campaign to expel priests, now including not only foreigners but two Salvadoreans: Fathers Inocencio and Hyginio Alas. As early as seven years before, Inocencio had been arrested for speaking as the church delegate to the first National Congress on Agrarian Reform. When the order for his assassination was revoked, he had been forced to drink a full quart of pure raw alcohol. He was then driven out into the mountainous countryside, stripped and left to die. He was nine days in an emergency center fighting for his life. For the next six years he had been the object of continuous death threats and propaganda against him in the press, on radio and television. He was brought to court for inciting the peasants to revolt, and, oddly, acquitted—"oddly," not because he was guilty but because the Salvadorean judiciary is as much an agent of the government as the army itself. His parish house was set on fire and later bombed. After continual arrests, he finally took refuge in the home of the papal nuncio and escaped to the U.S.

Throughout these pages one must consistently remind himself that what is described here did not take place hundreds of years ago or in an atheist iron curtain country. It took place in our own time and in a professedly Catholic country of the Western hemisphere.

7 Jun. 77: So many priests have been arrested, expelled, or "disappeared" that fifteen parishes are now left without priests. There are daily house searches and looting in the homes of men and women suspected of Marxist subversion. Parents place pictures of their "disappeared" children in the papers in the hope that someone released from prison can tell them that the children are still alive. Corpses have been seen floating in rivers, but no one dares retrieve them for fear of reprisal.

Meanwhile, ads from previously unknown organizations continued to call the Jesuits "the hangmen of bourgeois society." The ads go on to claim that the Jesuits have always been liars, false prophets and divisive. They are adept at manipulating people and institutions in order to obtain their secret purposes. They are hypocrites spreading the gospel of "St. Marx." They are communists who incite people to violence from the pulpits, lectures, and classes. It is not at all unlikely that out of their blind ambition and greed for power they themselves murdered Father Grande in order to reduce the country to a state of anarchy.

21 Jun. 77:

War Order No. 6
San Salvador, June 21, 1977.

The Supreme Command of the White Warriors Union (*Unión Guerrera Blanca—U.G.B.*) in the face' of the criminal persistence of those groups that, through the bloodying of our fatherland, plan to enslave it to international Communism orders:

1) All Jesuits without exception must leave the country forever within 30 days of this date. These miserable supporters of the murderous Popular Forces of Liberation have no reason to continue poisoning our people.

2) The religious orders and priests who are not agents of international communism have nothing to fear from us and can continue their work in complete tranquility. Our struggle is not against the Church but against Jesuit guerrillaism (*el guerrillerismo jesuitico.*

3) If our order is not obeyed within the indicated time, the immediate and systematic execution of all Jesuits who remain in the country will proceed until we have finished with all of them. Further: We warn A) all neighbors, B) parents and students, C) employees that if as of the indicated date there is disobedience, all Jesuit installations and places frequented by them will be considered military targets. Since this warning has been made with sufficient anticipation,

we will not be responsible for the death of third persons as a consequence of our operations.

4)   According to the circumstances, the U.G.B. reserves the initiative to effect operations before the deadline.

Love live the Commandos of Liberty!
War to the death with international Communism!
The Fatherland to Power!
White Warrior Union
W.W.U.

The deadline is July 20, 1977.

To this threat, the Jesuits responded: "The Jesuits will stay in El Salvador. We will not leave unless we are expelled or physically eliminated. Christian power is far stronger than a two-edged sword because it is based on the teachings of Jesus Christ. It is a power that neither money nor guns can destroy."

1 Jul. 77:   General Humberto Romero was sworn in as President of El Salvador. For the first time in the history of the country, the Roman Catholic archbishop was not present for the inauguration. Furthermore, Archbishop Romero made it clear that he would boycott any civil ceremony at which the president might appear. There were, of course, strong negative reactions to this announcement—from the landowners, the government, and from the papal nuncio. The Romero government promised that when they took power no priests would be killed or deported.

As the deadline approached for the "immediate and systematic execution" of the Jesuits as "agents of international communism," Jesuits in the U.S., particularly Fr. James Connor, S.J., and Fr. Simon Smith, S.J., in Washington, D.C. began a feverish campaign to keep the matter in the public press and before the eyes of the American government. Already two priests had been assassinated, eight arrested and tortured, fifteen expelled and five denied re-entry. The Jesuits feared that once the attention of the international press waned, the Romero government would feel free to slaughter even more indiscriminately. Congressman Donal Fraser initiated hearings on religious persecution in El Salvador. The Carter administration sent a stern warning through the State Department to President Romero. Romero promised that his government would "repress violence energetically no matter where it came from."

For their protection, Jesuits were accompanied everywhere by two or three laymen. They exchanged their clerical suits and collars for lay clothes. They traveled by day only in groups, tried to stay home at night, and did not answer doors except at prearranged signals.

The students at the *Colegio Externado* hung up a homemade sign which proclaimed: **"Christ said, 'Be joyous if they are persecuting you.!'"**

Ironically, most of the students of that high school used to be the sons of rich landowners. As one exiled Jesuit commented, "For years we have worked with the wealthy classes, but many of those who were our students are now our worst enemies." A Jesuit publication wrote: "Some who invited us yesterday to their table today seek our crucifixion. Some who yesterday enjoyed and boasted about the education we gave them and felt honored to have been associated with us today make accusations against us and drag our name down in shame . . . They are horrified that we urge them to consider that 'he who says he loves God whom he does not see, but does not love his brothers whom he does see, is a liar.'" (I John 4/20)

21 Jul. 77: A *New York Times* headline read: **"Jesuits remain in Salvador as Death Deadline Nears."** One of the Jesuits said, "We are trusting in God and, perhaps, the government."

The deadline date passed without incident. And the next day, and the next. President Romero seemed to have a great deal of persuasive power over the White Warriors Union.

26 Aug. 77: Two lay deacons, Felipe Chacòn and Serafin Vàsquez, were found executed in El Salitre. Chacòn's body showed that his skin had been torn from his face and his head scalped to delay identification, and Vasquez had been hacked to death with machetes in his home. A government release said that the men were cattle thieves who tried to ambush treasury agents. They were also accused of holding "secret political meetings with local peasants."

25 Nov. 77: The Church was surely not completely united against the injustices done to its fellow members. Father José Pineda, 29, and the leaders of the Brotherhood of the Holy Interment in the town of Quezaltepeque accused Archbishop Romero in *El Diario de Hoy* of "fomenting hatred between the classes and withdrawing from the norms of the Church to sow division among the people." It also claimed that connections could be found between the archbishop and the communists. The journal, *La Opiniòn,* ran inch-high headlines on its front page: **"In the deaths of three policemen, RESPONSIBILITY BELONGS TO MONSIGNOR ROMERO: The Archbishop Has Turned the Temple of God into a Sanctuary for Terrorism and a Refuge for Criminals."** Even in the U.S., the ultra-right-wing *Mindszenty Report*, in its October issue, heavily intimated that the incidents had been "orchestrated by the Jesuits themselves for publicity and to gain sympathy for their campaign against the government of El Salvador . . . It is characteristic of these Jesuits to get the drop on seekers after truth by accusing their opponents of the very crimes of which the Jesuits themselves are guilty . . . (All of which) leads to further questions about an organized campaign against the anti-Communist nations of Latin

America . . . The threat of communism in El Salvador and other nations is growing and being abetted by a number of revolutionary Marxist clergy who visualize Christ as a guerrilla leader."

22 Nov. 77:   Father Miguel Ventura, pastor of Osicala, three catechists, and his sexton, were tormented by security forces who raided the church and occupied the town while searching for accomplices of an alleged guerrilla. Father Ventura was tortured all day long; he was beaten in the stomach and the face; his hands were tied behind him and he was hoisted by his hands over a tree branch in his back yard; when he refused to confess to guerrilla links, the soldiers stuffed a rag in his mouth to drown out his cries and took him into the garage for futher torture. "I was hung up twice, for about five minutes each time," Fr. Ventura said later. "The first time I was thinking that no matter how bad the pain gets, I have to maintain my posture as a Catholic priest and not give in. But the second time, I couldn't think of anything but the pain. It was unbearable, and I was screaming." The three catechists were beaten and burned on the feet.

During the occupation of the town, soldiers confiscated Bibles and catechisms along with other papers, threw a group of worshipers out of the church, and forced open the sacristy looking for "subversive propaganda." When parishioners went for help to Bishop José Alvarez of San Miguel, he said he could not bring the matter to the local police commander because he was not familiar with the background of events. Bishop Alvarez holds the rank of colonel in the army of El Salvador.

After signing confessions, the priest and all but one of the laymen were released. The one detained has never been seen again. A month later, Fr. Ventura said in the U.S., "The tremendous poverty and misery of El Salvador are not unknown. But even worse is that when a man does learn to lift up his head and begin to think about who he is, he meets with worse oppression than that of hunger. He meets fear and constant threats. To speak of human rights in El Salvador is really to degrade the concept. They don't exist."

25 Nov. 77:   The government began to become worried. The landowners' paid advertisements in the papers began to hint that the root problem might be the government's inability to deal with the Marxist incursions of these revolutionary priests. Therefore: "In order to counteract the terrorist attacks and the provocation of international subversion, the Legislative Assembly today decreed the 'Law of Defense and Guarantee of Public Order.'" In effect, this law suspended all rights to strike, organize, assemble, protest, be judged by a jury. It made it a crime punishable by up to three years in jail to send out of the country information such as that contained in this book. For this reason—which still exists—many names and sources have been deleted in these pages.

12 Jan. 78:   Congressman Robert Drinan, S.J., and two other
                American experts on El Salvador concluded a five-day
investigation into the human rights violations in El Salvador. In the
usual one-inch headlines, *La Opiniòn* screamed: **"In this upheaval of the
public peace RESPONSIBILITY LIES WITH THE JESUITS."**
Subheads of articles within its pages included: **"Foreign Priests in El
Salvador with Contacts to the Terrorist International Mafia; Members
of the Society of Jesus, Orchestrators of the Campaign to Shame Our
Country; The Priest Drinan Brings Instructions from the Marxists to
Monsignor Romero; The Triangle of the Devil."** This Triangle, as an article inside the paper reveals, is composed of: resident foreign Jesuits,
Archbishop Romero, and the congressman-priest Drinan who is also a
"member of the international Jesuit syndicate."

On 10 January, Fr. Drinan had had a meeting with President
Romero:

Romero:

I invited the Archbishop to fill any vacancies with priests from abroad. I
said to give me a list of the vacancies and of the candidates to fill them.
Let me see where those candidates would come from, the countries and
churches where they are working. We would investigate and decide who
can come.

Drinan:

That is interference in the church. It is not for a president to say who is a
good priest and who is a bad priest.

Romero:

Yes, it is, if they interfere in the business of the government. Priests go
from one place to another and not in real discharge of religious duties.
They should have one jurisdiction in which they perform their functions.

Drinan:

That's not for you to say; that's for the archbishop to say.

Romero:

Is the clergy under the president or not? . . .

Drinan:

You say you have no political prisoners, but friends, parents, relatives
tell me the contrary. And dozens of people approach me on behalf of persons who have been killed or disappeared. You say you have no political
prisoners. Perhaps they are already dead.

I cannot guarantee one way or the other. But since July 1 it is my responsibility and no one has been detained since then.

In El Salvador—as elsewhere—many Christians do not realize that they attack Christ himself not only when they assassinate a priest or bomb a Church or trample the Eucharist underfoot, but just as effectively when they beat a peasant.

Rutilio Grande had always written out his homilies because, "if I don't, I'm bound to get carried away!" In response to those who attacked him for building small scripture communities he said:

The so-called Catholic Conservatives are preoccupied with a god of money and their own interests, a god made by human hands and plastered over with the blood of their own innocent brothers. They rise up thinking in the name of their almighty god, Money, without so much as a thought for the filthy, squalid, anemic poor millions of campesinos. Hypocrites! To call yourselves *Catholic* Conservatives is a lie. But I pardon you and forgive you your gratuitous and baseless attacks, and I give my life that you may be converted and saved by recognizing the injustices to God in this country.

Then, quite suddenly on that evening in March, Rutilio Grande was silenced. But not really. He had passed on his voice like a torch to the campesinos of El Salvador. After the siege of Aguilares a peasant who five years before had borne his despair in silence said:

What we learned from those soldiers is that no one and nothing can take away what we feel. This even strengthens us to see if we are really faithful to the Word of God and to his church, of which we also form a part. These times and these tests which God sends us shake up the church and take away what is unsure. Only what is really faithful to him and sure of his Word remains. So we must be constant in His Word and in prayer to God so that he will have mercy on his people and grant realization of the truth and repentance to those who persecute the church and torture Christians. This reminds me of when Saul persecuted the church and God granted him realization of the truth and repentance because of the prayer of Christians. Afterwards he was one of the most fervent apostles in God's apostolate.

Within seven months of Rutilio's assassination, thirty-three young men applied to enter the Central American Province of the Society of Jesus. That is surely a large number for a province which numbered only 250 men at Grande's death. It is surely a sign of something.

And it surely shows what a shy, self-doubting man can do when he forgets his own abilities and walks out onto the water with his eyes only on the Lord.

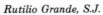
Rutilio Grande, S.J.

*Pictures on this page come from
the book* RUTILIO GRANDE:
Martir de la Evangelación Rural.

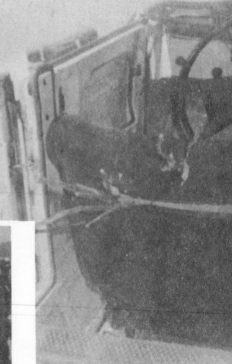

Back view of driver's seat.

Safari jeep as it landed after shots.

II

RHODESIA

JOHN   CONWAY,   S.J.

MARTIN   THOMAS,   S.J.

CHRISTOPHER   SHEPHERD — SMITH, S.J.

Time: 10:00 p.m., 6 February 1977
Place: St. Paul's Mission outside the
village of Musami, in the black
Tribal Reserve 45 miles northeast
of Salisbury, Rhodesia

*I only have escaped, alone, to tell
you.*
— Job, 1/16

Coped in morning mist, the massive bulwarks of the ancient city of Zimbabwe rise up out of the lush green jungle at the southeastern edge of the Rhodesian highveld—Zimbabwe—"The Great Stone House of the King." This huge edifice curves into a great oval whose walls stand thirty feet high, each stone exquisitely fitted to the next without any mortar. To the self-important European it is inconceivable that such an architectural feat, of such fantastic size and contour, could have been raised by "ignorant" black Bantu natives hundreds upon hundreds of years ago, without the benevolent guidance of white men. And yet, for centuries Zimbabwe has hulked high on its hill, enduring the lashing of monsoons, the lacerating heat, and the predatory hands of man.

Despite the green fortress of nearly impenetrable jungle, the mysteries of this ancient stronghold have lured adventurers—African, Muslim, Portuguese, and British—to hazard their lives to find its key, because, over all those years, the false legend persisted: Zimbabwe is the fabled land of Ophir, the palace of the Queen of Sheba, and the site of King Solomon's Mines.

In the mid-sixteenth century, drawn by the siren song of Solomon's treasures, the Portuguese began pressing into the forests in order to liberate the black Shona tribes from their Heart of Darkness, to shed the light of Christ on them and save their souls by freeing them from their gold. Very often these Europeans proved to be neither more intelligent nor more civilized nor more high-minded than the savages they came to domesticate, but a blunderbuss pitted against a handful of six-foot *assegai* war spears soon established quite satisfactorily the true superiority.

Although they found no gold to speak of, the Portuguese had discovered a land of fantasy: great rivers along whose mudbanks toothsome crocodiles momentarily snoozed in the hot sun; ungainly thousand-year-old baobabs, "upside-down trees," whose spindly branches look like roots reaching up from trunks ten feet thick; and a treasure of fabulous flowers flaming in the sharp white sunshine—lavender jacaranda trees, foxglove orchids, thistly purple infulsas six feet high. Much later, the British Doctor David Livingstone would discover the tiara of Zimbabwe—the mile-wide amethyst cascade of Victoria Falls, plunging 350 feet from the thrashing Zambezi, twice as high as Niagara. One uses the word "discover" as if a place cannot exist until a European has seen it with his own eyes. For centuries the Shona had called the great falls *Musi oa tunya*, "The Smoke that Thunders."

There is, of course, a serpent in every Eden. The intruders also discovered the anopheles mosquito and the tsetse fly which, respectively, shared malaria and sleeping sickness with their guests, no matter what their land of origin.

After the Portuguese, the first outsiders to challenge the Shona were other Africans. Fresh from conquests in Zululand (South Africa) the Matabele, "The People of the Long Shield," marched into southern Zimbabwe in search of a new home. The Matabele were born warriors, and no man was allowed to marry until he had "washed his spear in blood." Within a few years, far better armed and experienced in battle, the Matabele had reduced many of the southern Shona tribes to tribute-paying vassals and established a new capital at Bulawayo, "The Place of the Killing." If a Shona village refused to pay tribute, its men were slaughtered and the women and children enslaved. The Matabele raided far and wide to rustle cattle and to loot produce at harvest time, and their rapine sowed a blood-hatred between the Shona and the Matabele which lasts to this day.

When the Matabele chief Lobengula at last became chief of all Zimbabwe in 1870, he inherited a centralized tribal organization that had perfected the arts of war and plunder. But there were other warriors and plunderers to the south—white men—who, unlike the African planters and husbandmen, knew that the value of the land lay not in its forests and savannahs but beneath it: gold.

Today, except to black nationalists, the land locked between the Zambezi River on the north, Mozambique to the east, and South Africa and Botswana to the south is no longer called Zimbabwe. It is named, instead after still another legend: Cecil Rhodes—idealist, schemer, financial genius, statesman, bountiful philanthropist, diamond magnate, and unscrupulous empire builder.

In 1859 Rhodes encouraged and partially subsidized a trek from South Africa by the London Missionary Society to the court of King Lobengula in their hope of beginning a mission in Zimbabwe. In deference to the black king, these gentlemen had to approach his throne on their knees across the earthen floor of his *kraal*—which was thickly carpeted with new and ancient cow dung. Since cattle were the source of wealth, the thicker the carpet, the more awesome its owner. But the emissaries' conquest of fastidiousness succeeded, and they were somewhat reluctantly allowed to establish a mission station at Ingati. And into the hands of the missionary society's patrons, Cecil Rhodes and DeBeers, Ltd., King Lobengula unwittingly bartered away his birthright—all the metals beneath the ground in Zimbabwe. They were surely useless to him; and in exchange, he received a handsome reimbursement of $500 a month, a thousand rifles, and a gunboat. Five years later, the guns were rusting away because the British had not also agreed to teach the natives how to fire them or keep them in repair.

A year after this concession, ignoring Lobengula's protests, Rhodes sent an initial column consisting of the Pioneer Corps and an escort of five troops of British South African Police, supported by 200 Ngwato natives to occupy Mashonaland. This spearhead thrust far beyond the king's encampment into the central plateau and establish a fort at Salisbury. Thus began, in effect, a systematic undeclared war of conquest of the Shona and Matabele lands. Cecil Rhodes could well be piously grateful for that minor religious success of the London Missionary Society. Once again, the church had become the head of the spear, wielded in the hands of the predators. The dalliance of the church with Caesar has always been an unhappy one.

For the conquered, the conditions laid down by Rhodes belied his calm and benevolent assurances at the time of surrender. After the occupation, the majority of the police were disbanded, each member receiving 4,500 acres of Zimbabwe land at a small rent. Each of the troopers received 3,000 acres and 15 gold claims.

But Rhodesia was then a land without roads, without railways, without adequate supplies and with the ever-present danger of the dispossessed and humiliated natives all around them. The new white farmers lived in mud huts in isolated areas. Fort Salisbury was a shanty town. Not until a year after the occupation were women allowed to enter Rhodesia and begin to establish homes.

But with the same grim determination that moved settlers to open up the American West, the Rhodesian pioneers began carving settlements out of the veldt. They did not find the fabulous treasures of diamonds and gold their ancestors had found in South Africa, but the red earth was rich and fertile. And they found something as valuable as precious stones: ludicrously cheap African labor, black gold.

The conquered African tribes saw their ancestral lands confiscated, just as the American Indians had and, like the Indians, they were herded into reservations with poorer soil and inadequate water. Their resentment smoldered and grew, finally erupting six years after the occupation in two bloody rebellions. With great cost on both sides, the insurrections were quelled, but under the uneasy peace the hatred festered unhealed.

68

Slowly, Rhodesia began to emerge into the modern era—except of course for its original owners. From now on they were rigorously controlled. The white minority was determined to avert the threat of another black uprising and equally determined that the cheap black labor supply essential to its economy would not be disrupted. The majority of the natives, they believed, were still barbarian beneath the surface, and they considered it their paternal Christian obligation to suffer the burdens and responsibilities of ruling, in order to protect the simple black African folk from their own innate atrocity and ignorance.

The blacks found jobs as house-men and gardeners. Gradually, they were trained as carpenters and bricklayers. As far as possible, the churches tried to provide health services, and some inroads began to be made on the astonishingly high infant death rate. Education, however, was another question. There were some whites, to be sure, who were more than a bit hesitant to have too many uppity educated blacks spreading unhealthy ideas among the reserves. But the fault also lay with the black parents who could not understand why their children had to go to the white missionaries' schools. At the small native boarding schools, boys had to be locked in their huts at night to keep them from running away, and small black girls had almost to be forcibly abducted from their homes to be educated. Until 1946, government-run schools for Africans were limited to primary schools teaching the three R's and industrial courses.

By 1930, Africans (i.e., blacks as distinguished from whites or "Europeans") had been forbidden by law to settle in European areas; they could live on the premises of their white employers or in so-called urban "locations," but the "pass laws" outside those boundaries were very tight. All male Africans are still required to carry at all times a registration certificate if they want to remain working in any urban area. A black is not to be in the streets of a white area after dark. Finally, the Sedition Act made it illegal "to engender feelings of hostility between Europeans and others."

The hatred was silent and submerged. But it was seething.

This black and white Rhodesia is a land of paradoxes. In the unproductive lands below the highveld and in the malaria-infested swamps of the north, there are African villages virtually untouched by the twentieth century. At the same time, at the center of the country rises the jewel of Salisbury, one of the most beautiful small modern cities in the world. In the north, the dam at Lake Kariba in the Zambezi River holds back the world's largest man-made lake, a triumph of modern architectural ingenuity and British endurance. During construction the mercury boiled at 120°, day and night, so hot that workers had to carry their metal tools in pails of water. Perspiring a gallon of sweat a day, they endured tsetse flies, leopards, hyenas, cheetahs, and baboons; but they built their dam. At the same time, in villages hidden away in the jungle hills around the site, the drums beat imploring the forgiveness of the river god for this sacrilegious incursion and begging his punishment on these irreligious white barbarians. Apparently, their prayers were heard. Before the dam was completed, the rains beat down on the jungle, tributaries flash-flooded, and the great Zambezi hunched himself up and came thundering down on the white man's wall of reinforced concrete—110 feet over low-water level!

Cecil Rhodes once defined his policy for Rhodesia as "equal rights for every white man south of the Zambezi." Later, under pressure from his more liberal colleagues, he reluctantly amended "white" to "civilized." But he probably regarded the chance of black Africans becoming "civilized" as so unlikely that the two expressions seemed to him to say exactly the same thing. It is hard to realize that Rhodesia today is merely eighty years from the dung-strewn *kraal* of King Lobengula, and the greatest of the paradoxes is that the ruling white minority of this new country is now trying to lift itself up into the twenty-first century by keeping the subservient black minority back down in the nineteenth.

In Rhodesia, every man has a vote, provided he meets the property, educational, and occupational requirements. The problem is that most African children do not finish primary school, and only .05% complete secondary school. While white literacy is nearly 100%, African literacy is only 30%. If that were not protection enough, there are two voting rolls: the "A" roll from predominantly white districts which elects 50 members of parliament; the "B" roll from predominantly black districts which elects 15 members. Once again, "all animals are equal, but some animals are more equal than others."

The land is indeed divided with scrupulous equality into two distinct halves. The difficulty is that there are six million Africans for one half and only three hundred thousand Europeans for the other half. Moreover, the Tribal Trust Lands are less productive, overworked, overpopulated, while the European portion covers the fertile central highlands with farms averaging from 2,000 to 5,000 acres. There are some blacks whose sheer persistence and thrift have enabled families gradually to purchase their own land in the somewhat better "Purchase Areas." Their plots supply the owners with good food and a surplus to sell. These crop earnings enable them to hire brickmakers and to put up houses of sometimes six or seven rooms. The more prosperous African housewife scans her daily paper for bargains and takes the bus into town to shop and to visit her husband who works in town all week.

Yet fence-to-fence with these prosperous African farms are hundreds of dead little plots whose owners try to scrabble up a subsistence crop without sufficient water or fertilizer or knowledge of farming. Therefore, in order to eat and pay their taxes, many blacks are forced to work for less than whites in towns, in the mines, on large farms, and as domestic servants and laborers in the cities. But the majority return to the Tribal Lands after less than five years, after they've saved up just enough to pay their taxes and buy some tools and seed for the useless ground. In some African areas, 80% of the young men at any one time are away from their families working for the white men.

Because of family planning, the white population growth is only a little more than 1% a year, even with the influx of new Europeans. But the black population growth is 5% a year, because they try to have as many children as possible since so many of them die before maturity of malaria, parasites, tuberculosis, and malnutrition. Recently, the handful of educated blacks has begun to wonder if the new white interest in fostering birth control among the blacks might be motivated by something less than total altruism.

On the other hand, many Europeans are tempted to believe that black Africans are congenitally lazy. Such is not necessarily the truth. The stagnant pools of the Tribal Areas are infested with parasites which cause Snail Fever (*bilharzia*) which in great part accounts for the chronic lethargy of Africans. It is rarely fatal, but it is as enervating as anemia, and 90% of Rhodesia's black children are afflicted with it for life.

Even if it were generally available, the white man's medicine has little appeal for the African. Not only does he believe that it could be used as a weapon, but, more importantly, he believes that sickness never comes from natural causes. Rather, if he or his children are sick, it is because his ancestors are upset by his sins. Ancestor worship, at least roughly similar to the Christian "communion of saints," is virtually universal; the tribe consists not only of its living members but of its forebears as well, and the needs of the dead are very often more important than the needs of the living.

Furthermore, the gods or one's ancestors cannot be placated by direct contact through prayer; their wills can be changed only through the intercession of a medium. Therefore, every village has its "witch" doctor, with his headdress of feathers or fur and his necklaces of cowrie shells, who for a price will throw his collection of carved bones and read one's fortune. Or he may go into a trance and let the dead speak through his mouth. In the big towns, the witch doctor of the "location" wears the white coat of a medical doctor and has a very rich clientele among the Africans who have succeeded in the white man's world but have their roots still firmly implanted in the *kraal*. Nor is it any wiser to sneer at the witch doctor than it is to tempt the wrath of the Zambezi River god. Whether through the superstitious susceptibilities of their victims or through some actual ability to manipulate nature, the medium's curses are often very chillingly effective. In neighboring Zambia, a hospital was forced to build an extra wing just to accommodate the work of the witch doctors. It is too easy to sneer at these healers. Western doctors often don't know *why* their potions work; they just do. So, too, with the "witch" doctor.

Some jobs are reserved exclusively for whites. Black doctors, nurses, teachers, clergymen, and lawyers can serve only blacks, no matter how learned or wealthy they become and no matter what position they attain in their segregated communities. Blacks are paid less than whites, even for doing precisely the same job at the same location. On farms and in the mines, for exactly the same work, blacks receive $55 a month and whites receive $800 a month. What's more, there are 50,000 new black workers coming into the pool of potential workers every year, and there are just not enough jobs for them. Therefore, they are grudgingly willing to take less pay for the same job or, more likely, they will join the army. One of the greatest paradoxes in modern Rhodesia is that, in the war between the white supremacists and the new black guerrillas, one half the white man's army is black and two-thirds of his police force is black!

Galvanized by their common fear of the explosive power of six million black natives, the whites—rich and poor, British and German and Afrikaner, professionals and farmers, Catholics and Protestants and atheists—are as organically united together as the parts of a single human body. However, as in so many other such complex human situations, it is both unwise and unfair to oversimplify one side into ruthless and ogrish Simon Legrees and the other side into unstained

Topsies and Uncle Toms. From inside the skin and memories of the white Rhodesian, the roots of racism do not look as irrational as they might to an American college student 4,000 objective miles away.

To the eyes of a white Rhodesian, the Africans with whom he lives and works every day are only sixty years away from naked savagery. And surely they have been treated better than the Americans treated the aborigines from whom they took their land. What's more, every white Rhodesian over thirty-five remembers with a shudder the days of the Mau Mau, the occult and pitiless guerrillas who for eight gruesome years marauded the towns and plantations of nearby Kenya in the fifties, in a war in which thousands of Africans and Europeans were slaughtered. He looks to the new nations of Central Africa who have achieved early majority native rule: a parade of dictators, juntas, genocidal tribal wars, 28 coups which overthrew infant governments and 16 attempted coups. Kwame Nkrumah, the first president of Ghana, was ousted from office for extortion and corruption. In Uganda, Idi Amin Dada all by himself would be enough to convince a white Rhodesian that his Christian obligation is to save the Rhodesian blacks as well as its whites from such a holocaust. It is, as it has always been to British colonials, "the white man's burden."

To such a Rhodesian, Prime Minister Ian Smith, is the very embodiment of the charismatic savior. As a young man, Smith had been more interested in sports than in academic study. During World War II, he enlisted in the British Air Force as a fighter pilot and was shot down over North Africa. He was horribly burned and mutilated in the crash; his face and body were repaired by surgery, although to this day he is still partially paralyzed and is unable to smile. Patched together by army doctors, Smith once again indomitably flew missions over Italy. When he was shot down again, he found his way to a group of Italian partisans and continued to fight the war on the ground as a guerrilla. Such a man is not likely to be daunted by criticism, even from all the United Nations of the world.

As most segments of England's dying empire were gradually granted independence, Rhodesia's white minority also petitioned to become a separate nation. The British government, however, was unwilling to set Rhodesia free until it had set up a practicable mechanism for the gradual take-over of power by the black majority from the white minority. For years the two governments haggled, proposed and counter-proposed without success, until finally at 1:15 p.m. on 11 November 1965, Prime Minister Ian Smith took to the radio and announced to the entire country that, because of irreversible differences with the British government, the Rhodesian parliament had unilaterally divorced itself from the Commonwealth and had declared itself a separate republic.

Infuriated, the British sought and secured from all members of the United Nations an embargo against any trade with Rhodesia and a boycott against all of its products. Every nation in the world rescinded its recognition of Rhodesia, and all its consulates around the world were asked to withdraw. The Union of South Africa, itself not the most favored of nations within the world community, refused to take sides and, in effect, provided Rhodesia's only outlet to the sea. However, though all the world's nations had refused—at least publicly—to acknowledge even the existence of this new upstart state, one surely had to be practical. Most of the world's chromium was locked away in Rhodesia, and the world's cars would not sell without chrome. Bewilderingly, as with her Prime Minister in his days as a soldier, Rhodesia continued onward, battered but unbowed.

But the opposition to the white-supremacist government did not come merely from without. There had always been bands of black dissidents fighting an attack-and-run war against the white government, but they had always been containable. Now, however, their numbers began to swell, and their public notoriety was able to secure them outside help—from neighboring Zambia and Mozambique, from the Organization of African Unity, and most notably from the Soviet Union.

Paradoxically, the very word "Bantu" (ba, plural prefix + ntu, person) means a single person welded together out of many. But whereas the white minority is as inflexibly unified as a pillar, the black majority is split every-which-way in their reactions to one another and to the white rulers.

In the first place, there is a relatively recent fragmentation among blacks brought about by Rhodesia's emergence into a new and modern world. The majority of Africans follow the old ways, as indifferent to the politics of Salisbury as to those of Patagonia. At the other end of the spectrum, a very small black elite with education or money or both is highly sensitive both to the injustice of minority rule and to the precariousness of their own financial position if they call attention to that injustice. And in between the two is a large number, mostly illiterate young men, who find the old ways intolerable and the new ways inaccessible.

74

The older generation are mostly subsistence farmers out in the Tribal Lands, with very little if any contact with the white man and his lifestyle. For them, as it has always been, honor accrues to a man or woman with age and not with wealth, quality is more important than quantity, and a relative (even a dead one) has more influence on one's choices than a stranger in the capital. Furthermore, many of the rural blacks live in polygamous marriages so that the number of their relatives is innumerable. This custom of polygamy came about because, with all the wars over the centuries, a woman could not be assured of a mate unless she were willing to share a husband with other wives. As a result, a child in a village has always enjoyed the honest affection of the entire kinship group, and the loyalty of a Bantu clan is perhaps unequalled anywhere else in the world. More to the point in today's black guerrilla warfare, one family member must support another in *any* circumstance and, on his honor, must avenge any wrong done to a fellow clan member. The Bantu proverb says, "What a man does is of greater importance than what he knows."

At the other extreme in the black Rhodesia community, however, a new generation has begun to emerge from the mission schools, through secondary schools, and even through universities like Oxford. For them, intelligence demands that one submit the old uncritically accepted values to the cold light of academic logic and injustice. Perhaps one has an obligation to the tribe, but in the struggle for upward mobility he also has a prior obligation to himself. The old chiefs are no longer leaders of their people. The white men have very shrewdly made them part of the administrative structure, responsible for the blacks keeping the laws. Emasculated by the white men's paychecks, the black chief is as against black nationalism as the white government is.

Caught between these two radically different black worlds are the young. Those working on farms live in clusters isolated from one another and from the ways of home; those in town find that they cannot really fit in even with the blacks who have been assimilated into city ways. They move between two conflicting value systems without a firm hold on either. They share with one another a common frustration but, until recently, no realization of unity.

Thus there is a division among black Rhodesians between young and old and middle-aged, between urban wage earners and rural subsistence farmers, between the educated and the illiterate, between short-term urban laborers and the distrusted educated black elite whose only search seems for personal prestige, far distant from the problems of their less-advantaged black brothers.

The young black Rhodesian is angry, frustrated, inarticulate, confused. Like any of his brothers and sisters in urban ghettos all over the world, this makes him automatically ripe for propaganda. He is hungry for a way to vent his impotent rage at the difference between the home of the white lady whose lawn he tends and the verminous *kaia* made of clay and dung in which his mother kneads corn cakes for the bloated bellies of too many brothers and sisters.

There are many black leaders who seek the allegiance of these frustrated young people, but they themselves are disunited. Beneath this new modern division lies the centuries-old blood-feud between the Matabele and the Shona. The leader of the Matabele is Joshua Nkomo, a former welfare worker. Year after year since 1956, Nkomo and his followers have organized in defense of black rights and majority rule and in disloyal opposition to white supremacy. And year after year his organizations have been summarily and efficiently suppressed and outlawed. His most recent effort, the Zimbabwe African People's Union (ZAPU) was banned in 1962 and almost immediately set up exile headquarters in neighboring Zambia, where it enlists, equips, and trains dissident black guerrillas to infiltrate back into Rhodesia through the wilderness lands of the north.

The predominantly Shona group, the Zimbabwe African National Union (ZANU) under Rev. Ndabiningi Sithole broke away from Nkomo in 1963, after many of the intellectual Shona leaders had become distrustful of Nkomo's ability to lead. Recently, however, the hardening of the white government's opposition and then later its foot-dragging on majority rule have made the two outlaws and their guerrillas more aware of the wisdom of at least uneasy friendship.

Thus began a particularly dirty little war. The guerrilla radio from Zambia keeps repeating: "Rise up, black man! Form groups at night! Cut down the tobacco fields! Kill many cattle!" There is so much undeveloped land along the northern border at the Zambezi Escarpment that guerrillas can infiltrate with relative ease, and since 1972 warfare has been a way of life there.

Two elements of "the old way" have still not been eradicated from the young guerrillas, some of them as young as fourteen years old: first, the unquestioning loyalty of the clan and, second, a centuries-old belief bred into their bones since the dawn of time. From that clan loyalty, the insurgents can count on being hidden and protected by their innumerable relatives—even those relatives not in sympathy with their cause or their methods—because loyalty to one's family takes precedence over any ideology or patriotism or fear of reprisal.

Centuries-old beliefs tell even the oldest and most remote natives that the European lands and the new "protected areas" violate the dwelling places of guardian spirits. Besides that, the guerrillas have bribed or threatened mediums to tell their people that the ancestors favor the insurgents. As early in 1960, they had whispered rumors that the whites are cannibals, and in evidence they showed the smiling black face of a Bantu boy as the trade mark on cans of corned beef. The following year, ZAPU spread the story that an ancestral spirit had taken the shape of a sea monster and live in the welling lake behind an unfinished dam near Bulawayo; from that moment, no African would work there. Blacks fresh from the Tribal Lands were told that white doctors and their hospitals were slaughterhouses and that if a black man were found near Salisbury airport he would be turned into a pig and airfreighted for food to the foreign mercenaries in the Congo.

In guerrilla retaliation for "cooperation with the whites," a black school supervisor in the tribal area was tied to a stake and burned to death by the insurgents in front of his family, staff, and students. In other cases, grenades have been tied to the heads of tribesmen and the pins pulled. Other victims have been slowly bayoneted to death or limbs have been severed. Perhaps the worst atrocity of the war on the insurgent side occurred late in 1976, when 27 tea workers were gunned down in front of their wives and children on a white-owned estate in the Honde Valley, 140 miles east of Salisbury. The workers were told they were being punished for working for settlers.

The guerrillas have killed, raped, blown up, burned, tortured, and kidnapped non-combatants. Why would they kill their own people? Sometimes the people have been "caught in the crossfire" with government troops. More often, their torture has been used to instill terror and insure obedience or at least silent cooperation.

On the other side, the army and police—the majority of whom are black—torture non-combatants in order to get information about the guerrillas and their movements. 65,000 blacks have been relocated from the guerrilla-infiltrated Tribal Lands into "protected villages" with eight-foot fences; for a people used to roaming freely on the veld, these are little better than concentration camps. The motive, as the government claims, may well be to protect them from marauding terrorists, but these "protected" people are also no longer able to give aid to those same terrorists, and the "protected villages" are a shocking reminder of the "pacification areas" of Vietnam.

77

Government troops have orders to shoot to kill any African seen more than 50 meters from his or her dwelling between the curfew hours of six in the evening and five in the morning. Every week the regime reports the number of Africans killed "for violation of the curfew." No names are listed; in fact, it is a criminal offense to publish such names.

In one case, in July 1975, a black teacher named Makaya was returning with a friend from a drinking spree when the friend passed out. Mr. Makaya went home to fetch his wife to help him, and while the two were on their way back, they encountered government troops. Terrified at being caught outside during the curfew, the two began running and the security forces opened fire, killing the husband immediately. According to the Commission on Justice and Peace, the wife, who was eight months pregnant, was shot through the stomach. Miraculously, both mother and child survived.

The Commission has medical records, photographs, and affidavits to support allegations of torture of Africans, including beatings with hoses, water immersions, and the application of electric shock. Various methods of torture are alleged to Amnesty International. They include beating on the body with fists and sticks, beating on the soles of the feet with sticks, and the application of electric shocks by means of electrodes or cattle goads. In addition torture victims have been threatened with castration or immersed head first in barrels of water until unconscious. In 1975, the government introduced the Indemnity and Compensation Act which effectively absolves members of the security forces against prosecution for any actions carried out since 1 Dec 72 in the war zones.

On trees and posts throughout the country there are paper notices offering rewards of: "Not less than—
£ 5000 for information leading to the death or capture of a Senior Terrorist leader
£ 2500 for information leading to the death or capture of a Group Leader
£ 1000 for any trained terrorist
£ 500 for mines or heavy weapons
£ 300 for grenades or light weapons
Failure to do so can mean 20 years of hard labor!"

Every week white farmers are briefed by the military. Each "incident" is carefully described and the terrorists' *modus operandi* is studied. While their husbands are being briefed, the white wives practice pistol shooting.

One of the farmers, Archie Dagleish, is quoted by *The National Geographic*: "Eight people were in the house at the time. At 1:00 a.m. we were aroused by the barking of my dogs. Then a rocket exploded in a bedroom where a friend and his daughter were sleeping. Neither was killed, but she was injured very badly. We started getting automatic rifle fire, and I returned it. The terrorists threw grenades into the farm store and started burning down the compounds of my African workmen. They withdrew before the security forces arrived, but our men tracked them down. There were nine terrorists; we got every one."

One can perhaps understand the anger of the white Rhodesians—in somewhat the same terms one tries to understand the early American settlers, attacked by Indians trying to drive the intruders off land that once was theirs. But why do the white government's black soldiers and police also kill their own? Black civilians, the black soldiers say, are often "caught in the crossfire." As for the guerrillas, they could be hidden beside any road with automatic weapons, grenades, rocket launchers. They deserve no quarter. The people cannot go anywhere unarmed; white women are training themselves to kill any black man who moves on their plantations at night. As one black soldier said, "They are terrorists. We kill them wherever we find them and as fast as we find them." And another: "The terrorist goes into a village and says, 'Give me food'; and if the villagers have no food, he kills them. Is that freeing the country from the white man?"

And so there are black soldiers killing black guerrillas, and both killing black people. And white people. Recalling the days of Zimbabwe before the whites came, one black army man said, "What's new about that? We've been doing it for centuries."

The *New York Times* (14 February 1977) stated that, in the four years since the war began in late 1972, both sides have managed to kill 3,534 men and women: 2,364 insurgents, 847 black civilians (including 189 curfew breakers), 71 white civilians, and 252 members of the government security forces.

The most outspoken opponent of the racial policies of the Salisbury government had been Bishop Donal Lamont, O. Carm., of Umtali. He had written a pastoral letter condemning the land division of the Tribal Trust Lands and decided that "the Church has no choice but to support those who wish to be treated by the state as equal citizens." On 26 August 1976, Bishop Lamont was informed of four charges— two for not reporting terrorists in Roman Catholic missions, and two for advising missionaries not to inform on saboteurs—each charge carried with it the death penalty. His sentence was later reduced to ten and then four years. Finally, he was stripped of Rhodesian citizenship and deported back to Ireland.

In November of the previous year, a Father George had ridden away on his bicycle after saying Mass at Bondolsi Mission in southeast Rhodesia and was never seen again. On the 5th of December, the retired Bishop of Bulawayo, Adolf Schmitt, with Father Possenti Weggarten, principal of a secondary school, Sister Maria Francis, and Sister Ermenfried Knauer were stopped in their car on the main Victoria Falls road, asked for money, and shot. Sister Ermenfried survived the attack and said that the lone gunman had been a "terrorist." As in Vietnam, color is confusing in determining the enemy.

Rumors, perhaps unfounded, even began to circulate that many of the killings attributed to guerrillas were actually the work of the Selous Scouts, a counter-insurgency unit of black soldiers within the regular Rhodesian armed forces. In order to swing sympathies away from the insurgents and toward the white government, so the rumors go, the black army unit dresses in guerrilla camouflage uniforms, carries captured Soviet-made weapons, and attacks innocent villagers.

The Catholic Church in Rhodesia has been sharply critical of the white minority's racial policies. One African priest reputedly told his bishop that he had been threatened by one of the white members of the security forces: "You'd better watch out. One dead missionary is as good as a hundred dead terrorists to us." Many knowledgeable people, however, even of those whose sympathies are not with the white government, discount these rumors as sheer fabrication, a weapon straight out of a John Le Carré novel.

Whatever is the truth, it is without doubt that at the beginning of February, someone, somewhere, perhaps even on the spur of the moment, had resolved that it was time to kill another Catholic missionary.

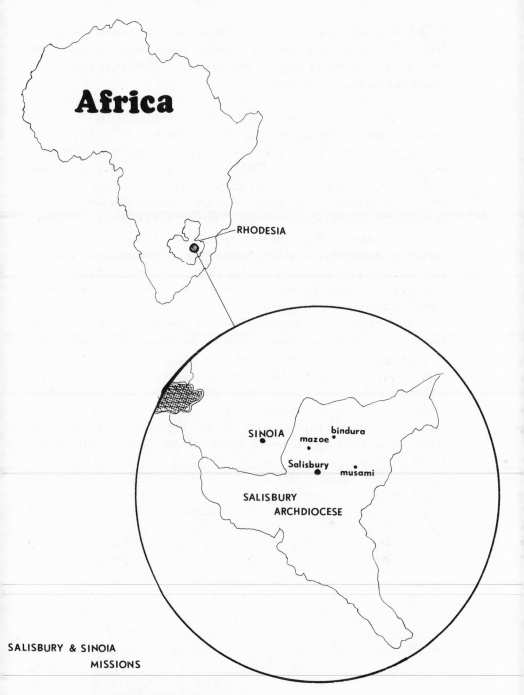

Africa

RHODESIA

SINOIA

mazoe

bindura

Salisbury

musami

SALISBURY
ARCHDIOCESE

SALISBURY & SINOIA
MISSIONS

RHODESIA

Mark Linder

81

31 December 1976,
7:30 a.m.

Gerry Finnieston was out of sorts this morning. He stepped out of the Jesuit community house at St. Paul's Mission in Musami to one more overcast day. The sky was leaden. Everything was heavy and sodden, a wretched stretch of steamy waiting before the inevitable drenching began again. Off to his left behind the administration block, wreaths of mist clung around the dorsal fin of Beta Hill and all along its flinty flanks. Up there in the rubbled lava, in a dozen caves and under overhangs, were prehistoric Bushman paintings sketched before Abraham had set out from Ur of the Chaldees to the land of Canaan. Days like this Finnieston felt like Abraham himself, only older. Happy New Year, he grumbled to no one at all. There's four days' holiday down the drain. Literally.

He walked down the slanted path from the community house and paused a moment at the central fish pond, looking down at orange carp darting unconcernedly among the weeds in the grey water. Hunh. Doesn't bother you at all, does it, all this wet?

He turned and walked along the main transverse road of the mission. He was glad one of the fathers had been off on a retreat and he could use his room for his four-day visit. It was nice to have a proper room rather than that little six-by-six guest hut next to the dining room. Nonetheless, he hadn't slept well at all. All those birds chattering and shrieking through the middle of the night. Puzzling. Before his transfer to Chishawasha, he'd worked at St. Paul's, Musami, for more years than he cared to count, and he couldn't remember such a lot of nocturnal cacophany. Sounded like there were spooked.

Four rainy days ago, Brother John Conway, his good friend, had rumbled into Chishawasha in his eight-ton lorry an hour after Finnieston's Sunday Masses and chauffeured him thus royally the 30-or-so miles to Musami for a holiday. Not at all mesmerized by his own blarney, Brother John had sounded like a travel agent, promising long walks and talks and swims and a chance to ring in the New Year with the old gang at Musami. As they'd ridden along, the hills had been cloaked in mist just as they were this morning, the road was slick with the last rain, and it was altogether a depressing day. But a day could hardly stay gloomy very long when one shared the cab of a truck with "Brada" John.

82

Tall, big-shouldered, jug-eared, and unassumingly happy, John Conway could charm a boulder into dancing with him. Even to the cautiously "proper" he was an exhilarating man to be with, and his big gap-toothed Irish grin was terminally infectious even on this somber day.

In the 22 years he had been in Rhodesia, John had been doctor, dentist, nurse, teacher, coach, garden farmer, builder of schools and playgrounds, and patcher-upper of all that and more. But, above all, he was "the truckdriver who loved children." They hung off him like the birds off St. Francis.

"They've made me move out of the community house, you know, Gerry," he said over the roar of the old engine. "Into that little rondavel hut behind the admin block—that one on the hill below the carpenter shop and the mill. I call it 'The Eagle's Nest,' but the rest call it 'Conway Castle.'

"You know how I've always run on about the mission's being too impersonal. Don't you think? I mean, the kids need a place to let go, a place to read and talk and tussle and play the record player as loud as they like. That's the real reason for the eviction notice, I think," he grinned, "the noise."

They moved across the line into the completely different world of the Tribal Trust Lands and trundled past a black township and a large African hotel. Prosperous looking place. Great deal of money for some in the African reserves. They passed an African bus, but other than that there was not much traffic nowadays, with the boycott and the shortage of petrol. And no one would stop for a car that seemed to have broken down. That trick of catching the Samaritan and then shooting him dead had been tried too often. But, no matter, John Conway would probably have stopped.

John was silent for a moment. "One day," he said quietly, "they'll come for us, you know, just as we are." He had said that before. Then suddenly he said, "Do you remember this song? 'Rose Ma-reeee, I love you! I'm aaawlways dreee-ming of you . . . !' "

They crossed the fine new bridge over the Nyagui River—at which many a farmer's thirsty cow had proved too much temptation for the crocodiles—and moved into Mangwende Reserve in which St. Paul's is located. It was perfectly ordered and peaceful along the wide tarred road under the lowering sky. No stranger could have believed you if you'd told him it was quite likely that behind the dripping bushes and trees, shadows moved stealthily carrying Russian machine guns. That was from old Tarzan movies and "Stanley and Livingstone."

They turned off finally on the sandy Zihunde strip road and bumped the six miles over the ruts and rocks to St. Paul's. Nestled amid the dripping jacaranda trees, the buildings were certainly unprepossessing. They were put together with their own home-made burnt bricks and were not about to win any architectural prizes. In fact, when Evelyn Waugh visited the mission years ago he had described them as "penetratingly drab." Not an unfair description, that. And yet the place is in itself a minor miracle, burgeoning up out of the African bush. From a single straw outstation of the Chishawasha mission, St. Paul's had grown to a hundred acres with a complex of primary schools for hundreds of black children and a secondary school which Gerry Finnieston himself had co-founded. One quarter of all the Catholic school children in the archdiocese were at St. Paul's. But there were also teacher-training and commercial schools, a novitiate for African sisters, a church large enough to hold 3,000 worshipers, and the pastoral focus of over 30 Mass stations covering 2,000 miles of the Reserve. Gerry Finnieston had arrived "home" for a holiday.

Later that Sunday evening before supper, Gerry had walked through the grazing lands beside the Shavanhohwe River. To the east was the mushroom shape of Ngomamhowa Mountain; ahead, the buildings of St. Paul's were silhouetted against the setting sun and the balancing rocks over behind the stadium. Then from behind him, he heard them—a procession of old vehicles, rattling up out of the gathering darkness. Musami's "Flying Squad," as he had named them when he was one of them, was returning to base.

They came at odd moments, Shep roaring by on his bike, then Marty Thomas on his. Twelve years Gerry had been one of them, before the motorbikes, thank God, grinding up the hill from the river in Conway's old Chev truck or the little Peugeot. At the mission they had a stable of odd vehicles whose mudgards and springs gave witness to the punishing roads their drivers had pushed them over for too many years. Today alone, each one of these relics had covered from 40 to 100 miles, with two or perhaps three Masses, baptisms, sick calls, and a round of settling disputes and counseling and encouraging. During the week, each of those drivers works in the schools or the teachers' college or the hospital, but at the end of the wearying week he piles into his car and off he goes, leaving any thought of leisure time behind.

They'd set out very early that morning; the roads are rough and there has to be plenty of lead-time. As the priest nears each center, he hoots his car horn; and once he arrives with the altar, the people begin setting it up and lining up for confessions. Catechists rehearse the people in the songs, give instruction classes for converts and those getting ready for First Communion. After Mass there may be a sodality meeting, baptisms, pre-marriage conferences. Then, the altar is packed up again, and the priest sets off for another center, perhaps making a detour to anoint someone sick. And then still another center. And then perhaps, home.

In the week that followed his arrival, there had been one sunny day, and Gerry and John Conway had taken good advantage of it to have a long walk and swim and just generally laze about. But even that one fine day had quickly closed in, and the rest of the days dragged by in dull, chill wetness, just like this dreary morning.

He pushed open the bottom of the stable-door of the lean-to dining room. The Dominican Sisters had apparently finished and were back in the convent, girding themselves for the day in the hospital. A few of the Jesuits were lingering over a last cup of coffee. As Gerry entered, the acting superior, Martin Thomas, bearded and kindly, was weaving a fantasy of words about the stars or paleontology or something. Martin was a romantic, with the heart and mind of a poet, but willingly shackled to 120 African schoolboy themes a week. And yet this morning Gerry sensed that Martin was not really wrapped up in his subject as usual but rather was juggling like Punch to keep everybody's mind distracted from something else. There was no reaction at all to his wistful meanderings; everyone's tolerantly muted sighs were telling him he wasn't being listened to. Finally, he shut up.

Father Dunstan Myerscough, the administrator of the community, graying hair neatly parted in the middle, sat quietly puffing his pipe. This airy stuff was not his line of country. He had work to do—the carpentry shop to check and then what he was happiest at: piloting the tractor up and down the neat furrows of the farm. So, what's a little wet? He rose from the table and moved to the door. "Good morning, Gerry." And he was gone.

"Good morning, Gerry! How 'bout a cuppa?" John Conway edged past the silent old TV set and went for the pot. As he went he launched into his regular morning summary of the news: "You know, I was noticing in that *Newsweek* you brought me, there's an American kid named . . . Cauthen, I think it is, or Crossen . . . who's the greatest horseman since the Apocalypse. He's only sixteen, and he drives through the whole pack of them and he's off!" And Conway was off, too, trying to find a handle for some exalted theme, his daily trick to get people talking. But gradually even his irrepressible effervescence was capped. No one was listening.

"Did you sleep well, Father?" This from young Shepherd-Smith, all liquid brown eyes, and serious, solicitous baby face. Hard to believe he was 34 and a priest. He was surely "an Israelite without guile."

"As a matter of fact, I didn't sleep well at all, Chris. The whole night long the birds were chattering away as if it were midday."

There was a silence for a moment.

"When I was a boy in Kenya during the Mau Mau," Shepherd-Smith went on helpfully, "that's the way the terrorists would signal one another in the dark and give one another orders and locations without anyone even realizing they were there." The others looked at one another uneasily, not quite having the courage to ask Chris to keep his history lessons to himself. "My mother and sister and I lived in an unprotected cottage in a dangerous bit of country, and we'd hear cries of birds and animals in the middle of the night. We were quite sure it was the Mau Mau."

Finnieston shivered just a touch and turned to the boyish young priest. "You mean you think those calls last night might have been terrorists?"

"I shouldn't be at all surprised. They're reconnoitering around here all the time. I'll tell you, when I go off on the motorbike on those back roads in the reserve, I don't feel very safe. Just before Christmas we had two incidents nearby. In one, the villagers were forced at gunpoint by the guerrillas to take what they liked from the local store. That means the trouble has reached us. We can expect more."

There was a pause. Then Martin Thomas stood up. "Well, it's time for me to hit the books, chaps." He and Finnieston walked out the door together. They stood on the path to the road for a moment, and Martin scratched his beard thoughtfully. "I know Conway's a pal of yours, but I wish he wouldn't give his 'talks' at breakfast."

"It seems you were all doing a bit of 'talking.' Are things as bad as that?"

"Shepherd-Smith is right. Things are different now. They're all around us. I shall be glad when the Superior returns from leave, and we can have some decisions made. I surely wouldn't want to have a puncture out on a reserve road far away from the mission. And we know many of the roads are mined. Things are different." He paused, "I'm rather sure the Sisters aren't aware of it, though. I've asked the community not to tell them. No need to worry them needlessly."

As they stood outside the lean-to, Sister Joseph cycled by them on her way over to the hospital, all starched and white. How do they keep those uniforms so white and unwrinkled in this heat? Forbidden by rule to perspire, perhaps. She smiled and waved but, oddly, did not stop. Sister Anna walked painfully past them, too, on her way to the hospital, but she did not stop either. She walked in a kind of dream of concentration, without saying a word. Perhaps she was praying. Or perhaps her arthritic pains were engulfing her again.

Or perhaps the Sisters knew more than the Jesuits suspected.

As they stepped into the road, Gerry said, "I think I'll have John Conway drive me back to Chishawasha early. This afternoon, I think, if that's all right with you."

"But you were going to stay for the New Year with us."

"I know, but there won't be much chance for the two of us to hike around or swim anymore, I'm sure. And . . ."

"Yes. We're all rather a bit edgy, too."

As they reached the central fish pond, Gerry Finnieston turned right to his room in the community house, and Martin Thomas moved painfully in the direction of the high school book bindery.

* * * * * * * *

Martin Thomas was a thinnish man in the prime of his years, softly smiling, but with deep-set, hooded eyes, darkly circled, which told anyone with sense that this man had known pain. He had entered the Society of Jesus as a boy of 17 and had spent 13 of his 45 years in Rhodesia. It was perhaps not precisely the career his father would have chosen; his father was a retired general of the British Army, General Sir Reginald Thomas, who had fought in South Africa in the Boer War and who now lived with his wife in the cultured and donnish atmosphere of Oxford.

It is difficult for a Jesuit from a working-class family to comprehend the sensitive antennae that have been bred into a man like Martin Thomas. In the Society of Jesus he is very often the previously privileged minority, and in the abrasions of this new melting pot he is, ironically, the one who must do all the conceding.

Perhaps he shouldn't have said that to Gerry Finnieston about Conway—a man so close to the earth and free of all his own inherited propriety. After all, John hadn't a mean bone in his body, and he was only trying—constantly—to bring out a little life and spontaneity in us strait-laced Saxons. The table talk in the Conway cottage in Tralee, with the praties passed round by loud-voiced boys, was a world away from the gentility of a general's table in Oxford. Now John Conway was his brother, and he truly loved him.

Martin was a thoroughbred, a man of incredible courtesy, almost a *noblesse oblige*. The founder of the Jesuits, Ignatius Loyola, had been like that. To some, Martin seemed almost diffident, always patiently and respectfully listening, weighing, and absorbing. He was an "easy" man, of deep and hard-won serenity. Long since, in the slow erosion of privilege which is the Jesuit course of study, he had learned the emptiness of mere "manners," and yet he had also penetrated to the reasons why a gentle-man treated paupers with the same reverence he gave a duke or a bishop: beneath this unpromising surface lurks Christ, the Lord.

To the unaware, Martin Thomas seemed unfailingly good-humored, never in the dumps. It seemed to cost him nothing, despite his bad health, to listen hour after hour to the pain of the boys, the sisters, the staff, the community, the villagers in so many mission stations. One wondered at how much such a seemingly shy man knew about the families in the reserve and how completely they trusted him.

It all seemed so simple for Martin. He was "one of those who finds it easy to get along with anybody at all;" he had a "gift" for making friends. As if it didn't cost. No matter how exhausted he was, he never hesitated to take a sick call, at any time of the night, even though many times it meant long distances from the mission on his motorbike and then on foot. On Sundays, he often came home later than the rest because people never seemed to bore him, and he lingered longer in conversation with the African villagers. And when he returned late Sunday nights, there were the eternal piles of exercise books all over his floor, waiting up for him. Very few knew how he dragged himself through Monday and Tuesday in a dull haze of fatigue.

After only two years in Rhodesia as an assistant, Martin had been made superior of the Mhondoro Mission, 150 miles southwest of Salisbury, the poorest station in the archdiocese. There he was alone with two very young African priests, in charge of the mission stations in an area of about 200 square miles. At the same time, he had to manage a primary school and a study group for boys who were still unable to enter secondary school but who could either board at the mission or complete courses with Martin by correspondence. He had been there for seven strenuous years, longer than he'd ever been stationed in one place as a Jesuit. Oddly, his Master of Novices had said Martin would never do any big job. The gift of prophecy is rare.

One Sunday evening after his rounds in the bush, Fr. Peter Kavuma returned to Mhondoro to find Martin with a black eye. It was highly unlikely that the perfect English gentleman had been in a bar fight! Martin told him that after Mass a madwoman had come to see him and became so abusive that he tried to push past her and get away. But she leaped on his back like a hellcat and proceeded to beat the living stuffings out him. Thus, the shiner.

Being superior had been a harness Martin neither sought nor particularly enjoyed. He was not a "forceful" man, although he could make up his mind and take action when it was called for. Just as Ignatius, he had a seemingly limitless tolerance, and yet beneath his gentility was the steel of conviction. He could tolerate fools unflinchingly but not forever.

Nor could he abide anything going to waste. He was an incorrigible collector of anything and everything and never threw anything away. He loved modifying machines with adapters and accessories, and he had so many wires hooked up to his tape recorder that it was beyond an expert to sort them out. And yet his machines did whatever Martin commanded them to do. If anyone needed anything impossible to find, the first place to go was Martin's room, where, from some deep recess, he could unearth anything from a pair of handcuffs to a leather nose guard to keep the rain off a cyclist's face.

Because books are hard to come by in the bush, they are as precious as limited editions—though not always treated as such by adolescent boys. So Martin set up a Book Hospital, and almost every Saturday morning he and two or three boys he had trained would deal with the casualties from the Junior School library of which he was in charge. Hour after hour he would labor like a plastic surgeon over war-weary, second-hand textbooks, so that many of the poorer students could have a reduction in book fees.

Money monopolizes the minds of poor men far more than rich men. All very well for the lilies of the field, but if one neither toils nor spins he must accustom himself to walking about naked as a lily. So poor men know the true value of a shilling. Martin often told the story of how he was once hitchhiking (not exactly encouraged by the superior) from Oxford to the theologate at Heythrop and was picked up by a chap who made £ 10,000 a year writing songs solely for Perry Como. That always seemed a bit disproportionate to Martin.

But the Lord did provide. Martin loved to tell the story of the preacher who thundered over his congregation the message of damnation for unrepentant sinners: "There will be weeping and gnashing of teeth!" he warned in a voice of doom. And from the suitably cowed worshipers came a pesky voice: "Han wha hif ya hain't got no teef?" Unruffled, the great voice boomed back, "Teeth will be provided!"

Through it all, Martin "studied things." He had a Lewis Carroll kind of mind, reveling in fantasy and paradox and esoteric stuff like ESP and water dowsing and hieroglyphics. He read widely: science fiction, historical novels, classics, "bloods" and especially poetry. And he delighted in words for their own sake, taking impish delight in peppering his English with Shonaisms. He was quite good in Shona, but often got into little confusions, as with the words *tsoka* (foot) and *tsoko* (monkey). One Sunday he gave the gospel a slightly new wrinkle by proclaiming that: "It is better to go into heaven with one monkey than to enter hell with two."

Like Conway, whose concrete chatter was always competing for air time with Marty's arcane meanderings, Martin Thomas loved to talk. In the seminary, he would pop into someone's room and talk all night if one would let him. It was said that sometimes a person honored by such a visit would end up by going to bed and asking Martin to put out the light when he'd finished talking.

Some of his fellow Jesuits in Rhodesia found it irritating that, with all the burning issues right under their noses, Martin would dodge all the life-and-death talk and take refuge in reminiscences! He never tired of the story of when he sneaked out of the seminary during theology to have dinner with his family in Oxford and had to borrow his brother's car to get back. But his brother, who was a doctor, needed the car first thing in the morning. So Martin got up for the chapel visit at 6:25 (at which superiors checked for the slugabeds) and then returned piously to his room, ostensibly for the hour of meditation. Quick as a squirrel, he was down the back stairs, out to the copse where he'd hidden the car, whipped down to Oxford, borrowed another car and tore back to the seminary as fast as electricity. At 7:30 he was kneeling at Mass, as pious as a first-time altar boy.

Martin's interests were astronomy and pre-history. The night sky was a constant delight for him, and he loved to predict exactly where the moon would be appearing on a given evening or to trace the lines of constellations for his hardly-interested brethren on the way back from the dining room to the community house. In a community too preoccupied with the practicalities of everyday work to savor the niceties of science, he was always being lured out onto an argumentative limb, only to realize that behind his back his less erudite brothers in Christ were gleefully sawing it off.

His great penance was teaching English to junior boys. For a man whose ear had been so sensitized to literature and whose conversation was always filigreed with whisps of great poetry, the prose of African children was a chore. Still, the government salary he earned as a teacher was very much needed by the mission; and although he did not particularly love teaching English to boys, he dearly loved the African boys.

Martin Thomas was a gentle man, not a volcanic preacher nor a political firebrand. His task in life was merely to serve the African people—as a teacher, counselor, father.

But at that very moment, as he walked to his book bindery wrapped in thought, he was being watched.

* * * * * * * *

17 January 1977,
10:00 p.m.

The January Jesuit Mission Meeting was finished, and Christopher Shepherd-Smith had decided to stay over in town and spend some time with his friends before motorcycling back to Musami. As he sat late in the evening in the kitchen with a friend with whom he'd gone through training, he felt really at home for the first time in a very long time.

For much of his life, Chris had been just a bit of an outsider. When he had left Africa for the novitiate, he'd been a British citizen, of course. But in England he was a colonial, surrounded by clipped Oxonian sophistication, and for five years he dearly longed for home. When he did come back to Salisbury as a seminarian, while most of his contemporaries were practice-teaching in secondary schools, he chose instead to attend the School of Social Service affiliated with the University of Rhodesia. For two years, working mainly with African fellow students, he'd studied Shona, sociology, and missiology. He also did practical work, which he loved, with delinquent African boys and needy families of the city. For a long time, too, he had worked at Fort Victoria, near Zimbabwe, doing a study of the living conditions and attitudes of black men and women working in the homes of white men and women. This had not been so easy. It was door-to-door convassing, and his innate shyness made it a torment to reach his finger out to one more bell, which would signal he-knew-not-what kind of encounter. What was worse, there was something deeply wrong about having to approach African servants first through their European mistresses and masters.

Then, too quickly, he had to return to London for theology. In his spare time he worked with elderly people and handicapped children. He was far more at ease with them than with theologizing; their hearts and needs were as open and uncomplicated as his own, and he responded to them as simply as a fellow alien manchild in a foreign and imperfect land.

Finally, in July 1974, he was ordained; and, within a month, he was on his way home. He was posted immediately to St. Paul's at Musami; and, with the oils of ordination scarcely dry on his hands, he was put in sole charge as pastor of 33 mission outposts scattered over 200 miles of bush. It was his first pastoral experience in a rural area, and the contrast between the poverty of the city and the poverty of the bush was appalling.

Except for Sundays, he was alone in the work, and one wonders what went through his mind in those endless hours alone, gunning his cycle over thousands of miles of sand and rock and brush, in fair weather and foul, going to meet strange black men and women whose lives were only one small step out of the Stone Age. Nothing in his training could have prepared him directly for all that—unless all of his training had prepared him. There had been nothing for it but to jump in at the deep end.

He was the youngest man at St. Paul's; at times the others seemed to react to him as if he were hardly a man at all. They didn't have to say it in words; he knew. The ironic thing was that *he* was the man of Africa, born and bred, and they were British; yet he seemed the "outsider." They were surely good men, gentle and generous with him—a bit too flippant for his taste at times and not at all as single-minded about the work in the reserve as he would have liked. On the other hand, he might perhaps have given them good reason to think him a

92

bit naive and over-eager. Was it that he was younger? Less experienced? Trained in a newer, more open way than their dour seminary years had been? Whatever it was about him, it seemed to him that his own self was what dried up the possibility of the one thing he most yearned for: a good friend with whom he could really share his ideas about theology and especially about his work. But he was the only Jesuit full-time out on the road; his week-long job was something the others merely dabbled at on Sunday. They were so completely tied up in the schools that he could hardly comprehend their table chatter of this boy's dyslexia and that teacher's punishments.

Myerscough was in his sixties and a former schoolmaster himself, and he got easily fed up with theorizing and abstractions. He was never happier than when he was out on the tractor, plowing the fields and placidly puffing away on his pipe. Thomas was a lovely chap, but he was so busy and, well, so "airy." He was completely involved in his own work and sickly on top of it, and one hated to bother him. Hackett had been very flattering about how well Chris was doing the job, but Hackett . . . well, Hackett was the superior, which was off-putting, and besides he was away on leave in England anyway.

The brothers were good, too, in their way. Conway was a gem and would listen for hours if you wanted, but one always felt like one of his kids—not condescended to, mind you, because John could never condescend to anyone, especially a child. But it was like talking theology to your mother; she hadn't the slightest idea what you were talking about, but she'd listen and smile; all the while you prattled on, you were absolutely sure you were loved. Conway didn't know the "new" theology; might even have been scandalized by it if he could fathom it. John read *Newsweek* and *Reader's Digest* and, of course, Kempis, which he quoted by the mile all the time he was cutting one's hair.

The sisters were kind, too, but again that was more "mothering." His only outlet was his lonely work, but a beautiful and joyous work with *his* African "children."

Here on this lovely January evening in town, though, it was different. He felt truly at ease with someone his own age, someone who grew up when TV and rockets to the moon were commonplace and not something out of a futuristic comic page. He felt snug.

His friend hit the saucer with his teacup. "Hey! You were a thousand miles away."

Chris smiled, caught daydreaming. "I was thinking about St. Paul's."

"I hear things are hotting up out there."

"They are, as a matter of fact, rather badly. The people suffer from it far more than we do, of course. The guerrillas have been about since early December, and the people have gotten under the crossfire between the terrorists and the security forces. I imagine that's another way of saying that, when they find the bodies, they don't know which side did it."

"But that must make you furious."

"Yes . . . that it happens. But I can't even pretend to grapple with the politics of it all—who's right, who's wrong. Of course, it's no good arguing politics in the first place, is it? So often people's politics are really just their irrational fears put into words. One can only show them that they're loved, fears and all."

"But, Chris, that's easier said than done, surely, when the people you care for are getting killed in the middle."

As Chris began to answer, there was a joy in his wide-open eyes which complicated men can never know. "But for the love of the Lord —and with the love of the Lord—*anything* is possible. You should see the Africans' faith! Pure, simple faith. One time I was with a man when he was dying; and, out of the blue, he said to me that he wanted to be baptized. Well, it had an amazing effect on the people; you should have seen them coming to Mass! The Holy Spirit is working out there!"

It was getting late. As they stood up, his friend's eye caught a picture of Our Lady in a newspaper on the table. "You know, Chris," he said, "Our Lady is near you and your people, too."

Chris chuckled excitedly. "She really is! Last month the Dominican Sisters got me five statues of the Blessed Mother. So I strapped them on my back and biked them out to five different locations in the reserve. Then I arranged that they be carried in procession from one house to another at fixed intervals so that the people could gather there in the evening and say the rosary together, as a community, you know. You wouldn't believe the things she's done. There are times when people who have been on bad terms come up to one another after the rosary and shake hands and forgive one another. Isn't that wonderful?"

Early next morning, Chris left for Musami, be-goggled, wearing his grey windbreaker. Pure, simple faith zooming off on a motorbike.

* * * * * * * *

It takes more words to explain a simple man than a complex man. It is a fascinating enterprise, like examining the smooth and simple planes of a Chinese puzzle box, knowing for certain that there must be a catch somewhere that will make the square pop open in a profusion of interesting facets.

If there is a word for Christopher Shepherd-Smith it might be "single-minded." He had a child-like simplicity, ingenuousness, and wonder in everything he said and did. Like a child, too, he felt the same complete and simple empathy when people he loved were unjustly hurt, and the same complete and simple anger when things "went wrong," when the world was wilfully distant from the Kingdom its Father had intended. Of such children, we are told, that Kingdom is made, and Chris' stubborn innocence was the very key to the hearts of the simple African dirt farmers he was so well-chosen to serve.

All good qualities, however, are really twins; each one is paired with its opposite shortcoming. Chris was single-minded; almost the only thought on his mind at any time was to serve the African people with his every and last breath. But as so often happens with uncomplicated people, Chris could often see *only* one side. Yet if you cannot see a problem as multi-faceted, with more than one plausible solution, you remain utterly innocent of the art—and the need—of compromise. As a result, Chris tended to be somewhat intolerant at times, impatient with the fact that the other Jesuits at the mission didn't have his young resilience, that they needed other interests and at least a few breaks from the work. Like so many young men in direct social work, Chris found it hard to understand how Jesuits of good conscience could devote their time to correcting verb tenses when people were starving a few miles away. Nor could he understand why others couldn't share his direct, uncomplicated view of things. He was still too young to see that the founding of the Kingdom of God on earth, albeit a matter of utterly pressing need, can nonetheless be measured only in millenia.

Chris read a good deal of theology but no novels or light reading at all (too wasteful of time); that, of course, made him unprepared and ill-at-ease with small talk and surely no match at all for Martin Thomas' verbal hegiras. Nor was he an intellectual. He had a simple, uncomplicated grasp of the gospels, and he was a "Pope's man." He read *L'Osservatore Romano* religiously, noted and adopted every word and instruction in his own life, and faithfully passed them along to the other members of the team. He was pious in a nice way, but obviously more than a touch strait-laced regarding adaptation of doctrine or—ugly word—compromise. It wasn't easy to discuss theology with him, even when one had the stamina; "he had his own wave-length, and it was difficult to tune him in."

One offshoot of his single-minded devotion was his orderliness; Chris was super-organized. Every last detail of his families, his converts, his candidates for baptism was scrupulously filed and cross-indexed. He devised all kinds of apparatus for catechetics and refined each aspect down to the minutest detail. But once again, the virtue of orderliness generates its opposite: inflexibility. Any pelagian of more experience knows too well that the more exquisitely detailed a plan is, the more chances multiply that the plan will at least partially fail. Perfectionism again.

Perhaps because he knew his already burdened brethren could offer little help for his pastoral work, Chris didn't like being helped. He knew exactly how he wanted things done. Thank you, but he could do it quite nicely by himself. And like all young men—especially young men "in charge" of something for the first time—he didn't welcome advice. This led sometimes to wordless antagonisms within the community. Nothing was said very often; he did not really sulk. But his jaw muscles were working stiffly, and the others knew that one or all of them were being "told."

Now, after two and a half years, though, all that was beginning to change. Chris had come to St. Paul's "very much the boy." Now he was learning ever so slowly to take himself less seriously, to tell stories about his own small failures and be able to laugh quite heartily at himself. (One senses, at least in some part, the sensitive hand of Conway in that.)

Chris had come to Musami like a brand new pair of shoes which have not been battered about enough to have some comfort and "give." But the work was beginning to undergird a measure of confidence in himself that he could indeed afford to bend a bit. He was beginning to make peace with life and with himself, midway between his abilities and his expectations.

Christopher Shepherd-Smith was just about ready to lay claim to the inheritance of his manhood. He was just that close to "being there."

* * * * * * * *

The Dominican Sisters went about their business as usual.

Sister Joseph Wilkinson was 58; she had come from Lancashire in England 37 years ago and had been a nurse and midwife all those years. She wasn't about to stop or even pause in her work because of all this foolishness. People were sick; something could be done about that. Along with her, Sister Anna, even at 75 and crippled with arthritis, hobbled over to the hospital every day she was able, to help wherever she could. It was good to keep busy.

The rest were teachers. Sister Ceslaus, 59, was a tall, comely woman who now taught swimming and photography to the African girls. She loved puttering around in the garden and filling every available space with bountiful jars of flowers. She had taught at most of the town schools in Rhodesia in her 41 years there. She was a fountain of joy and energy, tirelessly retelling to endless generations of saucer-eyed African children the adventures of Kalulu, the little hare, wisest of animals and surely the grandaddy of Uncle Remus' wily Br'er Rabbit.

Sister Epiphany was "our little old lady" (78) from Munich who had trained hundreds of African teachers in her 43 years on the mission. Even in so-called retirement, she was a wonderful example to everybody, always occupied in some way or other helping people, especially the girls in the home-craft classes. As long as she was being useful, she was perfectly happy.

Sister Magdala, from Kiel, West Germany, was the youngest of the nuns, 42, but had nonetheless spent 18 years in Rhodesia and was now superior of the sisters at Musami. Young and huge and beloved of her pupils, she had the right heart for Africa. She taught boys and girls in the secondary school, but she did even better multiplying her loving self by training African teachers. In those uneasy days, she spoke to a meeting of her fellow superiors of nuns: "Surely, we couldn't possibly forsake our people, whose lives are even more endangered than ours—having a brother or uncle or father on one side or the other, with the accompanying dangers. We may not abandon them." In her Office book she had written out a pledge to God, offering herself in place of those who might fear to stand in the front row.

They had never locked doors around the mission before. Now they were carefully checked every night. Merely a precaution. There was no real cause to fear that anyone would want to harm five women who, among them, had given 185 years of unself-conscious service to the black people of Africa.

* * * * * * * *

97

John Conway periodically stopped on his way back from Salisbury to see Gerry Finnieston, to go to confession, and give him an account of the latest alarums and excursions around St. Paul's. Today he had come only a few hundred yards down the Chishawasha road from the main highway when he spotted Gerry's car coming toward him. He slowed down and pulled to a stop on one side of the road; and, recognizing John's big 8-ton lorry, Gerry pulled up on the opposite side.

"Well, what are you doing here?"

The big Irishman swung lithely out of the cab, grinning. "I was on my way back from town, and I thought I'd stop for a chat."

"Well, we almost missed one another. I'm on my way into town to collect four petrol coupons."

They leaned against the car and chatted for a while, John telling him all the creepings and crawlings through the bushes that the children and the elders from the reserve had dutifully reported to "Brada."

John winked conspiratorially, "When they come, Conway will be ready to slip right past them, though."

"And how on earth do you plan to manage that?"

"I'll walk straight out of the Eagle's Nest and right through the lot of them—rigged up as a nun!"

The thought of this big raw-boned spalpeen, trailing yards of veil and skirt and walking smartly through a row of Russian machine guns, doubled Gerry Finnieston over with laughter. "Well," he said, recovering at last, "you certainly don't sound overly jumpy."

"I really don't think there's much to worry about, Gerry. Really. Certainly we've taken no sides, and we've done them no harm. Why would they want to come after us?"

Why indeed? Nonetheless, Gerry noticed that John was still wearing the Miraculous Medal he'd noticed before during his own visit to Musami at New Year's. He'd never worn one before. Christmas present, probably. Still . . . "John, the situation at Musami is serious. Take care. And let us take this opportunity of saying 'Goodbye.'"

They shook hands, got into their cars, and went their separate ways.

* * * * * * * *

When John Conway had arrived from England at Chishawasha Mission in 1954, he was given the red-carpet treatment. Father Mike Hannan, then in charge of all the Jesuit out-stations in Rhodesia, a man of crinkled face and infinite jest, had managed to scrounge up a remnant of red carpet and led Brother John grandly over it and through the portals of the mother mission. But in Rhodesia the red-carpet treatment doesn't last very long.

For less than a year, John was put in charge of the "intensive-care" section of the truck garden, and several times a week his produce was carted off to the various Jesuit houses of the district to provide provender for the troops. The path through his garden was the main path from the girls' boarding quarters to the school, and in a short time John knew each one by name and was greeting them in Shona, with just the slightest whisper of an Irish lilt. Within five months of his arrival in Rhodesia, however, he was transferred to the newly-founded mission at Wedza, to be jack-of-all-trades and especially to patch up their battle-weary vehicles and send them back into the fray.

Although he was an excellent bareback horseman, John Conway had practically grown up with a gearshift in his hand. As a boy, he had had to leave school early in order to help support a very large family, and he took a job bucking oil lorries round the Ring of Kerry on the west coast of Ireland. When the war broke out, although few Irishmen were eager to help Britain in much of anything, much less a war, John crossed over to England to work for a large construction company building airfields. The pay was good and helped the family back home. He made five to eight pounds a week and sent half of it home; if he missed a week, he sent his full salary the next week. But as the war ground onward and the reasons for fighting it became more compelling, John took a very hazardous job driving oil trucks through the worst days and nights of the Blitz. He had vivid memories of the Blackout, convoys of lorries inching their way along icy night roads in the pitch black, without lights. It was a tense few years, and on his evenings off he'd drop in at a pub for a few beers or into a town dance. By the end of the war, "The Kerry Dancer" could jitterbug better than any Yank in the place.

One day as he was driving through Bristol, he dropped into the Jesuit church; and, on his way out, the pamphlet rack caught his eye and he stopped to riffle through the booklets. One of them was about the life of the Jesuit brother, and he dropped his sixpence into the box and carried it off in his pocket. Three years later, with the war over and his brothers and sisters able to fend for themselves, he entered the Jesuit novitiate.

He fit the life like a piston in a valve, and he was "happy as a tick on a pig." He was set to work on the farm with old Brother Mannion, a slightly crustly old lad who used to plough with a horse which he treated as protectively as if she were the Queen Mum herself. But John had a way with horses and a way with the words, and before long he and Mannion had their heads together planning this and that, and Conway was on his way out into the field with the horse and plough.

And it was not merely the work he fit into but the spiritual life as well. The thirty days of silence and prayer of the Long Retreat were just so much familiar stuff to him, learned twenty-five years before at his mother's knee in Tralee.

When John touched down at Chishawasha and then was quickly sent off to the out-station at Wedza, he was by then well prepared for anything. And "anything" is precisely what he was given. The mission was a small collection of buildings and hen-houses, all roofed in corrugated asbestos. Within a month, John had solved the hospital's water problems by gerryrigging an ingenious water system, and the nursing nuns—all of them Irish—were completely in his debt and completely in thrall to his blarney.

His principal job was driving, picking up supplies, and above all coaxing the fathers' cars and motorbikes back into service and hauling the apostles out of the impossible positions they had landed themselves in during their week-long rounds of the bush.

But also he was the Boarding Master of the school and got to know hundreds of children on the station and out in the surrounding villages. He seemed tirelessly unable to get enough of kids. He would teach them and feed them and dance with them. He begged clothing for them and for his other poor. He built playgrounds for them—see-saws and swings and merry-go-rounds and basketball hoops and soccer pitches. He was the kind of unpretentious man who knows instinctively the needs and the ways of children, as Jesus did. He loved Wedza and was immersed in apostolic work there for six years.

Then in 1962 he was posted back to St. Paul's, Musami, where he rejoined his old pal Gerry Finnieston, who was principal there. He was kept busy with cars and gardens, which he looked after with his usual easy skill, but he was not quite doing the thing he was born to do. Then, out of the blue, came his great opportunity. The Musami superior had been ordered to start a sort of sub-mission or out-station or whatever-it-was-able-to-grow-into, at a place called Maramba, and he deputed John to "see to it." He was going to be the Founding Brother of a brand new mission, working alone in the bush many miles from Musami from Monday morning to Friday evening and returning to the mission for the weekends. And more chores.

Gerry Finnieston visited him many times out there and later wrote: "Maramba was a sort of Mission Impossible. It was 80 miles away from the main mission in an undeveloped Tribal Trust Land, inhabited by pagans and witch doctors and polygamists and undernourished children who had never been to school. To reach it, John traveled every week through Mrewa and its strip roads, then followed a fairly good gravel road lined with Methodist schools, then over the Makini-kini mountains along deteriorating roads, without stores or petrol stations, until he deviated from this and continued right through the uncut forests, eventually reaching the steep embankments of a river which was often in flood. Finally, he went down the embankment, through the river and up on the other side, then through miles of open fields without a single hut. It was a perilous journey along ways used only by miners and District Commissioners in four-wheel drive vehicles. John's transport was an old Chev truck that had seen better days.

"John had to see to the transportation of all building material for the new station and to the supervision of the builders. He started his Mission Impossible from nothing in the middle of the Rhodesian rainy season, and went there week after week in his old Chev, sleeping week-nights in the back of the truck. While the builders went on with their work, John gathered the children round him and began his community school where, in fluent Shona, he taught the children religion and how to read and write. He was a skilled pedagogue and catechist, and hundreds of children gathered round him and were formed into a Christian community.

"His fame grew and his medical skill improved. He studied dental surgery and purchased reliable dental equipment. He was no rough amateur here; his patients were given injections before extractions, and once he even injected himself and extracted his own tooth. I think of those sure hands of John and of his kindness and skill in treating his patients. I have seen him begin his clinic at five in the morning and was horrified at the cases he had to treat, screaming children, adults with terrible wounds and snake-bites and burns. All of them he treated with great skill and with a joke for everyone and a spoonful of sugar for the young ones. Once I went 20 miles beyond the out-station at

Maramba and was frequently asked when the Healer was due to arrive in their district."

Conway's people were mainly members of the Vapostore sect. "The Apostles," a mixture of Old and New Testament religion with their own bishops, each of whom had several wives. One of the tenets of the Vapostore was that they could not use medicine. But when one of the bishops got a toothache he would sneak over to the Brada's hut at four in the morning. John would whip out the tooth and manage to convince the bishop that a couple of aspirin could hardly be construed as medicine.

He kept a supply of very special medicine for the old grandmothers who came to him with a pain here and a pain there. "Well now, luv, I've got just the stuff for you. It's really strong and it'll cure what ails you in no time." Then he'd take them round the back of the hut and give them a pint or two of his own home brew.

The people were reluctant to take the children out of the fields and send them to school, and saw no reason whatsoever why the girls should go. Conway's chance came when there were three days of violent storms in the area, with lightning cracking and thunder fit to tear the top off the world. When it finally abated, some of the children came to see if Brada was all right. It was precisely what the Kerry Dancer had been waiting for.

"Well, I was scared half to death," he told them. "On the first night, I was sitting there saying my prayers and there was a knock on the door. 'Come in,' says I. But no one came in. So, with the fear quaking in my heart I walked over to the door, and took hold of the latch, and opened, and . . . what do you think was standing there?"

"What, Brada? What?"

"A great big fierce lion, that's what! Well, I ran quick as a bunny and hid under my bed. The next night, the same thing happened, and I bolted my door and shivered the whole night long under my bed, with that big old grandpapa lion standing outside my door. Oh, I was so scared."

"And what happened on the third night?"

"Well, on the third night, I wasn't quite quick enough. Just as I was about to slam the door, the lion got his shoulder in the doorway. And he said in this big, deep voice, 'Now wait a minute, Brada! Don't be afraid. I don't want to do you any harm. I just want you to take a message to my people.' So, he gave me the message, and then he went away."

"What was the message! What was the message!"

"The lion said to me, 'Tell my people: *hoyoko*! Beware! They must send their children to school!' And then he walked off into the trees without even saying goodbye. Now what do you think of that?"

The children were very suitably impressed and went off to tell their parents. Later in the day, a group of parents came to hear the story for themselves. They explained to the Brada, who was a European and did not know these things, that the lion was obviously the *mhondoro* or tribal spirit and that it was very important that Brada remember whether the lion went off to the right or to the left of his doorway. Now John knew that there was a medium of the spirit living on each side of his hut, and that either of them could become possessed of the *mhondoro* and confirm or deny the lion's message to the Brada for his people. So John pointed straight out the doorway. And from that day on, all the children were sent to school.

The mission grew. A formal school was eventually approved and opened, and certificated teachers came to reside at Maramba. For awhile, Fr. Berrell, a Jesuit studying anthropology, came to live with John and do research in the bush. He provided daily Mass and "a shot for the pot," which gave John a much improved standard of meals.

After four years of carving out a little village in the midst of nowhere and of the long weekend journeys to and from Musami, through rivers and over corrugated roads baked hard as iron in summer and a morass of gluey muck in the winter, John was called back to the African novitiate in Mazoe to teach the novices how to repair cars. But it was frustratingly tame and unchallenging work for him, and after a short time he was transferred again to the School of Social Work in the city. But he found it empty there, too; there were no children. So he went out and found them in the African "locations." Even then, though, John Conway was not a man for the sophisticated cage of a town caught up in modern industrial scrabbling and clutter. He was an Irish son of the soil and longed to be back in the open spaces of the bush and the simple life of the people of the real Africa. After two years of dogged service, he was finally reprieved and joyfully returned to Musami.

He was happy at Musami; it was home. He had now been in Rhodesia for fifteen years, and his knowledge of Shona and of the people were expert, and he devoted them might and main to his two favorite tasks: ministering to the cars and trucks that kept the priests able to carry the message to the people, and ministering to the children and the poor Africans he so obviously loved.

103

John was not a craftsman, but a patcher. His manner of finding if the electricity was on was not to go to the switch and test it but to stick a screwdriver into the plug and see if sparks flew. It was a method that ended him flat on his Galway Bay more than once. He didn't look for polish in a job but was more than happy if whatever-it-was worked, even for only a short time. He was a great believer in the "birds-of-the-air school of mechanics." At the mission, he was electrician, plumber, and sagittarius—in charge of the water supply. This involved frequent trips to the river about two miles away. If the lights went out even for a few seconds, the river pump would go off, and if the electricity failed because of a storm, Brother Conway had to stay up all night until the electricity came on again so he could restart the pump. Otherwise, all the dormitories and all the schools would have been without water.

His regular work, as with so many Jesuit brothers' work, was often interrupted by Mayday distress calls that assumed the proportions of an atomic attack and were surely more pressing than whatever he was involved in. Usually they were such urgencies as a schoolchild's trunk without a key. He had a box full of innumerable "magic" keys that seemed to open anything. If those failed, there was always a hammer and a screwdriver.

For the most part, "Brada" was imperturbable. Oh, he did mutter a bit when someone came to him at six o'clock in the evening to get him to fix a light switch—which had, of course, been broken since early morning. His style was always happy-go-lucky, admittedly not too highly organized, and more than amenable to interruption for a nice long chat. That, in its turn, got the members of the community a bit steamy, if a job John had promised was not quite ready as advertised, owing to a long bit of a blather with the children. But that was the price of having this lively, loving, indefatigable outsized leprechaun in their midst and at their behest. How could they get along or get around without him?

John's work as a trained mechanic was to set the fathers free to do the work that they had been specially trained to do. It is difficult to explain, even to a fellow Jesuit who is a priest and especially in these days since Vatican II when many brothers are becoming permanent deacons, why a man of John Conway's intelligence and obvious catechetical skill would remain "just" a brother. He would never consider acting as a preacher or a leader at the liturgy, though many thought he should. His conviction was that the chapel was where the priests did their work. He was a brother, not a father; brothers received their own graces and charisms, and fathers received theirs. The one thing that troubled him was that the shortage of brothers' vocations forced the fathers to do "brothers' work," tinkering with cars and patching up boilers, instead of the preaching and teaching they had spent nearly fifteen long years preparing themselves to do. It was a waste of talent, and that bothered him.

But there is a paradoxical twist even here. All the children called John "Brada," and he was surely known by more of the African parents than any other Jesuit on the mission. He was a delight to the mothers as he praised their children and crooned over their babies. "The stars are shining in your eyes, 'Amai'"—perfect blarney idiom in perfect Shona. He was a *fine* man, that nice "Brada." And so, ironically, all the Fathers were eventually called "Brada"—because they worked with John Conway.

No theological schooling or mechanical training, though, could have prepared John Conway to do what he did more superlatively than anything—and perhaps even than anybody—else: caring for the children and for the poor. At the end of school, all the children would come trooping into his workshop where he kept two picture books, one the story of Gulliver and the other the story of Bernadette of Lourdes. For an hour or so, he'd stop his work and tell them about their favorite pictures in fluent Shona.

He had the Irish gift for the story, and he'd mix a marvelous brew of saints, animals, and traditional African stories that held the shining little black faces agape with anticipation. Even adults would sit hanging on his every word. He told a story of ghosts he had seen one moonlit night, twelve of them, all black ghosts, marching gravely in single file down the dark halls of the community house. Solemn and ramrod-straight, they passed poor terrified "Brada" and walked right through the walls! They were carrying hoes on their shoulders and trooped along mistily across the lawn to the sacred tree—without so much as a whisper. There they gathered into a ceremonial circle and ever so slowly they began to dance. Round and round, round and round, they moved, sacrificing beer to the spirits of the tree. Then, quick as a wink, they disappeared: pffft! Brother had looked at his watch at that moment and . . . it had stopped! Midnight! All that was left round the sacred tree was the empty beer bottles the ghosts had used. "Now what do you think of that?" And in a flash of black legs they were out of the shop and across the fields to the "sacred" tree, and what do you think? There were the beer bottles!—John Conway did not just tell a story.

Conway Castle was a little mission all its own—library, school, catechetical center, pantry, loan company, clinic, and used-clothing outlet; don't ask where it all came from. He was the Pied Piper of Musami. It was rare to go into his room and not find some children there. It might be a little girl learning to write, or a little boy too poor to go to school, or a group of children looking through a picture book. On Sundays after Mass, there would be a crowd of kids in and around his little hut. The record player was blaring; small boys were kicking around a soccer ball; some were learning to read and write. But at the center of it all were the stories of Jesus.

John knew all the families around the mission and their individual triumphs and traumas, whose son had run off to the terrorists, whose son had joined the police. Many parcels of clothing sent from Germany to the Dominican Sisters somehow found their way into the hands of John Conway and were passed along to the neediest of them.

He had incredible stamina and was physically very fit. He thought nothing of swimming eighty lengths of the students' swimming pool, tirelessly timing himself, using an unpatented and inimitable stroke he'd learned in the great salt waves off Tralee. Nor did he seem to tire of offering wee sermons to his not-so-resilient brethren, especially the youngest, at dinner. It was his method of getting through the fronts people put up, especially the young who are so fearful of being discovered to be young. He considered it part of his vocation to get priests not to take themselves too seriously. "Tell me, Chris, what would you do if you were Pope?" or "Chris, have you ever been in love?" or "What is your philosophy for a happy life, Chris?" This, of course, was simply the excuse to tell you his own: "The secret of a happy life, Chris, is to have a noble cause to suffer for." At the time, it sounded a bit quaintly medieval and ingenuous.

John Conway was always so full of cheer, so ready to hop around in a little jig or to pull someone's leg, that he might seem to have been the perfect extrovert. On the contrary, if you lived with him you sensed that there was within him a deep reserve. Below the banter and fun and boisterousness there was hidden in him a deep center-place which rarely revealed itself except to one or two special friends. He had said to Gerry Finnieston once that a quick death at the hands of the terrorists would be a wonderful thing. At the same time, he looked forward to many years of work for the Society—although he wondered what possible use he could be. One frequently stopped into the chapel for a visit and saw him sitting there in the darkness, looking at God and letting God look at him. Doubtless, they spoke together from time to time of his usefulness.

What's more, he was a man able to spend five days a week, for three years, all alone, miles and miles from another white man. As with the shy Christopher Shepherd-Smith riding the endless trails alone, this big laughing Irishman was himself a bit of the outsider among these proper Britons. Beneath his stack of records for the children, there was a recording of rebel songs of the IRA he'd never dared play for the others. Somehow they wouldn't understand, having been free for so long, how thrilling and alive freedom can be, how it had to be celebrated all day long with laughter and music and dancing. The others knew—but did not really feel—the need of those young black boys out there in the darkness of the forests to be men, to be free. John Conway loved them in a far more vulnerable way than his brethren were able, and he understood.

* * * * * * *

6 February 1977,
7:45 p.m.

Dinner for the Jesuits and the Dominican Sisters was over, the dishes washed and stowed away, the cook gone home. Dunstan Myerscough, the minister of the St. Paul's community, went into the kitchen for a last look-round. He was, above all, a tidy man, his graying hair neatly furrowed exactly down the middle. As minister, he was in charge of buying, buildings, meals, and health. Dunstan had a good pair of hands; he was the one the artsy types had always depended upon for the sets and lighting of seminary shows. He was a careful, quiet, warm-hearted man. Well, then, everything tidied up. He clicked out the light, locked the kitchen, and went into the dining-television room. Rather shabby little place, he thought, by London standards—a few armchairs, but mostly hard upright ones, and an undersized TV set more than ten years old. Good enough for our needs, though.

St. Paul's, Musami

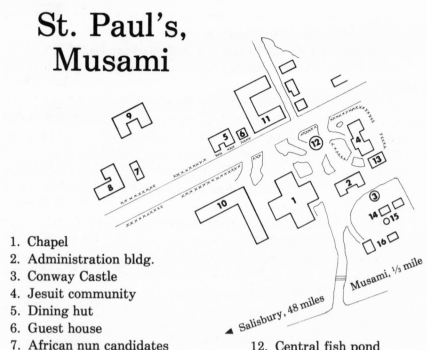

1. Chapel
2. Administration bldg.
3. Conway Castle
4. Jesuit community
5. Dining hut
6. Guest house
7. African nun candidates
8. African nuns
9. Dominican convent
10. Boys' dormitory and classrooms
11. Classrooms
12. Central fish pond
13. Garages
14. Carpenter shops
15. Water tower
16. African teachers' houses

Five of them were watching: young Chris, John Conway, and the three younger sisters, Ceslaus, Joseph, and the stout young superior, Magdala. Brother Adamson was out for a meeting with one of the African staff and his family. Chris had intended to go to Salisbury, but there was something wrong with his motorbike, so he'd decided for an easy evening at home. The old women, Anna and little Epiphany, were probably off in the convent saying their prayers and nearly ready to turn in.

"Anything good on?" Dunstan asked.

"It's 'The Sweeney,'" Conway called back without turning, "Good shoot-'em-up."

"Where's Martin?"

"Over in the community house, I suspect. You know Martin and the brainwashing telly!"

"Anything on the news?"

"Some Jewish chap named Ginzburg picked up in Moscow for sassing back the commissars. Odd name for a Russkie . . . Ginzburg. And the Americans are getting ready to perish of swine flu."

"Well, I think I'll leave you to your shoot-'em-up and do a bit more reading. See you tomorrow."

He closed the door on a chorus of "Good night, Dunstan" and "Good night, Father." They didn't turn as they spoke; some detective was careening down a London street with foreign agents after him, guns blazing. Silly stuff. Still, it would take their minds off things.

Myerscough stepped into the drying muddy road and past the little guest house, walking toward the pond. It had been a rather dull day, in both senses of the word. The sun had been trying to break through since morning and hadn't quite succeeded. But there had also been very little to do, especially for a Sunday. No one had gone out for Masses in the bush; there had been only the parish Mass. A couple of the fathers had been forbidden by the terrorists themselves during the week, and at all the stations the previous Sunday the faithful begged them, "Please do not come here next Sunday, Brada. Not safe to come here."

He walked by the broad path leading to the front entrance of the chapel, its corrugated iron roof catching the last glow of the dying day, and turned right up the path by the side chapel door, toward his room in the administration building. As he was about to go round to the back door, he noticed a light in Martin Thomas' room over in the west wing of the community house. Grading the endless papers, poor chap. A bit wordy, but a good, decent fellow, that Martin.

The old water tower on the hillock above Conway's rondavel glowered down on him in the gathering darkness as he climbed the stoop to the veranda outside his room and let himself in the back door.

A few pesky birds were squawking irritably back and forth to one another in the afterdusk. Otherwise it was peaceful.

* * * * * * * *

6 February 1977,
9:50 p.m.

Myerscough sat in his chair, slowly turning the pages of his book. He was in his shirtsleeves and soft slippers; his jacket, Roman collar and rabat were carefully hung away. Occasionally, he poked his glasses back up the bridge of his nose as he read, puffing contentedly on the old pipe. He chuckled to himself. The place was quiet as a monastery.

Suddenly he sat up with a start. He was nearly certain he had heard a very gentle knock on his door. Now, who the devil . . . Then, without getting up, he said in a somewhat hesitating voice, "Well . . . come in. Uh. What is it?"

But the door stayed closed. Myerscough grew a bit more tense. Slowly he rose from his chair. Then there was a small voice. "This is Sister Magdala, Father. Will you come? You're . . . wanted, please."

Myerscough let out a sigh of relief and reached for the door knob. Why couldn't people get sick at ten in the morning? "Where am I wan--- . . .?"

He pulled the door open and saw Sister Magdala, helplessly fat, her eyes agape with fear, suddenly shoved aside into the shadows of the corridor, and a grim-faced young terrorist in camouflage stood in front of him, his A-K rifle pointing directly at Myercough's chest. "Put your hands up! Right over your head!" Angrily the young African gestured the quaking nun back down the corridor toward the outer door; then he turned back to the priest. "All right, now you! Come out! Outside!"

Dumbfounded, the priest raised his hands and moved through the doorway into the hall. "Now, see, here . . ."

"Watch! Take off that watch!"

His heart thudding rapidly, Dunstan Myerscough began cautiously to lower his hands and reach for his watch, his eyes riveted on the guerrilla. He pulled at the band.

"Carefully! Very slowly. Take it off."

Very gingerly the priest handed over his watch.

"Now. Outside."

As they moved out the back door of the administration building, Myerscough saw Sister Magdala standing there on the stoop with Martin Thomas, his face taut-drawn and wary as a pointer. Two armed terrorists stood on either side of them. Off the stoop to his left by the end of the building he could make out John Conway in the dark, his big hands helplessly at his sides, smiling, looking warily to either side at the guerrillas guarding him. There was a flash of white uniform there, too, but Dunstan couldn't make out who it was.

"Now move!" They were shoved to their right along the veranda and turned around the north end of the administration block on the chapel side. Stumbling forward, Dunstan caught a glimpse behind him of Chris and the other two nuns, Ceslaus and Joseph, being shoved into line behind Conway. Good God, he thought, they've got us all. They must have reconnoitered very well; they knew exactly where we'd be! They must have broken into the dining room and gotten the five who'd been watching TV, then moved along the road to Martin's room and then to his own. He hadn't heard a rustle. Silent as panthers. They'd missed the old nuns. And for some reason they had none of the black sisters and none of the African teachers who lived on the mission grounds.

"You can let your hands down, but be careful." Perfect English without a trace of an accent. Mission trained? "Move along."

Myerscough had no idea how many there were. Eight? Ten? But the one barking the orders seemed to be the leader. As they reached the turn of the veranda the leader said, "Come on, come on, come on! We're not going to shoot you. We're just going to show you something."

Show us something. The terrorists had shown people unspeakably horrible "somethings" in the past four years. The children? The African teachers? Oh, God, not the little black postulants!

They shuffled awkwardly along past the side door of the chapel—"Quicker, quicker!"—but just as they came alongside the fish pond, Myerscough came up short and turned somewhat breathlessly and testily, "Look here, my friend, "I'm not as young as you are. I *can't* move any quicker."

For the first time the young man's teeth showed white against the darkness in a sneering smile, "You're not that old yet. Get moving." He prodded the priest again. "Here, wait a minute. Take those glasses off. Give me those glasses." Myerscough dutifully fumbled off his glasses. "Hand them back. Carefully!" The young man took them and shoved Myerscough forward again. Without his glasses, the priest aimed himself down the main road of the mission rather than walked.

It must have been shortly after ten by this time. It was quite overcast, a very, very faint moonlight obscured by light cloud. It was getting ready for a light rain at any moment. In the blanched light, without his glasses, the stubby hedges along the main road, the front of the church, the guest house and dining room looked to Myerscough like a photographic negative, all blacks and whites, details lapsed into a smear.

Ten yards or so beyond the dining hut they came to a break in the hedges on either side of the road. To the right, a little track led down to the quarters of the African sister candidates and beyond that the Dominican convent. In the field to the left stood some classroom buildings and the boys' and girls' dormitories—Surely, that's not what they're going to "show" us. They haven't harmed the children!

"All right, stop. Stay there." And so they stood in a sort of line: Martin Thomas by the opening in the hedge leading to the convents, Myerscough, Sister Joseph, still in her white hospital uniform, young Magdala, and Shepherd-Smith, faces frozen in a confusion of fear and courage, and finally by the opposite opening, Conway and then Sister Ceslaus.

As they stopped and turned, hearts still pounding, still completely mystified at what the next few moments would mean, they counted about ten terrorists talking in a bunch, nearly in front of the dining hut, ten yards away across the break in the hedge. Some were in camouflage, some not; and they seemed apprehensive, too, talking indistinguishably in loud whispers, seemingly unsure or undecided about what to do next. There was a man much older than the others, not in camouflage, in whom the others seemed to take great interest. Myerscough hadn't seen him before, and now at that distance and without his glasses, he couldn't tell if he were a local who had been spying for the insurgents, or someone in charge, or merely someone they'd picked up along the way. What's more, they were talking Shona; and, coming so recently from thirty years in South Africa, Myerscough couldn't understand a word of their argument.

And what on earth had they wanted with his glasses?

It wasn't many minutes later that there was a rustle in the darkness to their left, and two more armed terrorists appeared through the hedge into the half-light of the road, prodding along "the little old lady," Sister Epiphany. Sister Anna was nowhere in sight. At 78, Sister Epiphany could hardly keep her balance and tottered across the road into the arms of Sister Ceslaus at the opposite hedge. She was like a frail little bird startled from its nest.

They were now eight, lined up across the road from one hedge to the other. Their hearts ticked off an eternity in seconds—one, two, three heartbeats. Then more.

At irregular intervals two or three of the insurgents would come up to the opposite edge of the break in the hedge, five yards away, and raise their guns. Hearts stopped. Then one would snicker, lower his gun, and move back to the others. Then another would take his place. Over and over.

The leader had said on the way down, "We're not going to shoot you. We're going to show you something." Myerscough began to wonder: does this man mean what he said? Or is this the end? Or what is he going to show us? He'd showed us Sister Epiphany, and she was all right at the moment.

Suddenly one of the two men on guard stepped across the gap between the groups and went directly up to Martin Thomas. Everyone tensed. He pointed to Martin's grey whip-cord pants. "Take those off." Martin's face twisted with disbelief for a moment, and then he began clumsily to remove his trousers. "Now just push 'em across to me, slowly, very slowly." And the young man took the trousers and moved back to the larger group, without so much as a snigger or a further remark. Somebody else came and took his place across the gap.

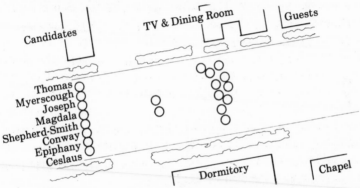

Father Thomas stood there, half-dressed, and Myerscough who was standing to his right was embarrassed for the poor man and moved to stand in front of him, to shield him if he could.

As the terrorist moved away with Martin Thomas's trousers over his shoulder, Christopher Shepherd-Smith leaned across Sister Magdala and Sister Joseph and said softly to Dunstan, "Would you give me absolution, Father?" And all the sisters turned around and, with their lips at least, said, "Please. Absolution, Father." So, very quietly, Dunstan Myerscough spoke the words and, watching the two guards every moment, moved his finger in the sign of the cross. Then he turned to Thomas and said, "Father, have you given me absolution?" Martin only nodded. Those were the only words they had spoken from the time the terrorists had collected Myerscough from his room. Not a sound otherwise. But Shepherd-Smith's request was Dunstan's first full realization that they were going to die.

113

Sister Joseph and Sister Epiphany were busy with their rosary beads. Myerscough couldn't see the others. The eight of them simply stood there, waiting, like strangers queued up for a bus. Absolute silence. It could all be just a scare; it still might well all blow over. They thought of how they would tell the story tomorrow—and for the rest of their lives. Perhaps. No one knew how much time had passed at the moment when three of the terrorists broke away from the farther group and somehow decisively took the places of the two guards. They knelt on one knee and raised their guns. The eight white men and women were transfixed. There was a loud call from the leader down the road near the dining hut.

"And after that loud call, I happened to be looking at the gun in the middle, and that started belching fire. Things are a little bit vague from that point. The next two or three minutes, insofar as I saw this belching fire, I sort of half-turned-round—I don't know whether instinctively or imagining I was hit or what—and flung myself to the ground. And apart from a short burst, as I thought then, from the three guns facing us—after a very short burst—there was silence. And then I heard running feet. And then there was a loud bang or explosion —I don't know how to explain it—from the south of our position. And . . . and then I heard more pounding of feet, going away. Then, dead quiet."

Myerscough lay still. He simply couldn't move; he felt paralyzed and dazed. He must have been wounded; he could feel the clothing next to his skin soaking with blood. Could a bullet have hit his spine? And then he came to his senses. He understood.

Slowly he edged himself forward and turned his head. Martin Thomas, Sister Joseph, and Sister Magdala lay all bloodied in a heap on top of him. He looked down the road. The terrorists had gone. Shuddering, he pushed his way out from under the bodies and stood up. One by one he went to the others. They were absolutely motionless and with—how could it be?—a wonderful look of peace on their faces. Except for Martin Thomas and little Sister Epiphany. When he first turned to Martin, that gentle man, there was a kind of gurgle in his throat, then a long sigh, then still. When he got to the little old nun there was a last gasping of breath, then still, perfectly still. "I think that neither Sister Epiphany nor Father Thomas had any consciousness left. There was just nature breathing its last."

Dunstan Myerscough stood there a moment in the dark night, breathing heavily, surrounded by the bloodied corpses of his friends.

There was nothing he could do for them; there was nothing he could do. Suddenly it began to rain softly, a misty drizzling rain. He gathered himself together and stumbled off like a drunken man through the gap on the east side of the road to the nearest building, the little hut where the African candidate sisters lived. He thought he'd remembered seeing the flicker of a light in there before. It was dark now, and deadly silent.

He opened the door and just put his head inside. "Can *anybody* give me a hand?" he pleaded. "I must do something with these bodies." But every bed was covered up. There wasn't a hair or a toe showing, and not a sound or a reply to his request. But the sheets trembled, and he knew they were alive, terrified. So he spoke into the darkness, still trembling himself, "Now it's all over. It's all quiet. You just go to sleep and don't worry. Don't . . . worry."

"So I closed the door and looked round about me, rather stupidly I must have seemed at that moment. I went back to the administration block near my room. The main office is there and there's a telephone in there. But first of all, I thought, no, I'd better move the bodies. Yes, the bodies. So we have a Datsun—I'm not sure if it's a ton or a half-ton truck. I wanted the keys to that to try and get the bodies in there. I hadn't quite decided where we could put them, but they certainly couldn't remain lying on the ground there.

"I couldn't find the keys for the truck. I searched the office, and I went back to my room. I was in that state then that I wasn't quite sure if I'd used the truck myself before and forgotten to put back the keys. There was a little Renault Six, a little station wagon, with all the seats in. Saw the key for that, and so I went back to the scene in the Renault. I got out of the car, and then I realized, well, how futile it is. How could I manage to do anything with seven bodies, by myself with a little Renault Six? I couldn't possibly get one of them in through the doors."

So, still dazed, he went back to the office and had another look for the keys to the truck. He pulled up everything on the desk. Useless. "Well," he thought, "I can't find them. I'll just . . . I'll just go back with the Renault there, and I may . . . I may be able to get them one at a time in the trunk. I've got to get them. They can't stay there. Not like that."

Half-blinded without his glasses and in a dizzying stupor of shock, he stumbled back out to the little Renault, parked next to the building at the head of the main drive into the mission. As he fumbled with the car door, he saw someone walking cautiously up the main road through the drizzling darkness. For an instant his heart clenched to a fist in his chest until he realized that it was Denis Adamson coming home from his meeting. He ran to Adamson and said, "Please, Brother, do you have the keys to the truck?" Adamson's mouth dropped open; Myerscough supposed he had heard the shooting and the explosion; he didn't realize then that his face and hands and clothes were reeking with blood.

"Yes," Adamson said numbly. "Why?"

"Well, I want them quickly, please."

"But what's the matter," he pleaded. "What's happened?"

Dunstan turned in helpless fury and pointed off toward the dining hut. "*That's* the matter. Down there, Brother," he said. "They've *all* been killed."

It hit Denis Adamson like a sledgehammer to the head. His eyes went wide with knowing and not knowing.

"Well, we managed to sustain brother a little bit, get him over his shock. I said, 'Will you please go and get the Datsun truck, and I'll come down in a minute and give you a hand.' So I went back into the office and phoned the police; but as I phoned them, a Greek store manager, a friend of the mission, was on the line apparently and could hear me trying to contact the authorities. 'I want the police, please!' And he said, 'Is that Musami? What's happened there?' And I said, 'Seven people killed. Would you please leave the line free, please? I must get the police and the army.' And the Greek man said, 'Well, we heard the shooting. Didn't you hear the police returning the fire from the township?' Well, I wasn't in a state to think back and reason that that was the cause of the explosion and the other heavy fire we'd all heard. I mean, I'd heard. I said, 'No, but please leave the line. Give me the line, please, so that I can get onto these . . .' And he said, 'Well, we have informed the police, and the police have informed the army. The army are in Marewe at the moment, but they've got the message and they're setting out at once.' Well, that meant that they would be approximately an hour coming from Marewe to Musami."

Dunstan cancelled the call, reminding the Greek man that he was to tell the police and the army that this was urgent and to come quickly. Then he got through to the mission superior, Father Patrick McNamara, in Salisbury. Mac asked if he should come up, but Dunstan told him not to. "First of all, there's a curfew, and, secondly, even if you do come out—which is rather rash—what possibly could you do? No. Leave it. Just get the news round, and would you please ring the Dominican motherhouse and tell them what has happened to them? Then if we could see you tomorrow . . ." And he hung up.

When Myerscough got the Renault back down to the break in the hedges, Brother Adamson was already there with the truck. As he drove up, Adamson shouted hoarsely, "Turn those lights out! It's not safe!" Dunstan got out of the little car. "Now, Brother, it's quite safe now. There's nothing else to worry about. We've got to move these bodies."

So they set to work. They got one body into the truck. It was terrible work. Just then, two of the African sisters came out and asked if they could help. "One was in her spotless white uniform. She was weeping uncontrollably, so we persuaded her to go back and accepted help from the other one, Sister Dominica, who was upset but still in control of herself, a really competent woman. So with the three of us, we managed to get two or three at a time into the truck, and we took them the short distance to the little guest house next to the dining room where it had all begun."

So as the very early morning wore on, struggling in the rain, they laid them all out on the floor of the guest house. They had no idea how long it took. One hour blurred into the next in a grisly nightmare. Finally, Dunstan Myerscough locked the door of the guest house behind them. By that time, Brother Adamson was beyond himself with nerves, ashen, and Sister Dominica was ready to collapse with strain and fatigue. The two of them took hold of Myerscough's arms as he made to go off down the road. "You can't go back to your room. You're going to come in at once," they said.

"Anyway, I was a bit beyond being nervous at that time, so I said, 'Well, I'll see you shortly. You put the cars away, and I've got something to do.' So I went down to the Dominican convent. I was wondering about Sister Anna, who had not been with us. But when I got to her room, her door was locked and her light was out, so I left that alone, but I went round and closed all the other doors of the Dominicans' rooms and put all the lights out and latched the front door. And then I went back to the community house, and I saw Father Thomas' door wide open and the light on. I turned out the light and locked the door and took the key away. And I put the other lights out round about—the outside lights round the community house.

"I went to my own room and closed my door, closed the office door, and put out all the lights round there. Then I went to find Brother

117

Adamson and Sister Dominica. They told me to come at once; there was an empty room in the convent of the African sisters. 'It's not safe anywhere else,' they said.

"Well, I wanted to go round to the boys' dormitory. I thought the explosion had come from around there or something had landed near there. But by this stage, I'm afraid it was almost to the stage of hysteria on the part of the brother and the sister. They were in tears. 'It's just not safe. You *cannot* go there!' Perhaps they were thinking more clearly than I, perhaps not. 'Well,' I said, 'all right, then. We'll leave that there. If anything had happened we probably would have heard by now.' So I went back to my room—no, they wouldn't let me go back to my room. I went with them to the African sisters' convent.

"It was a little back room. We daren't put the lights on. They seemed to think there might be somebody round or those people might come back again. And, as I say, there was a room there; one bed in it and a simple space on the floor. So Brother tried to persuade me to take the bed. 'I'm not in the bed mood, Brother. You get on the bed and go to sleep, and I'll sit down here.' So I lay down on the tiny little mat on the floor. It was pretty cold; it was concrete.

"Anyway, every quarter of an hour, Brother would touch my shoulder with his hand, shake me, and say, 'Shh! *Don't* snore!' So I said, 'Brother, I haven't been asleep. I wasn't snoring yet.' And he whispered hoarsely, 'No, you are. You're snoring. They're still out there. I've heard sounds outside.' And I said, 'Oh, it's just the rain. We're all right here, Brother, all right. I won't snore.' And this went on almost by the quarter-hour all night; 'You must keep quiet! There's somebody tapping at a window, and I heard a voice saying, 'Who's there?' We're not moving from here until it's broad daylight tomorrow! And so I said, 'Yes, well, it's all right, Brother.' And so we spent the night."

* * * * * * * *

7 February 1977,
Dawn

"Well, soon after five in the morning, I had had quite enough of that, so I got up as quietly as I could, but Brother heard me trying to open

118

the door. We had a short little argument there about the wisdom of going out in the dark. Finally I said, 'Well, I'm sorry. You can all stay here. I'm just going out to unlock the church. I'm going to call the girls. I'm going to have a wash. I haven't washed since that gruesome task.'

"So I went out and walked over to the church and opened the doors. And I thought, well, I'll have a very quick shave before I go and call the kitchen girls and ask them to get a fire going and get some coffee or something. And then, as I headed toward the administration block, I saw the army truck."

With infinite relief, he approached the truck. As the head of the security forces came forward to meet him, Dunstan was astonished to see that it was a boy he had taught in secondary school at St. Aidan's in South Africa. When they had greeted one another, Myerscough said, typically, "Now, before there's any real business, can we go and get some coffee? Can I go and clean myself up a little bit and get my shoes on and so forth?" So while the priest went off to change his clothes and wash the dried blood from his hands and arms, the security forces began to examine the grounds for tracks. The rain had grown heavy during the night and obliterated most of the footprints, but despite the rains there were still heavy bloodstains all over the killing ground.

When Myerscough returned to the dining room, several of the officers were inside drinking coffee, and John Potter, the police superintendent, had arrived. He informed them that a cattle herder and his brother had been found dead eight kilometers north of the mission; they had both been shot. Some of the soldiers had discovered spoor leading out into the hilly bushland east of the mission, and a party was sent to track them down. Then, the police asked Dunstan to perform the last painful chore, to go next door to the little guest hut and identify the bodies for them.

It was ghastly work, bringing back those horrifying hours, making the whole thing so unchangeably real. The corpses were all wounds, from head to foot. Several of them had broken ankles because, as the superintendent explained, it is impossible to hold an A-K rifle steady without a stand; they will rise by themselves and there's nothing one can do about it. So the gunman usually starts firing as low as possible to be sure of hitting the target.

Painful as it was to identify the bodies of his friends, there was one wonderful consolation about it for Myerscough. The previous night, as he had gone from one to the other, he had noticed the wonderful look of peace on all the faces except Martin Thomas and old Sister Epiphany. Now, as he went from body to body, telling the police their names, he noticed to his surprise that even they had "that same look of calm and peace, perfectly happy and at rest."

They came out of the guest hut and saw the police vans lined up to carry away the bodies. Solemn-faced little black boys and girls in grey trousers and blue shirts watched, eyes round with awe and hardly comprehending as the white plastic bags were carried on stretchers from the hut to the vans. With them was Tauya Chiveso, the black catechist who had worked for two and a half years with Christopher Shepherd-Smith, going from station to station. He held himself erect, face tensed with unconquered grief. But when they brought the young man's body out of the hut, he burst into tears and cried, "My priest! My priest!" and he collapsed into Myerscough's arms, sobbing.

A television truck had arrived from Salisbury and a busload of reporters, who were wandering around the tin-roofed buildings, taking notes. This was suddenly the first time in history that the world would know that the Musami Mission existed. It would probably as quickly forget.

In the investigation by the police and security forces, several interesting elements came to light. Myerscough was still convinced that there had been only one fusillade of bullets. But the army and police found 111 spent cartridges, some from RPD machine guns, some from A-K rifles. Unfortunately, it was impossible to discover where they had been fired from, owing to the fact that an enthusiastic young soldier had gone around picking them up and putting them in his cap.

Strangely, bullet holes were discovered in the peak of the chapel, 100 yards away and in a direction nearly 60° to the left of the missionaries. Ironic, too, that four bullets could penetrate two sheets of corrugated iron 100 yards distant and yet be held in the muscle of human bodies less than five yards away.

Sister Anna had been discovered safe and sound in her room that morning. At a little after ten the previous night, she had been sitting up in her bed reading when the door was flung open and a young African shouted at her, "Get out! Get out! You're going to be shot." 75 and cramped with arthritis, Sister Anna tried her best to get to the door but stumbled and fell to the floor. "Get up," the terrorist shouted at her.

120

But Sister Anna had taught African boys for forty years, and she looked up at him and said, "I'm an old lady. I have a sore leg, and I'm not young."

The young terrorist looked at her impatiently. "All right. Stay here and put out the light, and I will pretend I did not find you." He pulled her watch off her wrist and went next door to get Sister Epiphany. Sister Anna locked the door and turned out the lights. Later, she heard the shooting.

A young African candidate sister, Sister Emerentiana, told the investigators that sometime after 9:30, while their superior, Sister Monica was giving the candidates a conference, there was a knock on their door. Because of the hour and of the rumors that had been surrounding them for months, they were too frightened to open the door. They put out the lights and heard footsteps outside, running about, and voices calling back and forth to one another. When the intruders began beating down the door, the sisters opened it.

Two men came in and ordered the nuns to sit on their beds while they ransacked the room. Then they herded the sisters outside and hustled them up to the Dominican convent. They were ordered to stay outside by the door while the terrorists went inside, knocking on all the doors. They came out with old Sister Epiphany and ordered all the women to march back to the African candidates' hut. As they were being jostled along, Sister Monica summoned up all her courage and asked, "What do you want here?"

The answer was curt: "We want our country."

When they reached the small house, the black sisters were pushed inside and told not to come out, no matter what happened. They huddled into their beds, terrified to death of these awful men. Then they heard the shots. But they were too rigid with fear to find out what had happened. A few minutes later a voice that sounded like Father Myerscough asked for help, but they were afraid it was a trick. Then they heard the sound of a car, and then the truck. Finally, Brother Adamson came to get help, and two of the sisters went. They had no idea that anyone had been killed.

That morning, reporters asked Sister Anna if she would not leave Rhodesia and return to West Germany. "What good would that do?" she answered. "If I'm going to go, they'd come and find me wherever I am."

The following day, Tuesday, Dunstan Myerscough was summoned to attempt to identify four bodies of insurgents whom the security forces had shot sometime Monday evening. When he got there, they'd been dead over twenty-four hours, just lying there in the open covered with sheets. He thought one looked vaguely familiar, somewhat like the leader who had ordered him out of his room. But without his glasses, with only the faintest moonlight filtering through, he hadn't been able to see anything clearly. He was not sure.

A month later, in a subsequent terrorist attack on Riverbend Farm, a notebook was discovered describing the February 6 attack on St. Paul's Mission: "We reached there at 9:15, and we had a storming raid. We shot four Europeans who were priests. Sisters were five and altogether there were nine, eight dead. No comrades were injured in the action. We were very happy."

10 February 1977,
10:00 a.m.

The funeral Mass of the Resurrection was celebrated by Archbishop Patrick Chakaipa, the first black bishop of Rhodesia, on the grounds of the Dominican Motherhouse in Salisbury.

For two hours before the Mass, united in grief, white and black mourners passed by the coffins to pay their respects to seven martyrs of charity: Sister Ceslaus, that fountain of energy and stories for black children; Sister Epiphany, the little old lady, the teacher of so many teachers; Christopher Shepherd-Smith, who had finally laid hold of his manhood and took it with him when he died; Sister Magdala, who had prayed to take the place of those who might fear to stand in the front row; Sister Joseph, starched and unyielding; Martin Thomas, that lovely, gentle man; and John Conway, the Kerry Dancer, who now left so many African children orphaned. Not one of them had ever knowingly done anyone harm.

At the Offertory of the Mass, African men and women from the mission brought up small gifts of money as their *chichemo*, that is, the gift which says, "We mingle our tears with yours."

Later, Dunstan Myerscough was also asked if it would not be wiser if he returned to England. But he, who had come unscathed through a rain of a hundred bullets, intended to stay. "We Jesuits were brought up to be ready for it. We were never promised an easy passage. One day an end will come to this. I just hope and pray it will come soon."

Since that moment, three families of Protestant missionaries—men, women, and babies—have been slaughtered. Another Jesuit priest and brother were cut down by terrorists. Gus Donovan, the former superior of St. Paul's, has disappeared while on his rounds of the bush stations. And hundreds more Africans have been "caught in the crossfire."

Gerry Finnieston, after fifty years as a Jesuit, now sees Catholic missions closing all over Rhodesia—100 of the 300 stations have been forced to cease operations. Warnings have been sent to get out of the country or die; priests and nuns have had to leave all but a change of clothing behind and move to Salisbury. Young African seminarians have been sent orders to come home and join the resistance or their families will suffer. In one village, any man or woman who had a relative who had "gone over"—become a teacher or a policeman or the like—was lined up, 35 of them, and shot. Their bodies were thrown by the wayside and the other villagers were forbidden to bury them. They were to be left there till they rotted.

In his new station, Gerry is alone. He wanders over to his hut in the dark after supper. It is quiet, too quiet, only a dog barking. At what? It is so quiet you can hear that quiet. What's going on in the dark out there? People rarely come to visit anymore, and if they do, they are sure to leave well before supper. He understands. "Could be worse. Not much."

The end is not yet.

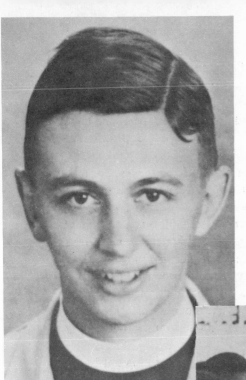

Fr. Martin Thomas

Fr. Christopher Shepherd-Smith

Br. John Conway

124

III

BRAZIL

JOHN—BOSCO BURNIER, S.J.

Time: 7:30 p.m., 11 October 1976
Place: The village of Ribeirão Bonito at the
eastern edge of the Mato Grosso, the
great frontier area of south-central
Brazil.

*You rich, see what you have stored
up for yourselves against the last days.
Here, crying aloud, are the wages you
withheld from the farmhands who
harvested your fields. The shouts of the
harvesters have reached the ears of the
Lord of Hosts. It was you who con-
demned the innocent man and killed
him. He offered you no resistance.*
                              —James 5/1-6

For hundreds of miles, Federal Highway BR-158 coils lazily through the wild outback of Mato Grasso, Brazil. Like a long, red-brown anaconda it oozes through the gnarled scrub, completely indifferent to the nameless little dun-colored towns that leech along its flanks. A few raw adobe and straw buildings clot around an open space here and there, way-stations lining the dirt highway, waiting dully for a bus or a truck to take advantage of their grubby wares. There's a gas station, repair shops with two or three skeletal carcasses of cars huddled around them, poorly-stocked stores, a few rough cantinas. There are a couple of whorehouses.

Each town is a place of indifference, a forgettable stop to relieve oneself on a long trip from somewhere important to somewhere temporarily more important. None of them is more than ten years old; the red dirt highway was not cut through the wilderness of the *sertão* until 1966. It exists for the big ranches, and the towns exist for the highway people and the ranch hands. Like all the Tombstones and Salt Licks and new This-es and Thats of the American old West, these dirty little Brazilian frontier towns would never snag the interest of even the most fastidious cartographer or reporter. Unless, of course, some stranger got himself murdered there and gave it at least a momentary fame.

For awhile, it seemed that Ribeirão Bonito, the town at Km 41 of Highway 158, would be just another of those towns. It had a lovely name, "Pretty Little River," certainly lovelier than its original name, "Pig Ravine." The river was indeed pretty, but all in all it was a little failure of a place. And then, on 11 October 1976, a generous little failure of a man named John-Bosco Burnier, S.J., attempted to stop the torture of two women there, and was shot by an arrogant little policeman. As one of the villagers said, "If it was one of the people of the town, that is something we're used to. It happens every day. But a priest! The police have gone too far." And suddenly that little man's death sparked Ribeirão Bonito into new life, more life than it had ever dreamed it possessed.

Other than the few tradesmen and the prostitutes, the people of Ribeirão Bonito are mostly *posseiros*, landless peasants, mestizos with

126

some Negroes and a few Indians, migrating west in search of land and food and away from the pestilent ant hills of the northeastern shanty-towns. They are truly pioneers in the roughhewn West, sturdy men and women, toughened by suffering back home and suffering out here in the bush. Some squatters farm nearby plots, but the soil is leached and unyielding, and even that is endangered by the encroachments of the ever-expanding large *fazendas*. These hugh plantations belong to cattle barons, whose expanding herds need from 20 to 30 acres of grazing land for each steer yearly. And they have hundreds of steers. Often the *posseiro* gets in the way of growth and progress.

There is not much that an illiterate squatter can do to prevent the inexorable advance of the *fazenda*, insatiably devouring little plots like his. Who is he to stand up to the powerful financiers and politicians of Rio and São Paulo, with the soldiers to enforce their desires? How could he hope to stop the multi-national corporations of Japan and Italy and America who buy up the land for grazing or cash crops or mineral speculation or merely for capital reserves? Even if he were to try, stupidly, to resist, the new owners would send their *capanga*, the company thug, to burn his hut and confiscate his harvest. And the owners also have at their command rural versions of the infamous urban "Death Squads" of Rio and Recife who come in the night to taunt and loot and kidnap and murder.

The police are no help; they are as much a curse as the bully boys of the *fazendeiro*. Because they make no more than $100 a month, the military police are, with few exceptions, on the rancher's payroll and often on his Death Squad. As one policeman said, "The squatters are of no value to the government. They serve no purpose. They have nothing and they're going nowhere." The bishop of Mato Grosso has written to the authorities about this pervasive injustice—to the Secretary of State Security, the Governor of Mato Grosso, the Minister of Justice, even the President himself—but it is shouting into the wind. In the end, the small subsistence farmer has no choice but to give up his home and his land and go to work for the big landowner as a contract laborer.

These temporary workers who come to towns like Ribeirão Bonito make a contract with the *fazenda* foreman to clear a certain amount of scrubland for a stipulated price—slashing down brush and trees and burning off the area to make away for grazing cattle. It is a hard life. Most of them are living away from their wives and families, like Okies, trying to make enough to keep their children alive. Conditions are

127

inhuman; wages are scandalously unjust. Sometimes workers will contract to clear a certain area, misjudge the time it will take and find themselves working endless hours for less and less money per hour. Money they must pay back for food and lodging often eats up all their earnings, leaving them with little or nothing to take home.

The ranch foreman is boss. The landowner gives him a certain amount of money, and he does the hiring and firing. Usually what he can make out of cheating or overworking or underfeeding his laborers stays in his own pocket. Needless to say, ranch foremen for the Mato Grosso are not ordinarily recruited from the Salvation Army.

During their contract period, the workers sometimes have Sunday off. For a few hours on a Saturday night, they head to a village like Ribeirão Bonito to let off steam and get drunk on *cachaca*, a clear fiery drink made from sugar which is lovingly called "the brandy of the poor," "thread of gold," "the little blonde." The local bar owner takes advantage of them with inflated prices, and they in turn take advantage of the local women. This is not the technicolor frontier of Miss Kitty and the Longbranch. It is a matter of dull and brutal coupling with dead-faced women trying to scrabble together a few pennies themselves to care for their own problems. When the farm contracts are terminated, the migrant workers move on to another ranch, and the prostitutes wait apathetically for the next contingent.

For tens of millions of Brazilians, life is dirty, hungry, cruel and short.

But today—11 October 1977—was a day to remember: a fiesta! Today was the first anniversary of the death of *their* martyr, John-Bosco Burnier, and the day of the dedication of their brand-new church. Today even the whores were smiling!

Visitors were everywhere. Peasant families from Agua Limpa and Mata da Banana, priests from Rio Grande do Sul and Marahanhaio, representatives from the Bororo and Xavante Indian peoples, bishops from all over Brazil, and Presbyterians and Pentecostals and Episcopalians and Methodists. Hundreds of them. Just before the procession, an auxiliary bishop from São Paulo had come up laughing from the creek, surrounded by children still dripping wet from their afternoon swim. All through the town firecrackers barked and sputtered up little fountains of russet dust. Such a bustle and commotion for the dedication of a single small church in the middle of nowhere!

They had talked for years about building a new church. The old one hardly deserved the name—two adobe walls, two open picketed sides, palm-thatched roof. Squatting in the corner of a raw dirt lot, it was hardly more than a rundown picnic pavilion in an old public park. They'd have to do something about it someday. Someday.

That day had come exactly a year ago today when the visiting priest had been murdered. That night the *posseiros* of Ribeirão Bonito had found there was more courage and power among them than they'd thought. Suddenly their dead-end lives had opened up. It had taken them only three months once the rainy season ended, working together in the strange new brotherhood born that night, to make the thousands of bricks, to hew out the roofbeams and raise the walls of this fine new church—tall and smooth-walled, its whitewash spanking-clean in the hot sunshine. As they worked they had sung together, matching their hammer blows and the scrape of their trowels to the rhythm of the song.

Let us make of our union our strength;
Let us make of our liberty our new home
On the land, which is God's and ours.
He who knows how to be a brother
Can stay.

The procession moved slowly from the weedy village soccer field along the wide dusty highway. At the head of the hundreds of singing people in their shabby Sunday best were Zé and Carlos carrying the cross, flanked by white-robed bishops. They moved past the newly built jail and saw the ruins of the old one where the priest had been shot down, the jail they themselves in an explosion of rage had torn down stone by stone with their own hands. In the doorway, part of the contingent of police reserves brought especially for today from Cuiabà huddled behind cement sacks. "Ha-*ha!*" shouted one of the men in the procession, "Wetting their pants!" And the laughter rolled up and down the line. One of the bishops seemed to be wiping sweat from his upper lip, but Carlos saw he was wiping away an unseemly guilty grin.

And the Mass began: " 'My dwelling place shall be built among you,' says the Lord. 'I will be your God, and you will be my people.' "

In a single year, something very important had happened to this nowhere place and its stalled lives. For the people of Ribeirão Bonito, today was a birthday.

And all of this new life had been brought to birth through the travail of a man they'd hardly known.

* * * * * * * *

It was perhaps unfair, or at least misleading to call John-Bosco Burnier a "generous little failure of a man." He did his best at every job he was ever given, but somehow each one of them was suffused with mediocrity, or less. And like Rutilio Grande, Burnier so longed to serve God greatly. Yet he was surely in no danger of becoming a legend in his own time. Until its last few hours, his life was pretty much a failure—not to serve, by any means—but to serve significantly, at least in his own eyes. Especially in the years after the turnabout of Vatican II, his faith became so disoriented that his service was often an act of dogged, uncomprehending loyalty and obedience, responding to challenges rather than offering them. And yet it is all the clumsy ordinariness which preceded his death that makes his martyrdom such a beautiful Cinderella story.

Many men and women felt orphaned by Vatican II. Later, when the Society of Jesus met in its 32nd General Congregation to revitalize itself according to the decrees of the Council, many older Jesuits were even further shocked at the dramatic changes within their own Order: the loss of uniformity and certitudes, the opening up and consequent "dilution" of seminary training, the erosion of the old customs, the old rituals and—it seemed—the old values. And all in the name of Jesus Christ! Unlike Rutilio Grande who finally found himself because of these changes, many other Jesuits began to feel like strangers in the very house they had given their lives to build. Such a man was John-Bosco Burnier.

He had been born in 1917 into a quite wealthy, quite conservative family in Juiz de Fora, 75 miles north of Rio de Janeiro. He was the middle child of nine; his father was a prominent engineer and his mother was the daughter of a respected doctor. In Brazil, where they labor over pedigrees with the punctiliousness of horse breeders, the Burniers were more than merely respectable. Their grandfather had been the engineer who built the great Central Railroad of Brazil, and their great-grandfather had been Dr. Michel Burnier, a famous lawyer and writer exiled from France during the Revolution. As the years went on, the "Michels" became "Miguels," and the Burniers became as thoroughly Brazilian as their neighbors. The family was unostentatiously comfortable with rank and money and with the privileges that accrue to both. And they were also a very religious family; three of the five boys became priests.

Two of the other Burnier boys and three of the girls were deaf-mutes. Senhora Burnier had prayed fervently to St. John Bosco during her fifth pregnancy that this child would not be impaired, and when he was born able to hear, she named him after the saint she knew had protected him. Living with so many handicapped children is a gift which often transforms the whole family. The other children are forced to make allowances, to protect, to rise above the petty taunts and cruelties from children who were not fortunate enough to learn compassion very early.

John-Bosco had gone to the archdiocese minor seminary for secondary school and, as a mere boy of 16, was sent by the Cardinal of Rio to study philosophy at the Gregorian University in Rome, the international seminary run by the Jesuits. After only two years there, he realized he was called to the Order and in 1936, with the blessings of the Cardinal, entered the Jesuit novitiate in Rio. Four years later, he was sent as a seminarian to teach in a high school. From 1936-1940 he not only taught Latin and Greek there, but also was prefect for the Aloisianum, a residence and meeting place for young men interested in entering the Society of Jesus. He was a quiet, studious young man, but he was also an excellent soccer player and organized the athletic activities for the high school boys. He had a deep, unobtrusive influence on those young men; one of them, Marcelo Azevedo, later became John-Bosco's own Jesuit provincial, and another, Luciano Mendes de Almeida, became that same auxiliary bishop of São Paulo who frolicked with the children of Ribeirão Bonito at the dedication of their church a year after John-Bosco's death.

Burnier began theology in Brazil, but a year later he was sent back to Rome to complete his Jesuit studies at the Gregorian. There he was ordained 27 July 1946, and two years later, having obtained his theological degree, he made tertianship at Gandia in Spain. Finally, after 15 years of study, he was ready to be put to work.

Throughout John-Bosco Burnier's life, one senses a strong undertone of sadly unfulfilled romanticism. The line between idealism and sentimentality is very broad and tenuous, but within his day-to-day work behind so many desks one catches a glimpse of Walter Mitty. His dreams never became foolishly dramatic, nor even explicitly stated, but in his letters they lurk between the lines: "To put an end to this long discussion, I underline the fact that the fulfillment of a complete renunciation of self implies for me, I believe, departure for a distant mission. I offer myself in a total gift to unite myself as an instrument to God, as our holy father St. Ignatius said. I feel my modest ability to serve will be augmented considerably if you will allow me to offer this

131

gift." It is a hope common perhaps to all of us that, if our talents were allowed to work themselves out in some exotic ambience, they would not look unpromising anymore.

All his life, Burnier had nurtured this somewhat quixotic dream of the foreign missions. For a Jesuit, there is no more romantic embodiment of the missions than their patron, the Jesuit Francis Xavier—the dashing sixteenth-century cavalier and intellectual whose heroic energies Ignatius Loyola had converted from the pursuit of power to the pursuit of service. For years this giant had walked the beaches of India ringing a little bell and preaching the gospel to children who couldn't understand a single word he said. Then suddenly, through motives not entirely altruistic on the part of the neophytes, the conversions had begun coming by the almost embarrassing thousands. Buoyed by this sudden success, Xavier had moved from India to Japan, laboriously wearing away the Oriental distaste and distrust for all things Western and raising up the seed of a new family of the church. Finally, he had died alone on the island of Sanchian, his eyes straining across the straits to the unfathomable mysteries of Cathay, unable to reach it.—Only the hardest of cynics could remain totally insensitive to the heroic lure of such a romantic life.

John-Bosco longed with a passion to go to Japan himself and throw in his lot with the missionaries among the poor. He begged his superiors to send him. Poor good little man, yearning to immolate himself heroically for God.

But there are two patrons of the missions: the *conquistador* Francis Xavier and the little cloistered Carmelite nun, Ste. Therese of Lisieux (Santa Terezinha), who also yearned to serve in the Indies but could only pray for the missioners, shut away from the world in her cell. For the next 16 years of his life, that was also the only service John-Bosco Burnier could give them. One suspects superiors reasoned that he wasn't a bold man, not particularly hardy or practical. On the other hand, he'd had four years in Rome, knew Italian, French, Spanish, English and had been an excellent student. He was an obedient man and it would do him good to have some experience of the official workings of the Order. So he was assigned by Fr. General John-Baptist Janssens to the central office of the Society of Jesus in Rome: Substitute Secretary to the Latin American Assistant to the General.

In Latin, the title sounds quite grand; it is surely impressively long. A brief Italian life of Burnier describes the central office as "a great intellectual beehive, with priests and brothers of every language and color" and calls Burnier's work "crucial and unheralded." Perhaps so. But in any bureaucracy, the length of the title is usually a quite trustworthy measurement of the holder's distance from the real center of power. Moreover, in response to a request for personal recollections about Burnier during research for this present book, not a single Jesuit who worked there with Burnier at the time could remember much at all about him.

For one thing, of course, it was a huge community. But the office itself, at least at the time, was a collection of excellent junior clerks, men who could remember files, letters, locations and dates with the speed of summer lightning, but not persons. This work was, in effect, high-level drudgery, and Burnier—as in everything—gave it the very best he had in him: four years of opening letters, drafting replies, filing copies, opening letters. . . .

That being the case, one wonders what the look must have been on his gentle pious face when the kind but somewhat flinty Father General informed him that the Society in Brazil had expanded so rapidly that he was dividing off a new vice-province of Minas-Goias, and that he was naming John-Bosco Burnier as its vice-provincial! Poor man. He had never once in his life been superior of anything, much less a brand-new vice-province with hundreds of men, three high schools, a university, a seminary, a center of social action, writers' houses and three parishes! And he had not been home for nine years! Nonsense. He had proven himself a calm and meticulous intermediary and had full knowledge (on paper) of every man and work in the new vice-province. Only an obedient man can command, after all. He pleaded his ineptitude, but Janssens, with a dispatch which precludes further argument or reasoning, replied: "Your reverence should not speak of his ineptitude; let him trust in God who gave the job to him and not to someone else." Those were times of enviable simplicity.

So, faithful as an ox, he returned to Brazil to take up the yoke of leadership. As one might have suspected, despite the best of hearts and with dauntless effort, he did not fulfill his new post overly well.

The formation of a new vice-province is always a shaky operation. As a result of the increase of available manpower and institutions in a large province, the central office in Rome sees promise that the province can be carved up into new administrative areas to shorten the lines of communication between individuals and their major superior. But it is only a promise. Once set on its own, the new entity can no longer depend on the financial backing of the former province nor on its larger pool of vocations; it must generate its own sources of both man-power and money. It is a precipitous business, especially for a man who has never been an administrator and never raised money in his life.

From the beginning, Burnier, in every way, had his limitations—to put it at its mildest. Like many men whose greatest virtue is uncritical obedience, he seemed to counterbalance his conspicuous spirituality with a conspicuous lack of foresight in practical affairs. He never seemed able to answer letters. Men waiting to be assigned to the next phase of training ended up assigning themselves and getting approval later. He shilly-shallied about decisions for fear of making a mistake and hurting the province, and then once he had made them became immovable about them. Some of them were disastrous. At the request of friends and benefactors in his home town, for instance, he trans-ferred the headquarters of the vice-province there and opened up a new high school in that city as well. What's more, because of the shortage of Jesuits, he himself volunteered to be its principal—on top of his work as vice-provincial!

He had the non-expert's inability to stand back from the whole work and achieve some kind of perspective and balanced view of the entire operation. Thus, he compromised some works and some financial resources set side for the training of scholastics. To his credit, at the first sign that the funds were taking a tailspin, he entrusted the finances to a properly experienced accountant. But after three years it became evident that his own assessment of his aptitude had been right all along, and that he would surely serve the Kingdom of God better anywhere else. That proved true only in a sense.

In 1959, when the master of novices for the province was elected to represent them at the 32nd Jesuit General Congregation, John-Bosco Burnier was named master of novices of the Brazilian Central Province.

In the Society of Jesus, there are only two offices to which a man may aspire: the post of minister, who assumes all the headaches of run-ning the community residence, and the post of master of novices. The reason is that, if he does, superiors can be sure that the man has either taken leave of his wits or has truly been called by God to that task.

The master of novices holds the future of his province in his hands. In what was—at the time—still a very isolated environment, he was for two years in sole charge of the formation of the young Jesuits who would eventually "become" the province. He was the one teacher of theology and spirituality, the one confessor, guide, and arbiter of manners and values. It was a sequestered but awesome burden. Unlike his filing days in Rome, this was truly a "crucial and unheralded" job. Not only is the master of novices the most focal person in the lives of his seminarians for two years, but he is also subject to the constant scrutiny and appraisal of the other members of the province. Each of them, when they come to the novitiate to visit or make their annual retreats, watches the young men to see if they are receiving the "proper" training he himself was given. For four hundred years they have gone back to their home communities muttering, "Things aren't what they used to be! They ought to get rid of that man!" What's more, Burnier was assigned to his post in the wake of Vatican II and during the very confusing days of the first session of the Society's own general congregation. When the liberals came to visit, they returned home muttering, "Antediluvian! Marching straight back to the 13th century! They ought to get rid of that man!"

During the years after World War II, in seminaries all over the world, superiors found a certain slackness in the incoming novices, a certain resistance to silence and recollection, a certain easement in the direction of the "world," brought about in great part by the increasing sophistication of the applicants regarding psychology, sociology, and so forth. For his part, John-Bosco Burnier was nothing if not a man of clear principles, and he wrote that, "No novice, through a lack of equilibrium or the spirit of obedience, ought to become useless or a burden to the Society." It was his task, he felt, to tighten things up.

There were some in the province who accused him of "integrism," that is, the conviction that there is one and only one "Catholic" way of going about any task: the way it has always been done. This seemed to fly in the face of the very definition of the word "catholic," which means universal, variegated, adaptable to any new culture or era. Nonetheless, Burnier was quite diffident and at times intransigent about implementing the innovations which his provincial proposed, at least in the manner of experiments. Again to his credit, hindsight tells us today that his hesitancy to join the pell-mell rush to change was not mere blind mulishness, nor were all the results of those changes unmixed blessings.

Moreover, he seemed to presume that the young men could be divided into "conservatives" and "progressives," with the former to be encouraged and the latter to be carefully changed. He did not immediately realize that this set up a barrier to real communication with them, and though they sincerely respected his deep spirituality and his

135

spirit of obedience in setting up the innovations he did implement, he himself began once again to suspect that he did not have the degree of competence for this office which his superiors had supposed.

The six years Burnier was master of novices were the most difficult of his life, a real "dark night" of his vocation and his love for the Society. The interval between the first and second sessions of the Congregation was particularly painful, simply because its deliberations were widely reported but not yet locked into law. Its requests for adaptation to modern times seemed to many, including Burnier, as almost an official surrender of all that the church and the Society of Jesus had struggled and suffered for since the Council of Trent. A Jesuit was now asked to reassess with a completely open mind all that the Society had been doing in education, in parishes, in seminaries, in community life. To many this "renewal" was actually a foolhardy rejection not merely of accidentals but of the very essence of Jesuit life. It was a threat to obedience, perhaps even an egalitarianism where every Jesuit no matter what his position or experience or mind-set had an equal say with his superiors in the discernment of the direction in which the Spirit was leading the Society today. A few even caught in these changes a vague whiff of communism.

For men like Burnier, it was a wrenching paradox—perhaps, he feared, even a contradiction: his vow of obedience to the Society and its Congregation seemed to be asking him to undermine that very vow of obedience! It was a crisis of alienation from the very authority for which he had had such unquestioning esteem since his entrance 30 years before. He had come from a traditional conservative family. He had been steeped in *"Romanità"*—the primacy of all directives emanating from Rome over any local or personal insights—by his studies at the Gregorian and his nine years there. He had been an unimpeachably good "company man." And now he felt betrayed.

Providentially, after six very harrowing and self-sacrificial years bearing the burden of the displeasure of nearly all in the province, he was transferred out as master of novices in December 1965. What was more, he was finally assigned to do the one job he had been telling his superiors all along that he was fitted for: working for the poor as a missionary. It was not to be Japan, but the frontier country of Mato Grosso. No matter; there were many immigrant Japanese settlers in the Brazilian outback, too. In remote areas, but he would find them! Nor was it the dramatic wilds of the Amazon country among naked stone-age Indians who had fled the incursions of the white man further and further into the jungle. It was only just on the edge of the true mission country of Diamantino, a parish near the city of Cuiabà, the capital of Mato Grosso, a city of 60,000 people. No matter; just let him get there and he would find a way to the Indians too!

It is hard even to guess the exhilarating thrill of freedom this new assignment brought to this good man. In the first place, it was the work he'd felt called to by God for thirty years. But also he was set free at last from shuffling paper, from bewildering budgets, from the formation of young men he no longer understood. And even better, he was freed from the incessant and seemingly inescapable antagonism between "the old way" and "the new way."

He wrote, "Personally, I cannot free myself from all that I identified myself with for the lat 29 years in the Society. There in the Mato Grosso, even if only on its edge in Cuiabà, there is no awareness of these debates, by which I never again want to allow myself to be disturbed. We are well off, away from all that, in the good company of the original Jesuits of the frontier."

"The old way" and "the new way" no longer mattered. In so many senses, John-Bosco Burnier was at last flying (on a bus) toward complete self-surrender to the poor and the outcasts of the wilderness.

* * * * * * * *

The trip from the East coast of Brazil to the interior of Mato Grosso is an immense journey backward in time. Burnier set out from the most modern metropolis in the world, the 21st-century city of Brasilia, and traveled through frontier cattle and mining towns almost exactly like those of the American wild West of hundreds of years ago, and finally, he hoped, to stone-age villages where Indians lived daily lives exactly as if all human history had never occurred.

For 400 years since the Portuguese invasion, the mountains along the coast had formed a fortress barrier that kept the population encamped along the eastern edge of the country. Today all along the Atlantic coastline there are glutted modern cities, 93% of the population. Half the people in South America live in Brazil, and yet most of them are crammed into that narrow coastal plain, "a gallon of people in a pint of land." And all the while, on the other side of the cordillera, stretches an empty land as large as the continental U.S. But for centuries only the hardiest, the hunted and the desperate dared probe into the *sertão*. Even today, when there are still only two people per square mile over the half-million square miles of the Mato Grosso, pioneers want only to stay out there long enough to strike it rich enough to move back to a luxury apartment in Rio or São Paulo. Very few do.

Half the rivers in the wild Mato Grosso flow to the north, into the vast 2000-mile Amazon basin, the richest and largest rain forest in the world, an ocean of eternal and boundless green covering almost half the area of Brazil and processing 15% of the world's oxygen. There is virtually no pollution whatsoever in the river; its waters are chemically purer than most American tap water. But it is inhumanly repellent wilderness, a steaming jungle of bawling alligators, gigantic leeches, anacondas twenty feet long and a foot thick, six-foot electric eels which can shock a man unconscious, wild peccary pigs to whom even jaguars give the right-of-way, and bloodthirsty mosquitoes. Over eons, the Indians have adapted to its horrors, but the white men find it a green hell.

The rest of the rivers of Mato Grosso flow to the South and empty into the Paraguay River. In the dry season, the lands of the Pantanal spread out in miles and miles of rich grazing land. But in the rainy season they are miles and miles of impassable swamp. There, a tourist can relax from his fishing and enjoy "The Show of the Piranhas," tiny savage-toothed fish which can devour an entire calf in seconds.

Between the Amazon and the Pantanal, the central highlands of Mato Grosso where Burnier was traveling offer endless arid stretches of dull-brown scrub, gnarled and stunted trees, and tall bitter tropical grasses, interrupted occasionally by stands of woodland which slope down to dull brown rivers like strips of suede. In winter, from mid-October to mid-April, the *sertão* gets more rain than the jungle; in summer, from mid-April to mid-October, the land is prostrate with heat. There has never been any rain in the Mato in July. The night clings like a wet straitjacket; the days are crematories. The valleys around streams are green even during the dry season, but the grass covering the rest of the *sertão* is coarse and unpalatable, and toward the end of the dry season the herds are skin and bone. And each year, because of the lack of railroads, hundreds of thousands of head are delivered to the East in three-month overland drives like those of the old American West. And as in the old West, the cattle drovers act as almost a private militia to the *fazendeiro*.

Brazil has rightly been called "The Awakening Giant," but of course when giants begin to stir, many tiny people will inevitably be crushed.

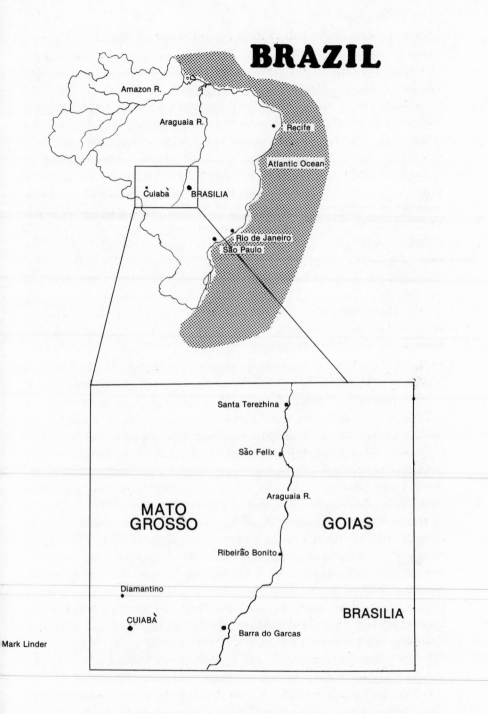

Mark Linder

139

Nonetheless, in 1955, President Juscelino Kubitschek persevered with messianic enthusiasm in his crusade to move the central government of the country from Rio de Janeiro to the rough interior of Goias, the state neighboring Mato Grosso. Brasilia was not to be the self-aggrandizing monument of a fanatical politician. This Federal District, a capital the size of Pennsylvania carved out of the wilderness, was to be both a symbol of a modern, dynamic nation but more importantly a stimulus to migration into the unused lands of the interior. The ultra-modern city itself is modeled on a jet plane: a fuselage mall from which modern apartments sweep away like wings; government buildings in the "nose"; shops and department stores in the center where the fusilage and wings meet.

While this space-age city was building in the middle of the wilderness, the road north from Rio to Brasilia was called "The Jaguar's Promenade." It was a pioneer town in the fullest and worst senses. It attracted the same adventurers and gamblers and prostitutes as the slowly emergent centers of the American West. But today time is telescoped: Brasilia went from jungle to frontier town to metropolis in only ten years! True, the plaster is already peeling off the walls in some of the ultra-modern buildings, but the move had broken the strangle-hold of the oligarchy headquartered in Rio, and made at least a momentary attempt to have the government represent all the people. That, too, has melted away under the pressure of ever more fascist governments. If nothing else, then, Brasilia has necessitated an explosion of road building and opened a rush of colonization of the outback, by both large international cartels and small squatter families. In 20 years, the population of the interior state of Goias has more than quadrupled from 40,000 in 1950 to 130,000 in 1970.

In the mid-70's, however, there was a kind of clashing of the tides of migration. Thousands of people began moving from the grinding rural poverty of the outback into the indescribably foul urban poverty of the *favela* shantytowns on the East coast. At the same time, other thousands were fleeing the squalor of the *favelas* to lay squatters' claims to the new lands in the West. For the squatters, it makes no more difference that the land they claim is Indians' land than it does to the large corporations or than it did to the noble American pioneers. There's plenty of land for all, and if the Indians don't like it, they can move. They seem hardly human anyway, if they're human at all.

When the Portuguese first landed in Brazil in the 16th century, there were probably more than three million Indians living there; by 1964, their numbers had been reduced to 200,000; by 1974, there were half that number. The original natives did not have the elaborate civilizations that the Spaniards had found in Mexico and Peru; there were nomads, living off the land, hunting and fishing, slashing and burning to cultivate the occasional patch of manioc root or sweet potatoes—just as many still do today. Because, like the American Indians, they had no central government, it has taken a troublesomely longer time to assimilate them or kill them off. Grimly stated, but true.

The Jesuits who had accompanied the invaders tried to protect the Indians from the predatory conquistadors by founding colonies or "reductions" hidden away in the forests of the interior. By 1622, they had secured the Indians' trust and had founded eleven of these large villages. But the Portuguese needed slave labor to cultivate and expand their great ranches and plantations, so they sent out bands of *paulistas*, the bandit dregs of São Paulo, to raid the Jesuit colonies and carry off Indian slaves. Actually, these new villages were a convenience to the slavers, since they had gathered the normally small nomadic groups into single locations.

In Guayira, in what is now the southern tip of Mato Grosso, the *paulistas* took 20,000 male prisoners, slaughtered women and children by cutting open their stomachs, and murdered the priests. At one time Indian mothers were killing their children rather than risk their growing up to face such horror. The Jesuits followed the Indians as they pushed further and further away from the slave gangs into the sertão, until the Portuguese and other Bourbon courts in Europe forced the pope to suppress the Society of Jesus entirely.

The greatest source of agony for the natives was the Portuguese failure to comprehend the Indian male's utter abhorrence for agricultural labor, which he considers women's work and therefore a symbolic emasculation. Incapable of submitting to the plantation system, the Indians fled or died. They buried themselves in the most inaccessible areas of the Amazon and the Mato Grosso. Those who stayed behind quickly died, since they had no resistance to the white man's gifts of alcohol, influenza, measles and smallpox.

With this failure, the Portuguese turned to the African slave trade which brought four million blacks chained in the holds of Brazilian caravels. Unlike the Indians, Africans were good workers and farmers, and gradually they were absorbed not only into the economy but into the people as well. Since for every ten men who sailed from Portugal in those early years there was only one woman emigrant, it was inevitable that there be a blending of the races. Moreover, once an elite society had been formed, the ideal Latin wife was aloof, domestic and above all chaste, by definition. Out of a sense of honor, a gentleman could not consort with the future brides of men of his own caste, and therefore the requirements of *machismo* demanded that he prove himself with Negro or Indian prostitutes and servants. Thus, we find what the Brazilians call the "whitening" of many of the other races.

Today, except for the Indians, there is very little if any racial prejudice in Brazil; most are *morenos*, dark-skinned whites, and what obvious racial differences there are express themselves in mutual exclusivity rather than in antagonism. The saying is: "A poor white is a black, and a rich black is a white." But the Indian is never rich.

Gradually, lured by the need for food and by a growing fascination with the white man's comforts and the money needed to achieve them, some Indians began to settle around the white man's towns in the outback and gradually began to master their pride and aversion to field work in order to buy the white man's goods. Late in the last century, Fr. Johann Bornstander, an Austrian Jesuit, made contact with a group of Indians around the town of Utiariti near the Bolivian border of Mato Grosso and began the first Jesuit mission out there since the suppression of the Society. He found human skulls encased in basketwork dangling from the roofs of the huts. The natives told him that parts of the bodies had been eaten but that they did not kill white men anymore for fear of reprisals from the machines which make the loud noise and kill.

At about the same time, gold and diamonds were discovered in Mato Grosso, and new hordes of adventurers flocked to the area around Cuiabà and Diamantino, disrupting the Indians once more and either massacring them or driving them even further into the bush. For awhile the coming of independence from Portugal and a surge of "noble savage" romanticism imported with refugees from the French Revolution finally brought a government attempt at understanding the Indians and securing their trust. But with the completion of a telegraph line to Cuiabà, fresh farming settlers swarmed into the wilderness, and antagonism between the settlers and the original owners flared up once again. One terrible story from 1890 tells of a white farmer who had employed 200 Indians and had no further need of them. He arranged a fiesta for them and poisoned them all. Such civilized savagery is not merely a matter of the past. Even today Indians are given poisoned food and infected clothing as gifts,

142

machine-gunned and dynamited from the air. Attempts have also been made to foster inter-tribal wars to save the settlers the expense and bother of killing off the Indians themselves.

The few Indians who submit to the white man's power become marginalized workers living near towns or wander, sick and starving, along the roads that have torn up the very reservations the white man had given them.

There are basically three reasons for the present-day extinction of the Brazilian Indians other than the natural process of "whitening." The first is disease: although the Indian has been able to survive for centuries in the nightmarish environment of the Amazon, he has no defense against the white man's diseases. Today, even a kind missionary with a severe head cold can decimate an isolated Indian village. The second reason is starvation—of both body and spirit. Driven from their hunting grounds, even if into reservations, they are left suffering from physical malnutrition and psychological disorientation. Many no longer have the will to live.

The third reason is simply organized genocide; the Brazilian Indians are dying out because they are being systematically exterminated by road builders, land speculators and cattle barons.

Lucien Bodard, in his book *Le Massacre des Indiens* describes a raid in the 1960's by a professional gang led by one Chico Luis which completely wiped out the Cintas Largas tribe in Amazonas. The pleadings of old women, the sobs of children did not seem to bother them. Girls were raped, then killed. The assassins laughed. Today, the skeletons of slaughtered Indians are still laid out in backwoods towns for sale to timber workers and rubber tappers looking for souvenirs to take home to their families and friends.

In a world where multi-million-dollar dams are halted half-completed to prevent the extinction of a species of inedible fish, 87 Brazilian Indian tribes which existed before history began have been completely annihilated in the last 50 years.

When the great Transamazon Highway, the pride of Brazil, was being built from Brasilia to the borders of Peru, engineers found that the best route went through the new Xingu Indian Reservation, a state park the size of Ireland. The solution to the problem was expeditious and simple: merely take back the southern half of the park and move the already confused Indians to another area with even more land just to the South. But the land the Indians lost was dense forest, and the land they were given was worthless swamp. Along the new road came more fortune seekers, speculators in tin, rubber and land. They shot Indians on sight, even on the reserve, just as a precaution.

The white man's manifest destiny is toward progress, and therefore he must rationalize that Might makes Right, that the Indian is sub-human, and that reports of his cannibalism and vice justify his extinction.

It is hard to put oneself inside the naked skin of an Indian, who never in his life has seen a white man, when suddenly he hears in the distance the unearthly sounds of bulldozers, power saws and dynamite. His curiosity draws him closer, and peering from the brush he sees great noisy monsters, growling and belching smoke, which scythe down trees a thousand years old as if they were not even there. At night while the machines sleep, he creeps out fearfully to touch their still-warm flanks, but the pale men encased in cloth raise the sticks which cough out fire and make the terrible thundering noise. Birds and monkeys scream and scatter. The sticks hurl stones at unimaginable speed that tear and shred the leaves. Sometimes the stones rip right through flesh and men die. There is no choice but to flee. Until there is no place left to flee.

Other than the missionaries, the only significant attempt to halt this genocide was begun by Candido Rondon, himself partly Indian. As a boy and young man he had worked cutting telegraph lines through the Mato Grosso. But at the age of 25, sickened by the unspeakable atrocities perpetrated without apparent scruple against the Indians—whose only crime was "being there"—he resolved to devote his life to their defense. Rondon died in 1956 at the age of 91, after receiving the Nobel Peace Prize for his attempts to establish peaceful relations with the Indians and after his hypocritically grateful country had named one of the backwoods states Rondonia in his honor. He had been instrumental in founding a government agency, the Indian Protection Service, to defend the Indians against the incursions of white men bringing them civilization and death. His constant warning to his teams had always been, "Die if you must, but never kill."

The method of the pacification teams, exemplified in the selfless and tireless work of the Villas-Boas brothers, Orlando and Claudio, re-quired endless amounts of time and patience—to say nothing of raw courage. First, since many of the tribes have never been seen by a white man and are known only from reports by other Indians, they must be found, in areas where the team knows a large conglomerate is planning a new road or telegraph line or ranch. The spotter plane terri-fies the villagers in the very act of discovering them, but once they are

144

located, a team of whites and acculturated Indians sets up camp near the village and begins making a great deal of noise. The Indians are wary as rabbits, and they have a saying that "the man who comes noisily means peace." The ultimate act of trust, of course, is when the Indian will let you hold his weapons. But that is far off at this point; the tribe will not even let the team see them.

The team leaves gifts of tools and trinkets halfway between the two camps and walks away from them. Even here, however, they must be meticulously careful; the Indians might place a different meaning on the gifts than the team intends—they have a horror of human images, apparently, and mirrors have been left shattered and dolls decapitated and their heads hung in the trees. Any small thing might be misconstrued and trigger a massacre of the small team, isolated hundreds of miles from any hope of help.

Silent as ghosts, the Indians retrieve the trinkets unobserved and, after a few days of more and more gifts, they begin to leave their own gifts in exchange: headdresses, seeds, arrows. They also leave little hints about preferred gifts they have noticed in the camp: clever imitations of axes, scissors, needles made out of leaves.

Finally, for a few days, they let themselves be seen—a party of Indians, naked and painted, staring across the clearing without speaking a word. Then, if the team is lucky, the Indians come closer and the leaders of the two groups reach out trembling hands, across milleniums of history, and touch.

Then all hell breaks loose. The whole tribe, without the women, comes into camp and takes over. Apparently believing that these white men have been offering them obsequious homage with all their presents, they make off with anything that pleases them—usually at least every pot in the camp; if anything annoys them, they break it. And the team is most willing to let them have anything that takes their fancy, since a refusal might mean their own deaths. Then, gradually, the tribe allows the team to go hunting with them and even carry their weapons for them, like newly acquired servants. Finally they let the team visit their own village, but only after the Indians are sure that they have pacified the white men.

This trust of the white men, however, can be dangerous. The Indian is as simple as a child, and once the trust has been established, he acts upon it without the slightest question. And as the Indians range further into the white man's territory, they wander guilelessly along the highway and stop trucks, placidly expecting the same kind of handouts they've gotten from the team. If the driver panics and shoots or tries to run them down, he himself could be killed or cause the slaughter of everyone in the nearest white settlement.

Fortunately, Candido Rondon died before it became clear how incapable his successors were of living up to his ideals. Except for such unimpeachable parties as the Villas-Boas teams, most of the teams became horribly corrupted. Inadequate funding by a cost-conscious government led to staffing many of the teams with the wrong kind of men, toughs and renegades in need of even inadequate money or a remote place like the jungle to escape the law. Finally, in 1968, the Brazilian government itself was forced to admit that the Indian Protection Service had become a sinkhole of corruption, theft, rapine and murder. The dream of Rondon had been degraded into a modern equivalent of the 16th-century *paulistas*. The Service was dissolved and replaced by the National Indian Foundation (FUNAI). Its declared objective was respect for the Indian people and their customs and a guarantee that they would have permanent possession of their own land. However, the large conglomerates and the small squatters did not agree. The rapacious need of the corporations demanded more land. The thousands of workers who laid the Transamazon Highway were also promised land instead of higher wages, and in one year alone, 5,000 white squatters invaded the land set aside for the tribes. In 1972, Antonio Cotrim resigned from FUNAI, condemning it as "an instrument of government hypocrisy and a grave-digger for the Indians."

There are really two ways to treat the Indian problem in Brazil. One way is the way of Rondon and the two (original) Indian protective agencies: to allow and defend the Indian's right to preserve his own culture, isolated from the so-called civilizing forces and diseases of the white man, in reservations that are preserved inviolate by an honorable government. The other way is, whether he likes it or not: assimilation of the Indian into the mass of Brazilian society. Mauricio Rangel Reis, the Minister of the Interior who controls FUNAI has said, "We believe that the ideal of preserving the Indian population within its own habitat is very beautiful, but unrealistic." General Bandeira de Mellor, the new president of FUNAI, put it perhaps more clearly: "We must not let an isolated minority impede Brazil's progress." At the bottom line, economic considerations come before anything else.

The result is pitiful. The *caboclos*, acculturated Indians of the interior, have become an illiterate mixed breed of subsistence farmers, squatters, migrants moving here and there around the outback to the boom crops on the large plantations, low-level ranch hands, rubber tappers, road laborers. Many of them, in search of anything better, end up in the shantytowns of Rio and São Paulo and Recife. Like Civil War slaves set free in the city, they are lost, still waiting for the government to be for them what the pacification teams had led them to expect.

More and more, the boys and men are wearing shorts, and the girls and women put on dresses for everyday, reserving painted nudity for festivals. They have eaten the fruit of the Tree of Knowledge, and they have been taught shame. Yearly, their needs grow: medicine, ammunition to hunt food for the tribe, hammocks and mosquito netting to avoid insect bites that will bring diseases to which their ancestors had been immune for centuries. Meanwhile, the Indian values—self-sufficiency won from life in the forest, a sense of freedom and independence—are traits which civilized men and women are working very hard to cure them of.

* * * * * * * *

12 March 1966,
6:30 a.m.

John-Bosco bumped along in the ancient bus on the long last leg of the journey to Cuiabà, across the endless virgin sertão. A rather tired old virgin she was, mile on endless mile of arid land peppercorned with tough scrub and grass. The previous night the passengers were to have stopped overnight in an inn at Alto-Garças, just inside Mato Grosso, but the bus had broken down, and it had taken a mechanic four hours to fix it. They had spent the night in the bus at a crossroads near Maneiros. This morning the arthritic old carry-all had coughed its way through Alto-Garças at 6:00, precisely the time they would have been scheduled to leave there—if they'd ever arrived.

The bus was still better than the train. In the first place it was cheaper. In the second it gave a much better chance for him to get to know the poor *posseiros* and Indians who couldn't afford the train. And even with the breakdowns the bus was better; it wasn't unusual, he'd heard, for rail passengers to be herded off the old narrow-gauge

147

train and forced to cut wood to get up steam in the boilers!

All along this thousand-mile road across the center of Brazil, there were only three cities. The other stops were no more than little clusters of gas stations and cantinas with perhaps a bed-and-breakfast place. Burnier chuckled to himself. Outside the cities, don't expect to have traveler's checks cashed or even a bed with clean sheets and no bugs. No doubt about it: he had just shed a hundred and fifty years of history. He did not mind at all. It was a rugged life, but far simpler than the one he'd left behind him. Or so he thought at the time.

Along the road, between what passed for villages, there were the wretched mud-and-wattle huts of the squatters. In front of each one stood a dirty tangle of big-bellied children, their mouths sagging open, picking their noses dully and staring at the big machine as it passed. One needn't be a doctor to know that they were filled with Chagas disease and snail fever parasites. Their parents and all the older children, illiterate and exhausted every waking hour and aged before their thirties, had been lured to the *sertão* from the shantytowns of the coast to find the acres of indescribably rich land promised free by the posters and radio offers. What they found was the sun-blistered wilderness from which they relentlessly tried to coax a few patches of food to subsist on: corn and manioc—a root something like a sweet potato, which fills the stomach but has hardly any nourishment whatsoever. But the amount of manioc they can grow on an acre is ten times what the same acre would yield in rice and potatoes and twenty times what it would yield in beans.

A large number of children mean so much more to be grown, but it is good to have so many. One or two will inevitably die; one takes that for granted. And the family needs workers. No man wants to work alone. There are too many ways in which the breadwinner could be struck down if he were alone—the bite of a venomous snake or an alligator or a jaguar, a falling tree, or the bully boys from the *fazenda* trying to force him off the land he has so conveniently cleared.

The squatter, even with a piece of his own land, has to take many jobs in order to piece out a livelihood for himself and his family. The most obvious is to accept part-time work on the great plantation at the peak seasons, along with the migrant workers and the *fazenda's* share-croppers.

In the Mato Grosso, 10% of the landowners own 45% of the land. Some plantations are as large as a small European country; 40,000 of them are over 2,500 acres and 62 of them are 250,000 acres. Each. A

Florida concern, for example, purchased 10,000 acres of outback, sight unseen, in the certainty that the teeming multitudes of the coastal cities would continue to emigrate west, that the military regime would continue to attract foreign investors, and that land prices would go up.

The prices are laughable. In 1960 the outgoing governor of Mato Grosso sold three million (3,000,000) acres of land—in violation of the law which recognizes squatters' rights—to São Paulo cattle and lumber interests for $1.00 per thousand (1,000) acres. That is one-tenth of a penny per acre. In 1965, the purchaser hired soldiers on active duty to help dispossess the squatters.

Local military police commanders continue the strong-arm methods, sending tractors to plow under the peasants' crops, break down their fences and destroy their homes, in scenes painfully duplicating those in *The Grapes of Wrath*. In March 1972, three carloads of uniformed men with machine guns arrived to arrest masons who were building a squatters' clinic for Fr. François Jentel in Santa Terezinha, Mato Grosso. But the peasants used their hunting guns to drive off the soldiers, wounding seven or eight. Next day the newspapers in Cuiabà reported that Fr. Jentel himself had laid about him with a machine gun, wounding eleven soldiers. Jentel was given ten years for subversion.

Brazilians say that they "collect the fruit without planting the tree." They have a national itch to skim off quick profits instead of laying down a foundation for the future. This is proven true not only in their treatment of the Indians but also of the squatters and migrants and sharecroppers. Notoriously the landowner connives to manipulate the terms of the workers' contracts against them so that often, instead of being better off for his labor, the day worker ends up deeply in debt to the *fazendeiro*. It is even worse for the landless sharecropper who receives his food, tools, hut, clothing and medical care on credit through the noblesse of the owner. In some places, armed men patrol the roads and fields at night to make sure that indebted workers do not try to decamp under cover of darkness.

The confusing terms of the oral agreement with the owner usually guarantee, also, that the *fazendeiro* may buy any surplus of the sharecropper at his option—at the lowest market price level of the year. The peasants are locked into debt since, for them, the monetary system is often abolished on the plantation and they are paid in tokens for the company store, which controls the prices of goods. For the sharecropper, in 90% of the cases, this means he gives at least one half of his harvest automatically to the plantation owner; for the wage worker it means that out of his $1.40 per day, he must kick back 30% to the store and to the foreman for the privilege of being chosen to work.

It is not slavery, but it surely is a captive labor force. If you ask a sharecropper or contract worker what he does for a living, he replies most often, *"Existe de favor"*; his existence is a privilege given him by the landlord.

The work day begins in the dark, between 4:30 and 5:00 in the morning. With a swish of cold water over his face, the laborer, young or old, crams into his mouth a bit of anything left over from the previous nights' meal, and walks to the fields to work from sun to sun, ten hours a day in the winter and twelve hours a day in the summer. At 8:30 he pauses for a cup of *rios*, the bitterest coffee sold. At noon, if he is working his own patch, he eats a lunch of manioc paste brought to the fields by the youngest child. After lunch, incapable even of moving under the lacerating sun, he takes a siesta. An hour later he is at work again.

At sundown he returns for the best meal of the day. Outside the hut is a short stump, the mortar at which the woman husks rice from the company store and batters it to powder with a pestle of wood. Beans simmer on the stove all afternoon, cooked to a paste and poured over the rice. Manioc flour is added until a dough ball can be formed with the fingers and popped into the mouth. Forks and spoons are among the many luxuries the squatters lack.

The children have gone to bed by 8:30, on mats of woven straw on the beaten earth. By ten, no one is awake in the house. The backbreaking day begins again too soon.

And these were to be John-Bosco Burnier's people.

Dom Pedro Casaldàliga, Bishop of São Felix in the northern Mato Grosso, has written: "The humblest and most difficult job for a Brazilian priest is in Mato Grosso, working for a people dragged and carried along on a wave of poverty, solitude and crime. Mato Grosso is still a land without law. One could call it the 'State Dumping Ground': no administrative understructure, no organization of labor, no state control. The power of law enforcement is too strong and too limited. The peasant's life is to be born and to die, to be killed without any fundamental rights—in the Mato Grosso, these words go together with a stupefying naturalness."

Outside the city of Cuiabà is a stone marker which declares to the passerby that he is at that moment in the exact geographical center of South America. At last, after thirty years of loyal work and dogged hope, John-Bosco Burnier had arrived: he was now a priest of the Mato Grosso poor.

Naturally a man who had waited for so long to do missionary work was eager to plunge into "the real thing," something remote and dramatic. But that was not meant to be. The real missionary work is not what is written up in mission magazines, whose editors must depend on colorful pictures of Indians in full costume to catch the attention of readers accustomed to TV. The real mission work would be too repetitiously loathesome. The mission support must depend on a few romantic stories culled from endless days of "business as usual."

Burnier had been hoping to leave Cuiabà almost immediately for the more remote area of Diamantino, within a week or two of his arrival. But the immediate needs of the Jesuit parish of Our Lady of the Rosary and the shortage of manpower necessitated his staying there for six months. It was a very large parish, part in the city but part also out in the suburban and rural areas. Except for a very few, it was dishearteningly poor, thousands of fortune hunters finding the pot at the end of the rainbow not only empty but owned by the elite few.

John-Bosco occupied himself with helping the poorest of them in their hovels and in roving the mission stations in the backlands of the parish. One aspect of his life there tells more of the man than anything that has been yet said about him in these pages. The veteran of the mission was Brother Nicholas Ritter, S.J., who had worked as factotum in the Mato Grosso for thirty years. Now he was stricken and a paralytic. For six months, Burnier stretched his hammock every night in Brother Ritter's room and helped him with whatever he needed during the night. Even after spending almost the entire night with the old man, Burnier did his full day's work without any mention of fatigue. He dressed Brother Nicholas, helped him eat, read articles to him from magazines, took him for long strolls in his wheelchair, making him laugh with jokes that both of them knew were a bit lame themselves. He brought the old man, almost totally immobile, to all the community functions and treated him with immense sensitivity and tenderness. Let anyone who has done the same even for a day and still gone smiling to work the next morning try to criticize the kind of man John-Bosco Burnier was.

He was learning. He began to understand that great service to God is not gauged by newsworthiness. As he wrote: "The history of salva-

151

tion is nothing more than the accumulation of the responses of individual men and women to the call of their baptism."

For the next couple of years he seems to have acted as a kind of "ambassador without portfolio." He was more than a thousand miles away from his provincial in an area where, during the rainy season, letters usually take about three months to arrive from the coast, and he was therefore in a sense forced to make up his own orders as he went along. When he had first been assigned to the mission, before he had really seen it or understood it, he had somewhat reluctantly agreed with his provincial that at the age of 53 it would be inadvisable to jump feet-first into the extremely rigorous life of full-time work with the Indians in the wilds of the jungle. Far more prudent if he content himself with working with the poor of Cuiabà and with the acculturated Indians nearby.

Before his first year was up, he was moved to the minor seminary in Diamantino as spiritual director and teacher of natural science and music. At the headwaters of the Paraguay River, Diamantino is only 200 kms from Cuiabà, but the trip inevitably takes five hours because of the execrable condition of the roads. The town is the northern limit of effective settlement on the borderland of the equatorial forest, little more than a cluster of hamlets of men and women left stranded when the gold and diamond fields ran out. Until the discovery of the great Kimberley mines in Africa in 1870, Diamantino had been the diamond center of the world. Now it is no more than the children of prospectors eking out a meager existence panning worked-out streams and growing subsistence crops. Besides these there are a few little manufacturing concerns powered by mules or oxen or waterwheels, since there is little or no electricity, depending on the vagaries of the weather. Private land companies have begun colonization schemes in tracts along this forest rim of Mato Grosso. But, although some of the few settlements seem fairly successful, certain of the speculators' promises must be held suspect. Most of their circulars guarantee 100% annual profits on plantation crops. Not in Diamantino.

As with so many other good sheltered Christians, Burnier found that actual contact with the irremediably poor over a period of time tends to begin liberalizing even the most ardent conservative. These people are so clearly unable to help themselves that larger and more organized groups simply must intervene in order to keep them from perishing or continuing to live lives of dull agony.

His work with the Indians seems to have begun as a kind of side-job apostolate, but gradually it began to occupy more and more of his time

152

and attention. Once he began to comprehend the Indians' needs and what seemed to him "the practical abandonment of the Indian sector" both by the church and the government, he offered to do the job full-time and even insisted, uncharacteristically, to the superior that he be designated to work directly with the Indians. This critical decision, he wrote, left him "marvelously at peace!"

Beginning in 1969, then, although he kept his base in Diamantino, he detached himself completely from his seminary work in order to work full-time with the Indians. He wrote in a letter of 26 June 1969, "I came to Mato Grosso at an age at which it would not be normal to face the backlands. I was almost 49. But God gave me the courage to face it. I began rather modestly in the back trenches of the parish of Diamantino, trying to liberate a younger man who would be more able to cope with the front lines. But it happens that the parishes around here are well organized and taken care of, and when I'd been here awhile, I began to see the pressing need to fill a hole in the vanguard. And how well I get on with the climate here! I got ten years younger after one month spent in the backlands of Rio Ferro. I am now assigned to 'The Flying Mission'—the one that moves around—for the Indians. Till now I have worked in the minor seminary."

The month he speaks of was work with Fr. Antonio Iasi. "I continue my missionary struggle. Lately I have been assigned to help Fr. Iasi to take care of some Indians who have only recently come into contact with civilization. They are called 'Wooden Lips' because of a disc inserted in the lower lip to distend it and make a man more threatening to his enemies. But since this is probably the last generation of warriors, the custom no longer has any function and it is dying out. It was precisely this curiosity that led FUNAI to show them off in Rio. The result was that one got contaminated and passed the measles on to the others which caused the death of 58 Indians. Fr. Iasi, with great competence and not the slightest fear, was able to help them with food and medicine. The epidemic practically stopped, with the death of only one more child. All the older people were saved.

"I passed some time there with the Indians: 13 grown-ups and 22 children. They are enchanting. I was amazed to see in them the same vivacity of any Rio child, but with the mentality of the Indian, though. But what cleverness and capacity for feeling! I had to be always making up games to entertain them. I was astonished at my talents as a clown, which I had never had occasion to use before! I think I was a success.

"I am back at Diamantino now, taking care of trying to feed that village. Here we have more resources, but since they burned the fields, they have already gone back to their normal activities of fishing and hunting. It is possible that in a week or two I have to go back to being a clown for the children."

So John-Bosco Burnier, who had been so disturbed by the interventions of Vatican II and the 32nd Congregation, began to show a quiet force for change, trying to set up some cultural mechanism to help two isolated locations of Bakairi Indians. "We ought not to be precipitous and impose our teaching of the faith on these people," he wrote. "We carry on our backs an historic sin, which can be overcome only with the testimony of our lives." He went on to explain that what he meant by "historic sin" was all the stored-up theological and philosophical presuppositions of the established churches, the uncritical alignment of the powers of the churches with the elite who were responsible for this inhuman exploitation of the helpless.

After his first two-week experience of living shoulder-to-shoulder with 34 Indians in a "transition settlement," he realized that a good heart and willing hands were not enough. He needed to take courses in anthropology and study the Indian culture; he was not a young man anymore and he hadn't the time to learn it all from scratch himself. Therefore he began to take one-week courses whenever he could, either in nearby Goiânia or in São Paulo when he returned home for periodic rest leaves.

There were three basic problems for a man in this mission: the language, the Indians' symbols and presuppositions, and the methods of evangelizing them in the context of their desperate poverty.

The language was the most critical problem, and a chaotic one at that. In the wilds of Mato Grosso there are at least 30 different Indian tribes, each with its own dialect and three or four language groups. Some fluency was absolutely essential. "In order to live with them permanently, the language is of capital importance. Otherwise, there is not a hope of understanding the mentality of the tribe or of helping them in their need. I beg the Holy Spirit to grant me the gift of the Bakairi language so that I can be of some little help to his poor people."

It was his greatest problem, but he worked at it—without a tape recorder to train his hearing, struggling against the Bakairi childrens' boredom at constantly repeating things for him, and the constant difficulty of understanding quick running conversations. But gradually he began to break through, if only in a little way, always feeling like a retarded child in the midst of an exclusive pre-historic club.

There was difficulty, too, in finding points of meaningful contact between Western symbols and Indian symbols, especially in the Mass and sacraments. As was noted earlier, the Indians have deep and unpredictable aversions to objects that whites take for granted, like mirrors and dolls. The sexual mores of the tribe, too, caused problems. Despite their partial acculturation, the Indians' custom since time immemorial had been to go about constantly and unabashedly naked; for a shy ascetic like Burnier that was at times unnerving. With the more primitive Indians, lovemaking took place in the middle of the common hut; if a man and woman wanted one another, even though married to others, they would go to the middle of the hut and copulate in front of everyone. Other Indians were more discreet, but sexual morality still seemed to be taken far too seriously by the whites.

An expectant mother is allowed to abort herself with herbs and drugs if she chooses. In some tribes there is a traditional practice of limiting families to three children; the fourth child is strangled at birth. For others, multiple births are considered unlucky; the mother clubs all but one child to death. Yet the Indians are extremely fond of children and cherish all of them indiscriminately, with little regard for their often uncertain parentage. They expect without question that they will behave well, and the children are never quarrelsome. This behavior of the Indians often displays a kind of contradictory union of innocence and savagery. There is, for instance, a tradition in some tribes that when a young mother dies, the small children who depended on her must be killed. The claim is that since every young child needs a mother, it is a kindness to spare these children the curse of a motherless existence.

For Burnier himself and even more for his few young converts, all this often became painful. But Burnier realized the need for patience, for repeated visits to establish trust and friendship and an openness to the gospel. He was unlearning a great deal, principally that the truth cannot be imposed from without.

Missionary method was never really a problem for Burnier. Principally there are two general ways of trying to help people inured to exploitation. One is the method of public denunciation, working on the grand scale, attempting to stir up public opinion and secure political action to alleviate the dehumanization of the dispossessed. The other way, equally necessary, is far humbler and far more appealing to Burnier's own character; it consists simply in assimilating oneself into the concrete lives of the exploited and trying to help solve far smaller everyday problems. It is, in a sense, the method of Christ's own incarnation: leaving behind the privileges of divinity and taking on the burden of man's sweat and pain and uncertainty.

This is not easy, not even for a man like Burnier, who one would have believed was thoroughly freed from "the world" by his years of asceticism. Not so. He noted: "Every missionary has to undertake a real brainwashing from his own hidden materialism, his own secularist biases. The greatest difficulty of all is to be open-minded enough to accept the right to diversity." It must be remembered once again that this was the man who, in a very true sense, had fled into the wilderness to escape the creative conflicts unleashed by Vatican II. Now he was faced with a conflict between "civilization," with its manners and customs and acceptable behavior, and the life of the Indian he hoped to evangelize—whose manners and customs and acceptable behavior had ante-dated those of the white men by milleniums. And not all of the customs one has uncritically accepted from society are always the only legitimate ways of dealing with human life.

"The church," he wrote, "is not catholic because she has imposed her language and customs on all nations, but because she has assimilated the languages and customs of all nations." This is no small step for the minor Roman bureaucrat and the unbending master of novices. As he shuttled back and forth—at one time both patient and feverishly eager—making new contacts, new beginnings, new studies in order to insert himself more fully into the life of the Indian and thus gain a foothold for the gospel, John-Bosco Burnier had never been happier in his life.

* * * * * * * *

The two Bakairi villages were small: 107 people at Santana, near Nobres just south of Diamantino, and 230 at Simoes Lopes, much further away near the town of Chapada dos Guimarães. The Indians living there were themselves quite small, little more than five feet tall, but barrel-chested and muscular. They had hooded and lashless almond eyes, spatulate noses, coarse black hair.

For centuries these people had lived by slash-and-burn, cutting out a piece of forest to clear space for sweet potatoes and corn. The men cleared the land and left the women to plant and tend it while they were off hunting or fishing. When the women wanted Brazil nuts, they simply walked into the woods and burned down the tree. They also cultivated manioc root which they preserved by rolling them into large balls to be smoked and then boiled non-stop for several days. The finished product looked like black cheese but it kept indefinitely. They took a supply of these balls on their travels, softening them in water into a sticky paste and then cooking them into pancakes. From manioc, once the poison has been removed, they still make a kind of alcoholic drink which they leave to ferment in open pots. Any passerby is expected to help the process along by taking a mouthful, mixing it with his own saliva, and returning it to the pot.

They lived in large communal haystack houses, big enough for several families each, arranged around a central area with an obligatory guest house in the middle. Gradually, the hunters had to go further and further to find game, so each year in May or June, the group simply moved from the weed-infested plots to a new place, burned off the underbrush, poked holes in the soil, dropped in the seeds, and waited.

Finally, the white men caught up with them and there was nowhere else to move. The Bakairi for whom Burnier was working lived now at the very edges of the mainstream of the outback Brazilian world: paid workers, herding someone else's goats or clearing someone else's fields, living in mud huts by the side of the raw highway. The Fazenda Rio Novo near Santana had had a processing plant and rubber plantation which employed many Bakairi, but it was sold to cattle ranchers and already the steers were being driven onto the Indians' fields to eat up the sprouts.

At Santana the Indians had a 100-acre communal farm; each of the eleven families worked five acres of its own and the rest was farmed by the unmarried young men. They had great hopes not only of meeting their own needs for the year but producing a small cash crop to sell. But as Ascelino Rodriguez, the captain of the reservation, told Burnier, "The beans are only a hope. The Indian agent has not even brought the seeds yet from Cuiabà. And the earth must help us, too. Beans do not do well around here."

Ascelino's dream was to have a school for the children. "But teachers do not want to come because they think we are wild Indians. And if they come, they do not stay very long. Right away, they want to go back to the city. Here in the woods it is too quiet for them."

"They live in penury," John-Bosco wrote, "a habitual mentality of begging, either from the mission or from the FUNAI. Some Indians are ready to return to the jungle, away from the white men, as long as they can take a radio and a watch and a bicycle. There is in them a tension between the Indian life and the plantation worker's life. They yearn not to lose contact with their own tribe, but in many ways they begin to imitate the life of the white worker, since they are continually under the influence of the little nearby factory where they went in search of paid work. This tension creates in them a new instability—crushed by the desire to imitate the whites and their inability to get enough wages to do it." He had found, once again, the struggle between "the old way" and "the new way."

Burnier did not enjoy baptisms by the thousands, as Xavier had. But he loved the simple people, especially the little children, and he was always ready to carry timber and straw for the Indian farmers in his noisy Toyota pickup. The Indians used the straw of buriti trees to thatch their huts, but there wasn't a tree for miles and the Bakairi had no vehicles at all, not even an ox-cart.

The priest had brought them the sisters to take care of their teeth and to teach the women how to make clothes. He bought goods wholesale in Cuiabà—ropes to make hammocks, oil, sugar, salt, soap, batteries—and sold them to the Indians for what it cost him. It was immeasurably cheaper than the plantation store, and the owners were not pleased.

He was a man of infinite patience, and one wonders how much the Indians used him. There would have been no malice in it. Since time beyond memory they had been used to wandering the land, taking from it and giving little or nothing in return. They had no idea of private property, which explains their bewilderment at the incursions of the white men. Now, as Burnier himself noted, they had become full-time beggars some of them, mystified at the need to pay. And why should not the white man give them something for dispossessing them?

Burnier was also good-hearted, though he still was not well-organized in practical matters. Setting out for a trip of several weeks to villages all over the mission, he never forgot to pack the Mass kit, but he often forgot the rice and beans! One time he left his glasses back in Diamantino and found himself at a baptism of two young men of Santana a hundred miles away. At such times he simply had to forego liturgical exactness.

He wrote to his sister, "I am so slow-witted and confused about packing things into the Toyota, and it always happens that a third of what I have to take to the *sertão* gets forgotten—including the rice, beans, cooking oil, salt, sugar. One time it was my hat, another time my boots, another time the flashlight. Till now I haven't forgotten the hosts, wine, chalice or holy oils, but one time I did forget the missal. I had to write out a Eucharistic Prayer from memory. It came out with some variations!"

One of his friends wrote of him, "His room was the living idea of disorder. Everything on the floor or on the bed, the table heaped up with stuff, and with his lack of good local memory, many times it took him an awful long time to find something he needed. I think it was rather early that he rejected that worthless touch of social class you call a bed and changed instead to a hammock. He carried around a sack with some pieces of clothing, a few toilet articles, hammock, rope and a rumpled tent. Shirts! I have seen him many times with some shirts that had belonged to much fatter original owners. And shoes. I don't know where he ever got them so twisted, and he never shined them."

But he had more important things on his mind than housekeeping. And did he move! "This is my program for the present: July 13-16, farms on the bank of the Paranatinga; July 16-26, to the Bakairi at Simoes Lopes; July 17-31, Diamantino; Aug. 1-2, travel to Campo Grande; Aug. 3-18, course in Ethnology; Aug. 25, meeting of the missionaries in Utiariti with the Indians of the River Juruena; get back to Diamantino by Sept. 14; again with the Bakairi the latter half of September and October.

"They tell me that the old go on remembering only old times! I don't feel old in any way—aside from my well-counted 54 years. And I work here in the outback with the enthusiasm of a young man. I can still walk 12 miles at a marching pace of about four miles an hour." Gasp!

The roads were a problem. They just didn't exist. Just the two tracks in the grass where previous vehicles had passed, once you got off the main, also unpaved, roads. When it rained, you simply went around the deep mud and built up a by-way. In the dry season, you rode a washboard. Very rarely could you go over 35 miles an hour.

There was a bus which went every other day from Cuiabà which left him 110 kilometers from his missions. From there it was hitching rides. The jeep he had inherited with the mission had gone well past senility, and it took him five years to beg money from his family and a group of German Catholics back East for a new one, which was really second-hand and under his ministrations became fifth-hand rather quickly.

He tried constantly to lead the Indians to consider the message of the gospels. Ironically, his greatest obstacle in evangelization was the corruption of Catholicism the Brazilian Indians and squatters had already been exposed to. "Catholicism among the Indians began with contact with the rural religiosity of the *fazenda* of the region, in particular regarding devotional prayer and songs the workers had half-learned from some itinerant missionary traveling around from his parish on a visit of obligation." It was a Christianity contaminated with syncretism—a mixtum-gatherum of Bible stories, magic, voodoo brought by the black slaves from Dahomey, fetishes, African gods and Indian spirits. Curing played an important part in this folk religion, since doctors are scarce and diseases are plentiful.

Out in the forest, the Indian himself had had no concept of a total God, but rather felt and continues to feel influenced by his own spirit-saints. Luck or sickness are not meted out to the Indian because of his virtues or sins but as the result of the individual's confidence in himself and his spirits or his lack of it. These fears and tensions can be expunged only by songs, dances and rituals presided over by mediums and witch doctors, which re-establish his confidence and therefore his luck.

The missionary thus has his work more than cut out for him: to struggle not only against paganism and its witch doctors but also against the Indians' own false ideas about Catholicism. It is an uphill struggle, especially when it must be carried on in a language which makes one constantly certain that he is neither understanding nor being understood.

In a letter of 1 February 1970, he points out an ironic note to his provincial, Marcelo Azevedo, which underlines the remoteness of his work and his independence of superiors back on the coast. He says that the yearly catalogue listing the assignments and addresses of all the Jesuits in the province "became a dead letter in my case last year. I had to substitute for the pastor of Paranatinga (in the high backlands near the headwaters of the Xingu River) from October '68 to July '69, and for the pastor of Marilandia-Afonso from August '69 to November '69. In fact, I would still have been out there in the woods if a disagreeable incident had not occurred which made me leave my field work. But I continue to give any collaboration to the Indian work that I can, here at the base of operations."

In another letter he expresses a certain sadness about the apparent lack of sympathy for the mission among the Jesuits back home. "In general I am well, somewhat sad to see that this missionary job is generally so little understood by our men. The visit of the provincial of the Southern Province which we looked forward to so much was a great disappointment for many of us. Not because he was not good and insightful, because he is a good man. But because it seems that he did not understand what it was all about. When he hurried off early, on the eve of the feast of St. Ignatius, so as not to be late arriving for the dinner at Anhanguera, it of course caused the worst impression among the men. But then, as we jokingly say out here, 'Well, that shows we're on the mission!'"

In the same letter he says that he is going to visit the following month with 40 Japanese families, 375 miles north of Diamantino, who had not seen a priest in three years. He would probably spend most of Lent with them and then most of the following summer. Perhaps it surprises foreigners that there are so many Japanese settlers in Brazil: the largest concentration of Japanese anywhere outside the home country. There are, in fact, three and a half times as many Japanese in Brazil as there are surviving Indians. Although three-quarters of them are concentrated back in São Paulo, the rest—emigrating from their own overcrowded little islands—arrived in droves within the borders of the Mato Grosso, ordinarily as managers of farms. They have also succeeded in obtaining their own land grants from the government, but only on the puzzling condition that they pass themselves off as "health services." Most of them are quickly assimilated into Brazilian life nowadays, and many of the young are baptized Catholics. "So you see," Burnier concluded, "I finally did become a missionary to the Japanese! Out here in the Mato Grosso!"

The work was wearing and short on dramatic results, but he was very much at peace. Nonetheless, there was the occasional twinge of homesickness for his large family and for people he had loved all his life. "Only the certainty of the future reunion guaranteed us by Jesus Christ can comfort us when we are so long separated from our dear ones. But not even that future victory can block out completely the pain of homesickness. It lessens it; it doesn't wipe it out."

The dealings of FUNAI with the Indians had begun to arouse distrust even as far away as Brasilia. Instead of civilizing the Indians, many of the teams had brought a savagery worse than the natives' own, since it was abetted by civilization's worst weapons—alcoholism, prostitution and contagion which were leading to the decimation of the tribes. To take up where the FUNAI had so painfully failed the dream of its founder, the church had set up the Missionary Indian Council (CIMI) to use the same methods of approaching and establishing trust with the Indians that Rondon had elaborated. John-Bosco was not only the delegate elected from the northwestern district of Mato Grosso to CIMI, but over the course of ten years' work with the Indians had become a man of convictions far different from those which he had carried with him from the coast to the frontier.

It was at Burnier's urging that the priests of CIMI began to merge Indian customs into the liturgy where it was appropriate. It comes as rather a surprise to find among the notes of the quintessentially submissive Burnier: "We must adapt ourselves to the culture of the Indian in order to transmit the gospel, or to discover within the life of the Indians the gospel values. With what right can there be uniform direction in liturgy and moral codes given from Rome?"

In another place, his notes become even stronger: "We cannot consent to the destruction of an entire people, to a situation of such palpable injustice! The greatest difficulty in saving the Indians comes from legal blocks and bureaucracy which impede every attempt at direct action. We must fight an open struggle, without truce, with all the licit means at our disposal. When working against false authorities and false justice, we are conscience-bound to oppose it with our protests, with public expression of our opposition—even at the risk of exposing ourselves to incomprehension on the part of authority or even to personal reprisals. 'The apostle's task is to provoke people to become aware of their own situation and to take over their own true liberation; evangelization demands the liberation of the land.'"

On his journey to the Mato Grosso, John-Bosco Burnier had come a long, long way.

---

15 July 1976,
Morning

One of Burnier's closest friends in CIMI was a very energetic young Salesian priest, Rodolfo Lunkenbein, 34. With the strong backing of Bishop Casaldàliga, Lunkenbein had convinced FUNAI to allow him to gather several small tribes of Bororos Indians into a single colony in the forest near Meruri. The advantages were many: a place to live together in a way they had known all their lives, a sense of security from the ranch toughs, and a fragile hope that together their tribe would not dwindle into nothingness. What's more the men could still seek at least some temporary work during peak seasons on the nearby ranches, while the women cultivated a small patch of land in the reserve. An agrarian school was set up to teach both men and women how to cultivate more effectively and how to vary their diet. A dispensary began to save at least some of the Indian children from the parasites that yearly carried off so many. And more important to Lunkenbein, the Indians began to understand and defend their rights as human beings and as fellow Christians with their Christian exploiters. Later, he hoped, they would work for recognition from the state as an authoritative and effective voice of the Indian in Mato Grosso.

The set-up was ideal for all concerned. Except for the cattlemen. Those Indians were squatting on valuable land, adjacent to pastures. Something had to be done about them and about that priest who was teaching them communism and resistance to the law.—The scenario might seem to some to be as simple-minded as the clichés of an old Western movie, but it was and is nevertheless real. And it was and is backed by the muscle and guns of the bosses' trusted cowhands.

One morning in July, 1976, a gang of sixty armed men broke into the mission settlement. An astonished land surveyor stood gaping at the intruders, his hand suspended in mid-air next to his tripod. The ranch hands pushed past him, throwing the tripod across the clearing. Father Gonçalo came running from the main hut. The ranchers surrounded him and began pummeling him with their fists and their rifle butts. Lunkenbein and Laurenço, the Indian leader, came rushing up from the fields.

"What's all this about? What are you men doing here?" Indian men and women gathered from the huts and fields and huddled behind the husky bearded young priest.

"What are *you* doing here? You're trespassing against the ranchers, that's what you're doing! This place you've got here is against the law about occupation of land."

Lunkenbein did not react. He turned to the Indians instead. "Don't be afraid. I will talk to the *civilizados*." Then he turned to the cowboys. "This land was given to these people by the government. Your trespassing is an affront to these Indians. This is their land. You can't take away their rights. If there has been any violation it has sprung from the blind land-grabbing of the *fazendeiros.* . . ."

163

Suddenly there were shots. Laurenço was shot in the chest. An Indian boy named Simão was fatally wounded, and when his mother, Tereza, ran to rescue him, she was also shot. One of the Indians opened fire and killed one of the ranch hands. Then the Indians fled screaming, and the cowboys fled in the opposite direction leaving behind their own man.

And young Father Rodolfo Lunkenbein lay dying in a pool of blood.

Reporting the news to his provincial, Burnier wrote, "Who could have had ill will for such a man, who had worked with such abnegation, doing his unpublicized and humble work in the backwaters of the Mato Grosso, with the esteem and affection of the Indians and of the poor people all around the region?" And he concluded, "After him, who will be next?"

* * * * * * * *

*22 September 1976,
1:00 p.m.*

Adriano Hipolito is Bishop of Nova Iguaçu, a shantytown section of Rio de Janeiro. Like so many other Brazilian bishops he had spoken out against the death squads of police who marauded the impoverished slum dwellers. On this afternoon he left his office with his nephew and his nephew's fiancée. They had driven only a few blocks in their Volkswagen when they were stopped by two cars. Five or six armed men jumped out and forced the bishop and his nephew from their car. The bishop was then shoved into the back seat of the kidnappers' car, and the young man and woman were left to fend for themselves. Where could they go? To the police? To lodge a complaint against the police?

Bishop Hipolito was blindfolded, handcuffed and forced down to the floor of the car so that passersby could not see him as the car sped past.

Half an hour or so later, the kidnappers stopped the car and stripped the bishop completely naked. They tried, unsuccessfully, to force him to drink a full bottle of rum. They shouted repeatedly that they were the "Brazilian Anti-communist Alliance," that the bishop was a "communist traitor" and that the bishop of the neighboring diocese would be next.

Then they sprayed the bishop's naked body with red ink and dropped him at the end of a street in the neighborhood of Jacarapagua.

Some men found the bishop, loaned him some clothes and carried him to the nearest parish. The bishop called the authorities and made a formal statement. He was told that his car had been blown up in front of the office of the National Council of Brazilian Bishops.

Up to now, the Brazilian police, so efficient in ferreting out subversives and pimps, have not been able to find any leads regarding Bishop Hipolito's kidnappers.

---

10 October 1977,
4:30 p.m.

John Bosco sat reading his Latin breviary in the quiet little garden of the house of Claretians in São Felix. He felt very content. Here it was October already and it had hardly rained at all. That downpour yesterday, but little more. And he had just helped to plant a mango tree in the garden, a kind of green memento of his visit. That was nice. It would be a good day tomorrow, too, they said, for the next leg of his long, long journey back to Diamantino. Nearly nine hundred miles by bus.

Exactly a week ago he had flown from Cuiabà to the northeasternmost corner of Mato Grosso for the annual meeting of the CIMI leaders of the area of São Felix. It had been held in the town of Santa Terezinha, named for the little French patroness of the missions. It had been a sad time, in a way. This was the first time the conference had been held without young Rodolfo Lunkenbein.

The plane fare had been exorbitant, but as regional director of CIMI he certainly had to attend, and at 59, after ten years in the bush, the old bones and innards weren't up to the bus ride both ways. The return trip would be penance enough! But it would be broken into stages. He had come down by outboard canoe with Bishop Casaldàliga two days ago from Santa Terezinha. That, too, had been a treat! Since his boyhood he had heard the legends of heroic battles of cowboys and Indians along the northern reaches of the Araguaia River. It had been a wonderful few days.

165

The meetings had been in the old parish house and church of Fr. François Jentel, who had become a legend himself in his fearless defense of the rights of his Indians. The participants of the conference had been four Tapirapè Indians with their wives and children plus the members of the prelature (an area not yet a diocese) who worked directly in the service of the Indians. The talk had ranged back and forth and up and down for three whole days: practical political problems, like culture shock, the right to land, problems of education, the encroachment on Indian territory for tourism such as the new Hotel Luctuante; practical social problems, most importantly the dialogue between the Tapirapè and the Karajà, a neighboring tribe currently suffering even more than they; and finally religious questions like the true call of Baptism to the full Christian life. It had been an exhilarating time, speaking simply and realistically with others as passionately dedicated to the same things he knew so well and cared so much about.

On the 7th, after the intensive sessions were over, he and Dom Pedro had been invited to the Tapirapè village within the fabled swamp of the Mondrongo. The moon shone cleanly in the cloudless night sky, as they made their way in fragile boats between moon-washed branches, sweating and joking with the Indian guides. When they arrived at the village, they entered the new *takana*, the central hut, and sat on the straw-strewn floor for a wonderful *batepopo*, a "chattering." For hours they sat there in a primitive hut surrounded by jungle, the soft strumming of guitars outside, talking with the Indians about the aspirations of the tribe and its rights and what it meant to be a Christian—without at the same time ceasing to be an Indian. As they walked back to the guest hut very late in the evening, Burnier had turned to the bishop with a smile: "Now that was a wonderful conversation, Pedro!"

The following morning, the bishop and Burnier had sat cross-legged on the mats of the *takana* with the Indians of Tapirapè and offered Mass together. Aptly, after the *batepopo* the night before, the gospel text had been: "Father, I thank you that you have hidden these truths from the wise and revealed them to the little ones." After Mass, they stayed exactly where they were and shared the noon meal together as well. Then they took the two priests to the motorized dugout for the six-hour trip south on the Araguaia to São Felix. As they entered the boat, the villagers presented John-Bosco with a ceremonial necklace in token of their friendship and in gratitude for his coming.

For the last stretch of the hundred-mile trip from the north, they'd been drenched to the skin in the open canoe by a sudden downpour, but

John-Bosco had not minded a bit, warmed by the memories of the past five days. And for two days more he had lazed sinfully about the Claretian residence, reading and praying. And planting mango trees! He had originally intended to leave the day after the boat trip, on a bus for Barro do Garças, halfway back on the long trip to Diamantino. But the bishop had very wisely prevailed on him to rest up a few more days while he himself caught up on some paper work and then, instead of going all the way to Barra in one stretch, he could go half that distance with the bishop to a little roadside village where the two of them would celebrate the patronal feast with the villagers and baptize the children.

That would be better. It would delay his return home, but it was worth it. It's a long, dirty trip on an unpaved road, and it would be far more pleasant to share the dust and conversation with the young bishop. And he had the rest of this pleasant evening to relax. Tomorrow, at six in the morning, he and the bishop would board the express Xavante Bus to the little roadside village of Ribeirão Bonito. It had a pretty name.

* * * * * * * *

Like his friend and fellow bishop of Recife, Dom Helder da Camara, Bishop Pedro Casaldàliga is indeed a legend in his own time. At 49, slender, bespectabled and unpretentious, he might be taken for a poet (which he is) who had wandered into the wilds of the Mato Grosso by mistake—were it not that his face is weathered by ten years of working and eating and dressing and living like the peasants and Indians he serves. When he smiles, he looks like a lanky boy. When he is thinking, there is a no-nonsense look to the man which has kept soldiers and governors at bay more than once.

Dom Pedro grew up in Catalonia in Spain when it was under communist domination during the Spanish Civil War (1936-1939). As a boy of ten he went to confession in stables and received the Eucharist at secret Masses. His Uncle Luis, a priest, was executed by the Reds in a concentration camp. (And yet more than once in the recent past, Brazilians of both state and church have called Dom Pedro himself a communist.)

After his ordination, Casaldàliga became involved in the cursillo movement, in writing radio programs and in editing a magazine, *El Iris de Paz*—a job from which he was fired for describing a social

167

pronouncement of the Spanish bishops as a "disappointing document."

He had come to the Mato Grosso as a Claretian priest in 1968 for reasons quite different from those of John-Bosco Burnier: he was looking for a place to make Vatican II work.

He found it. Within three years he had been chosen the first bishop of the prelature of São Felix, a territory of 150,000 square kilometers (about the size of the entire state of Michigan) with a mere 100,000 people. Most of the villages have no electricity, no surfaced roads, no newspapers, no radio or television or telephones. If the people were to be reached by the gospel, the gospel would have to come by pickup and bus and on foot.

Communications were a problem, but not the main problem. With the advent of the military regime in 1964, the government had encouraged multi-national companies to buy up large tracts of (as far as they knew or cared) unused land in the Brazilian *sertão*. It was a method of development which tightened the belts of the poor to allow the rich to grow still fatter. Since then, the Brazilian GNP has grown at the astonishing rate of 10% yearly, and the income of the richest has grown an even more remarkable 60%. On the contrary, the workers' earnings have dropped nearly 40% in those same ten years.

The new bishop of São Felix fought the resultant takeovers and dispossessions and appealed to the government to protect the rights of the small landowners. He went unheeded, but he had certainly gotten the government's attention. The peasants of his prelature have continued to be harassed and evicted; the parochial schools have been closed as agents of subversion; foreign priests have been expelled from the area. Because he himself is a foreigner, Casaldàliga is always in danger of expulsion "to reduce social tension." He has been placed under house arrest more than once; there is a price on his head for any gunman willing to take the risk of cutting him down.

In 1973, his house was surrounded and searched. He and his staff of 20 priests, nuns and lay people were questioned and some beaten up. The nuns' infirmary was declared illegal and replaced by a medical station. Casaldàliga was again arrested for his defense of Fr. François Jentel of his prelature who had been sentenced to a ten-year prison term on the charge of sedition.

In 1974, military personnel again invaded and ransacked the bishop's residence. They arrested, beat and tortured four priests who were there and temporarily held the bishop prisoner. Periodically, red paint is splashed on the whitewashed walls of his "cathedral."

After a pastoral letter in which he called for the "demythification of private property," as if it automatically justified even the hoarding of millions of acres of unused lands while peasants and Indians starved, he was accused by the press of being a "communist subversive, fomenting armed struggle." Nor was he exempt from attack even from one of his fellow bishops, a substantial landholder in his own right. This bishop had written an anti-communist catechism in which he admits sadly that there are indeed priests and bishops who are "agitators among workmen against their employers, helping the peasants invade others' property, communists within the ranks of the clergy, like Judas in the midst of the apostles."

But Pedro Casaldàliga stays on. He has become one of the flock he himself describes: "A simple and hardy people, migrants wandering in search of a destiny, driven by need, lacking preparation, with hammocks on their backs, numerous children, a skeletal horse, and four cooking pots in the saddle bag."

They are like the Okies of the Depression pressing doggedly toward the dream of California, like the Pilgrims enduring the hostile Atlantic to reach America, like the children of the Exodus on their desert march to Canaan.

And as they go, they sing a song their bishop, Dom Pedro, wrote for them:

We're a people of persons;
We're a people of God.
We want land on earth;
We already have land in heaven.

* * * * * * *

11 October 1977,
6:45 p.m.

Another garden, not so nice as the one the previous evening, more like the vegetable patch for the mission team at Ribeirão Bonito. They were good people here at this outpost: Fr. Maximino Parèdes, a Claretian, the village's first permanent priest; the French sisters, Irma and

Beatrice; young Dr. Luis who lived with his wife and baby in the hut next door; and a teacher-volunteer from São Paulo, a young man who looked about twenty or so. They all looked so young.

John-Bosco sat there in the flickering twilight in a cowhide chair near the well. Someone was sprinkling the garden, but he couldn't see who it was. The bishop was finishing his bath. That well was well used! Bad pun, but he chuckled anyway. One of the sisters was preparing supper.

John-Bosco sat with his book on his lap, but he was not reading. He was praying, remembering the day.

He and Dom Pedro had arrived in Ribeirão Bonito on the bus from São Felix at about one that afternoon. It had indeed been a dirty, dusty trip, seven hours bouncing along, but it had been fascinating to see how much this place was like Diamantino—and yet how different. And of course there had been the privilege of riding with Pedro. Such a surprising, charismatic young man. Young? Well, ten years younger than he, but skinny as a boy. Burnier chuckled again to himself and patted his little pot belly. I *look* more like a bishop than he does! But, thank God, it's he and not I. Tomorrow, I will be on my way to Barra and then Cuiabà and then Diamantino. And then off to the Bakairi villages. That's where I belong.

They had been met at the bus by the team and some of the villagers, but they were hustled off to wash seven hours of red dust from themselves and have some lunch. People dropped in to the little kitchen, some of them encouraging the bishop in his suggestion for building a new church. Granted that the good Jesus had been content to be born in a stable, but that was many years ago. He surely deserved better from the people of Ribeirão Bonito.

There were darker topics, too.

The entire town was on edge. In the first place, it had always been outlaw country. No one was inordinately curious about where his neighbors had come from or how they had made their living there. But they were used to that. Now things were even more tense. For the last few months, a policeman named Felix, a young tough, had been arbitrarily grabbing the villagers and roughing them up. The gun on his hip was his justification.

But two weeks ago he had gone to the neighboring village of Cascalheira, less than two miles away, and stopped at the little farm of Jovino Barbosa. He began to abuse Jovino's two sons in front of their father—no one knew why, something about stealing—and then began to threaten to kill them. Old Jovino went into the hut and reappeared with his ancient carbine. He shot Corporal Felix where he stood.

There was nothing for the old man and his sons to do but run.

The little police outpost had called for reinforcements from outside. When they arrived—in numbers—they seized people at random, questioned them about the whereabouts of the Barbosas, beat up some, tortured others. The warning signals to the villagers were clear: tell us where old Barbosa is or every one of you will get some of the same. But how could they tell the police what they did not know?

The police had gone back to the Barbosa place for Margarida, old Jovino's sister, and Santana, the wife of his elder son. When they took the two women into custody, they burned their fields, their supplies and their hut. Everyone presumed the two women were now in the tiny village jail. Some people said that they had heard screams. No one could be sure. Perhaps the women had been released and gone off into hiding with the men.

Late in the afternoon of the bishop's arrival in Ribeirão Bonito, the villagers had begun to gather at the river to bless the water for the next day's baptisms. It would be their patronal feast of Nuestra Señora Aparecida, who was also the patroness of all Brazil. The villagers grouped together near the stream in the shimmering heat. The men doffed their hats, some holding their babies, others watching the children darting among the legs of the adults and peering out at the visiting priests. Father Parèdes, bearded and solemnly handsome as a picture of the Lord himself, took the pot of water the women had drawn and give a short homily. He spoke of the water of the river which gave life and a name to their town now becoming the water of baptism which would give new life to the spirit, a life which will survive even death. As the young priest blessed the water, John-Bosco closed his eyes and prayed for these poor hunted people and for his Indians, who shared the same torment a thousand miles away.

Then the procession had returned with the baptismal water to the church, singing as they went. The highway was dusty, thicketed, lined with dead cars and garbage. They passed the little police station, white-washed brick, squatting cleanly among the weeds inside its barbed wire fence.

They could not see the iron chains embedded in the brick or the blood-stained walls inside. The little jail had always been used mainly for drunks, and they of course could not remember. Or for a *posseiro* who would not surrender his land to the *fazendeiro*, and he dared not

171

talk. The military police were paid under the table by the landowners to be both convincing and thorough.

Nor could the people in the procession see Margarida Barbosa, a gag in her mouth to stifle her screams as the procession passed, needles jammed underneath her fingernails and into her breasts, kneeling on soda bottle caps with her two arms outstretched, a pistol at each ear. She had been there a week without food or water, trying to tell the soldiers she did not know where her brother was. But that was not the worst. The procession also could not see little Santana, who had had a baby two weeks before, cowering, dazed, in the corner. They could not know that she had been raped, and then raped again, and then raped again, by Corporal Ezy Ramaltho Feitosa, by Corporal Juraci, by Corporal Messias, and by two ranch foremen. They could not even have suspected. Even beasts could not have done that. And the jail was silent. The surly young guards looked out at them indifferently, but warily. And the procession had passed. Singing.

When the service was over, the pastoral team and its two guests had come home to wash up, get a bit of supper, and then return to the straw chapel for Mass at 7:30. John-Bosco looked at the little stucco parish house. It was modest, three bedrooms, a kitchen, a small sitting room, and off the kitchen Dr. Luis's tiny clinic. It was . . . .

Suddenly there was a commotion inside the house. The young teacher had run in and the bishop was trying to calm him. As John-Bosco entered he was sitting there telling the others who had gathered in the kitchen. About five people had heard the screaming all the way out in the road: "Please! Don't beat me again! I don't know! Please!" And somehow, someone had found out the whole story—the beating, the bottle caps, the needles, the rapes.

The bishop straightened up from beside the young man. He looked slim and stern and fearful. For some reason, he thought, over the last three days, either from telepathy or some grace, he had prayed more than ever before and had offered to the Lord whatever would come. This was a duty he had to discharge. He felt profoundly the threat to Ribeirão Bonito and Cascalheira, to the pastoral team and yes, to himself. There was, after all, a price on his head. Perhaps tonight someone would claim it.

"Dom Pedro," the young teacher said, "let me go with you."

Casaldàliga shook his head. The boy was very young, and afterward he would still be in the town, and the police would make him a target. "Stay here. It is too dangerous."

Then John-Bosco stepped forward, slope-shouldered, squat, surely unpromising for pitched battle, but with the resolute calm of a man who has learned to look squarely back at life. "I will go with you." Not brave. But determined.

Surely they would not harm John-Bosco, Casaldàliga thought. He is not on the parish team and he's no part of this conflict either with the authorities or the police or the *fazendas*. John-Bosco would be safe, and two voices would be stronger than one.

Dom Pedro nodded, and the two men walked out into the red smear of dusk.

* * * * * * * *

In Brazil, it is not at all unusual for the civilized to torture the uncivilized—peasants, Indians, and those suspected of fomenting communism at the expense of private enterprise. The quintessential reality before which all others must bow is "National Security." The existence of the State, its internal development, its ability to resist any internal forces of disintegration—all require central control of every political force. If National Security comes into conflict with individual security, it is the individual who must yield to the myth of the people, since the State is the only ultimate guarantee of individual liberty in the first place.—The argument is admittedly somewhat circular.

Except for the difference in the amount of land per person, the political situation in Brazil is a mirror image of the one in El Salvador. "National Security" really means not the security of the nation—the people—but the security of a stable central control mechanism for the sake of the Economy. As in so many other places in the world today, therefore, anything said or done in the name of the Economy eliminates any further argument and any individual rights which would interfere with it. It is the same mutation of fascism as in El Salvador, in the hands not of a single Führer or Duce or Caudillo, but of a collective composed of rural landowners, the urban bourgeoisie, and most importantly the military.

The owners of the huge rural plantations are the local "bosses" of their areas; the peasants are deeply in debt to them, and therefore they control all local politics, such as they are. Because he is so overwhelmingly in control of the local economy, the *fazendeiro*—like the owners of the great Bonanza ranches of the American West—is far more influential than any local official, whom he usually chooses. As such, he is easily able to control the local police and augment them with his own private security forces.

The urban elite Establishment is held together, as in El Salvador, by strong family and godparentage ties, and its members make use of these relationships extensively in their business and government dealings. They would sooner rely on an unqualified relative than on a qualified stranger. What's more, the generals and archbishops and businessmen all come from this same complex of interwoven families. Their major interest is to produce export goods cheaply, massively and highly profitably, and therefore they automatically must lessen the buying power of internal workers. To make the minimum wage necessary for essentials, a father of two in São Paulo would have to earn $100 a week; the average unskilled worker, however, makes $66 a week. To buy the essentials, he would have to work 18 hours a day, six days a week.

The third and most important part of the Establishment is the army. In 1937, when Hitler and Mussolini were at their peak, President Getulio Vargas stampeded Congress to suppress the Constitution. Then he sent the army to suppress Congress. From that point on he began consciously to model the Brazilian government on European fascism: beefing up the security police, replacing provincial governors with hand-picked bosses, unifying the disparate states into a single Economy. Workers' and peasants' organizations were created and controlled from above and therefore inevitably expressed the needs of the exploiters rather than their own members' needs.

In 1964 the army again seized direct control of power in a bloodless coup—even though the generals had always been the real final arbiters in all political matters for the last 100 years. In 1969 they again closed down Congress. Their primary goal was to secure the confidence of foreign investors by proving the country's stability. In order to be certain of that, they had to eliminate all dissent, political debate and expressions of grievance. They had three very effective means to achieve that appearance of unanimity: deprivation of political rights for all those opposed to government policy, control of elections, and torture.

Within a week of the 1964 coup, the government had rounded up and arrested more than 7,000 people of other political viewpoints than its own. 375 of the country's most influential political and intellectual leaders were not jailed but were instead deprived of all political rights as citizens. Among them were three former presidents, including

Kubitschek, peasant leaders, economists, architects, supreme court justices, senators, and journalists.

Elections were brought under control by changing the process of choosing the president and others from direct election by the people to indirect election by the hand-picked members of Congress. Control of the ballot was also assured by the fact that the literacy requirement for voting excluded 50% of all Brazilians from the suffrage. In reaction to this ludicrous pretense at democracy, 40% of the ballots cast in the 1972 elections were either marked abstentions or were left blank or were cast for "Sujismundo," a government-created cartoon character who was the symbol of a nationwide cleanliness campaign. In the capital of Bahia State, a wildcat who had escaped from the city zoo during the election received 5,000 votes.

Therefore, because illiteracy and slow communications kept most of the citizens from knowing—or caring—what the government did, a small group of determined men could control the affairs of the country without general consent—or even knowledge. Government censorship of the press also helped. This Establishment is well aware of the needs of the elite minority, but is aware of the needs of the majority only insofar as they help or hinder the needs of the elite. "The Nation" is identified with the Establishment's governmental structure; therefore, any criticism against the current government is treason against one's country. The ordinary citizens, especially the poorest, who foolishly refuse to cooperate or who actively seek to hinder the intentions of the Establishment face the ultimate and ordinarily quite successful persuasion: torture.

Article 5 of the Brazilian Constitution states: "No one shall be submitted to torture or to cruel, inhuman or degrading treatment or punishment." But the Constitution has been suppressed in the name of National Security. Amnesty International has documented proof of more than a thousand cases of torture. The International Commission of Jurists states that "torture has become a systematic and scientifically developed practice," and that Commission was refused government permission to investigate the Brazilian prison system.

The number of people jailed on suspicion alone just in São Paulo numbered 28,000 in the first two months of 1977. In the same two months, 41 death squad assassinations were carried out in the Novo Iguaçu shantytown of Rio. Many of the bodies showed they had been tortured before they died. People listed "dead in traffic accidents" have been delivered to their next of kin with a single round hole in the middle of the forehead.

175

In the last 20 years the death squads, a loose organization of policemen, has killed more than 3,000 supposed petty criminals who have tried to muscle in on the drug, prostitution and gambling rackets—controlled by the death squad members themselves. These squads have also proved handy in cases of overly voluble political dissidents. Some of their victims have also apparently been innocent bystanders mistakenly identified to their executioners. Elenil Alves de Carvalho, a 35-year-old electrician with no record or political affiliation, was picked up by the death squad on his way to work. The next day his bullet-ridden body was found along with the body of a 12-year-old street vendor who had been shot twice in the head. As one resident of the Rio ghetto (where infant mortality is placed at 40%) put it philosophically: "You can divide the population into two parts: those who have been assaulted and those who are going to be."

By law, the police can hold any individual up to 30 days incommunicado and up to 60 days without being charged. These prisoners often are held so long that they simply become "non-facts." Moreover, they can count on fellow prisoners (some of them plants) to crack the resistance of those arrested. Let the experience of one American Oblate priest stand for countless hundreds of cases:

Every day, along with an American Mennonite volunteer named Tom Capuano, Fr. Lawrence Rosebaugh, O.M.I., used to push a cart through the open market of Recife picking up food discarded by the vendors. They lived their lives among the poor, and each evening they built a fire in the street and made a large pot of soup from the bruised produce. As the crowd of starving people gathered round, drawn by the smell, the priest and his friend shared what they had. But at about 11:30 on the morning of 15 May 1977, they were stopped with their cart by two well-dressed men with police identification. The police asked whose cart it was, where their license was, where they'd gotten the money for the cart. The priest told the detective who they were and what their work was.

"You're a priest? The long hair, those clothes . . . you look like a pair of dirty hippies. Cart's stolen, most likely. And you're not foreigners either. You speak Portuguese better than we do. Pack of lies. Pair of commies."

They were handcuffed and taken to jail. Two other policemen took charge of them. One belted Capuano in the side of the head with the stock of his shotgun and then jammed it into his ribs. In the follow-through he jabbed his gun butt into Father Rosebaugh's belly, sending him reeling against the wall. Their names were taken; they were stripped naked and shoved into a cell with 15 other naked men.

Before they were even settled, a young man came up to the two new-comers and ordered them to stand. He flexed his muscles and began attacking them with karate moves, to the head, to the shoulder, to the pit of the stomach. "Sit down," he ordered, "against the wall." He looked around to see if he had everyone's attention and then turned back to Rosebaugh and Capuano. "You like men? Well, you better, because in here everyone has a 'woman,' and you better have one by tonight. And you know what? If you don't cooperate, you're going to eat shit. You got that? Shit!"

When they went for food—a small handful of mashed cornmeal and a piece of raw meat the size of a thumb, the karate expert ordered one young man to get down on his knees and lick corn mash from the floor like a dog. He told Rosebaugh that he had been in this jail over a year, which was impossible. Men in there less than a month had become dehydrated and emaciated, and this thug was in better shape than a light-heavyweight fighter.

That night they slept in a cell with 37 men. The heat was stifling, the bodies jammed together. One man had to curl himself around the vile toilet hole. Because the air on the floor was unbearable, Rosebaugh spent the night standing up. Fights broke out. In the morning a new prisoner was thrown in covered with bloody welts from whips made of ropes laced with metal.

After three days, in a state of semi-shock, they were led out. Not a word of where they were being taken. Then, right in the area by the reception desk, while their clothes were being returned to them, they saw an adolescent boy standing with his hands gripping the guardrail and a stocky policeman with a thick board about two feet square. As they watched, hardly believing what they saw, the policeman raised the board and brought it down with all the force he could muster on the boy's hands. Six, seven, eight times. And then more. Each time a scream echoed throughout the jail. Then another officer leaning against the wall, dark sunglasses masking his eyes, moved forward and with explosive force smashed a metal wastebasket against the side of the boy's face. Numbly, the two Americans were led out. They had no idea what the boy's crime had been.

Father Rosebaugh was one of the lucky ones. One Brazilian, 33, who tried to organize laborers—not to strike, but merely to sign a petition for better working conditions—was struck with wooden clubs, burned with cigarettes, had wires wrapped around his toes and stretched up around his testicles, given electric shocks and died in convulsions. In November 1969, the Archbishop of Ribeirão Preto excommunicated the chief of police for "using electric shock torture on an imprisoned mother superior of a convent" who was accused of harboring fugitive guerrillas. As was said, Amnesty International has documented at least 1,000 detentions and tortures over the past decade.

Whenever a story of torture manages to get through the heavy screen of censorship into the press, a government functionary is quoted as declaring it "a lamentable but isolated case." The basic justification of the authorities for these activities is quite simple: "Don't these arrests prove that those priests and agitators are communists?" If the government is unquestionably right, the punishment proves the crime.

A young man in prison smuggled out a note with a released prisoner: "Only the mystery of Calvary makes us understand what it means, before God, to be hung up naked, like pigs in a butcher shop."

Even for the non-believer or the marginal Christian, the church is the only voice able to stand up to the inhumanity of legalized terrorism. With the suppression of all political opposition, the church—at least part of it—has been drawn in to fill the political vacuum. In this largest Roman Catholic country in the world, the government is more than willing to support the church's stances which lead to better morality and order, but as in tiny Roman Catholic El Salvador, they would be more than happy to have the priest stay in his sanctuary. The higher-placed one is in the government or economic structure, the less his actions for the good of the country can be hampered by conventional morality.

Some of the clergy seem to agree; many are confused by two conflicting loyalties; and, especially since Vatican II and Medellin, a growing number are beginning to resist unthinking conformism.

The rapacious Portuguese conquest of Brazil in the 16th century could be justified only under the pretense that its primary motivation was to bring the Indians into the church. Since then, at least until the early 1960's, the church and state had continued for four centuries mutually to reinforce once another. The *fazenda* had always supported the only priest in the area. He was dependent on the plantation for his sustenance, and therefore only the most high-minded and courageous or foolish cleric would have dared to criticize the often questionable activities of its owner. Moreover, as the naturalist Louis Agassiz observed somewhat sweepingly in 1868, "The ignorance of the clergy is universal."

The purpose of the church in the eyes of its principal supporters was to facilitate a spirit of prayer and acceptance of one's lot on the part of the native and lower classes, to care for such enterprises as hospitals and orphanages, and to educate the sons of the rich. For the 67 years of the Portuguese Empire and for the following century of the Republic, the church and the obligatory Portuguese language were the two most cohesive forces in the country. Over those many years, while endless revolutions crashed like thunderstorms in neighboring countries, and while the forces of liberalism, egalitarianism and republicanism were growing all over South America, Brazil had relative peace. The majority of its people were almost completely safely illiterate, and the country was divided between a few very rich families and countless millions of miserably poor families. For many, even many churchmen, it seemed "that's just the way things are."

The falling-out between church and state began in the early 30's with the fascist takeover of Getulio Vargas. Some churchmen began to see, against this repressive background, how much the tradition-bound church had contributed to an oppression that had been less evident until it was institutionalized. They began to open their eyes to the imbalance between the wealthy industrial South and the rest of the country. They saw privilege for the powerful and injustice for the poor in the urban *favelas* and the rural *fazendas*. Moreover, within the church itself, the more observant saw some frightening portents. The average size of a parish in the Mato Grosso was 300 square miles, with the faithful seeing a priest only once or twice a year, if at all. In urban slums, fewer than 3% of the adult shanty dwellers attended mass, while middle-class and upper-class parishes boasted 50% weekly attendance. There was an average of one priest for every 8,000 professed Catholics. As recently as the early 60's, one half of Brazil's new priests were foreigners.

Finally, because of the official church's apparent insensitivity to even their spiritual needs, many of the poorer Brazilian Catholics had gone over to the "Afro-Brazilian spiritualist cults." During the original conquest of the country, Indians and African slaves were routinely baptized without anything like an authentic personal conversion and with little instruction. Therefore, needful of a way of expressing their own spiritual lives, but fearful of repression by the official church, they have turned to a kind of paganism camouflaged under the guise of Christian devotions, especially to the saints. The two most influential are *Macumba* and *Umbanda*. There are 30,000 voodoo centers in Rio alone, and it is estimated that the number of nominally Catholic Brazilians from all social levels who belong to them is 55 million!

The repressive military takeover in 1964 coincided with a movement on the part of the universal church in precisely the opposite direction. Pope John's *Mater et Magistra* and *Pacem in Terris* and Pope Paul's *Populorum Progressio* discussed the painful rise of the working class and its human rights, the evils of colonialism, the problems of under-developed countries and the dignity of the laborer and the primacy of his rights over those of the Economy. In response to the lack of those human and Christian values in Latin America, a whole new school of "Liberation Theology" was emerging, based on Christ's liberation of mankind from slavery to other men as well as from slavery to sin. The Second Vatican Council was a ringing reversal of the church's century-old position of authoritarianism.

Motivated by these papal and magisterial urgings to reconsider and reform, the Latin American bishops at Medellin came out four-square for the oppressed and against the oppressors, many of whom were in all senses "pillars of the church." The National Conference of Brazilian Bishops, although representing the views of a small dynamic core of bishops, became the policy-making body for the whole Brazilian hier-archy. They issued statements condemning the fact that only the poor are arrested and that money is more important than the person to many so-called Christians, that the police criminals such as the death squads seemed immune to punishment, that the expulsion of Indians and squatters found in the way of massive business operations was not only tolerated by the government but encouraged. "We cannot talk of the concrete human condition and leave it somehow in a kind of 'spiritual place.' For us, the spiritual plans of God converge within every concrete human being, in all of his dimensions. It is our specific right and duty to treat as pastors all human problems—economic, political and social."

During the takeover of 1964, Dom Helder da Camara was tactfully replaced as secretary general of the Bishops' Conference. His views had by no means been those of all the country's bishops, some of whom were honestly thankful that the coup had brought things back to "where they belonged." Eugenio Cardinal Sales of Rio, for instance, said to a group of police chiefs in October 1973, "In the world today, an authority for repression is necessary as a consequence of sin. Everyone sees in the police a representative of order and security."

But despite that setback, the progressive wing of the church began to regain momentum. In 1969, they issued a declaration deploring terrorist movements, unsubstantiated imprisonment, and torture. This represented the opinion of only 25 bishops and two cardinals out of 215. But four years later, the Conference issued another declaration of human rights which representated the signed opinion of 80% of the bishops. This staying power is in great part due to the indomitability of such men as Bishop Camara in the cities and Bishop Casaldàliga in the rural areas.

Camara wrote: "Under the pretext of saving the country from communism, is it not possible that we cover the track of internal colonialism and keep the marginal citizens—millions of Brazilians—in a subhuman condition? It is foolish to treat as 'communist subversion' every defense of those who have no voice and every form of solidarity with the oppressed. It is only peace that we seek in all our pastoral activity. But we don't want the peace of the cemetery; we want the peace which defends life in all its physical and moral aspects."

Since 1969 Camara has been effectively silenced. Nothing can be published by him or about him, except attacks—against which he is allowed no defense. In May 1969 when one of the priests of his diocese was tortured and hanged from a tree, he said, "We live under suspicion. We live surrounded by espionage. From time to time we have to go to prison and grind out self-critical confessions."

Casaldàliga, too, tries to stir his people to liberate themselves, at the very least from their own self-detestation. "The gates may be open, but only you can walk out." But he, too, is suspect, even by some of his fellow activists, as being a bit "out there." And he writes poetry to boot!

The church in Brazil has paid for its defense of the defenseless. In the three years between 1968 and 1971, a total of 28 priests were imprisoned by the government on various charges of subversion. In a single year, 1969-70, 405 missionaries were expelled from Brazil.

* * * * * * * *

The two men—the slender younger man who looked like a priest, and the portly older man who looked like a bishop—walked the 300 yards from the parish house to the field where the jail sat silently in the darkening evening. It was an open lot of rough grass, edged with scruffy trees; the center of the field, around the jail, had been worn to dirt. It was perhaps a quarter-acre fenced in by stakes, pointed at both ends and bound together by lines of barbed wire.

The building was nearly brand new, ten feet by twenty, its sloping lean-to roof making it look like half a house, its clean whitewash making it seem more a dispensary than a charnel house. But in foot-high letters on the white wall it forthrightly declared itself: **DELE-GACIA de POLICIA**. There were two doors, one to the small room with a desk and cot for the policeman on duty, the other to the jail cell.

As the two priests climbed the little rise to the fence, they saw Corporal Juraci quickly closing the gate from the outside. He squinted fearfully into the gathering darkness in their direction and then ran.

Inside the enclosure they saw a broken spindle chair canted against the wall of the jail. Outside the doors, a white-necked peccary pig snorted angrily in the dirt. One of the soldiers had sneered unguardedly to a villager in the cantina that they put the pig outside every evening because it disturbed the rest of the two lady prisoners.

The two men came to the gate. A sinister feeling had invaded this lovely night. It would be so nice to have been somewhere else, to have been without the burden of serving. But when they got to the gate, it was padlocked.

"Hello?" No answer. Not even a moan, at least that they could hear. The two men looked at one another. Probably only one man left inside now that Juraci had left, and he was afraid to face them alone. There was a hut nearby and they walked over to find out what was going on. The peasants knew nothing. The priests decided to wait. Mass was at 7:30, but this was surely more important for the moment. Maximino could take care of the Mass. But not five minutes later they heard the engine of a pickup grinding up the little hill to the gate of the jail compound.

There were three military policemen in the little truck which belonged to a man nicknamed Bracinho, "Little Right Hand Man." He was the *bate-pau* for the military police, that is, their beat-the-woods, their informer. At the wheel was a boy who looked about twelve, Bracinho's son, Genivaldo. The corporal had brought reinforcements, Corporal Messias and Corporal Ezy Feitosa. The pickup passed through the gate and stopped by the jail; the men got out. Casaldàliga and Burnier left the hut and walked toward the gate. The air was suddenly very cold.

"The fear seemed almost palpable when we entered the gate. I was leading and Fr. John-Bosco was behind as we walked through the fence and toward the little jail and into the almost tangibly aggressive attitude of the policemen. The air was explosive, and I saw the glint of the revolver that the soldier Ezy Feitosa eased out of his belt."

The three soldiers stood in an arc in front of the two doors of the jail, as if daring anyone to enter. They were very young; Feitosa couldn't be more than 25 or so. But they were very powerful boys to the middle-aged men who walked toward them across the open space of their compound. They had guns.

"What the hell do you two want?"

With an emptiness at the pit of his stomach, Casaldàliga reached out his hand. "We are Bishop Casaldàliga and Father John-Bosco Burnier." His hand hung for a moment in mid-air, uselessly, and then dropped to his side.

"Yeah. The commies. So?"

"What you are doing to those women is not worthy of the uniform you wear. I protest in their name, in the name of the gospel."

The corporal, Feitosa, looked at his two buddies and sniggered. "Get lost. Go mind your own business, commie." He hefted his pistol and turned to the others for approval. They grinned at one another, like street toughs blocking a sidewalk.

"Listen to me," the bishop pleaded. "What you're doing is illegal. These two women had nothing to do with what you want to solve. They are only members of the family of the man you suspect. You have no reason to torture them. Please, what you're doing . . . ."

"Don't tell me what I'm doing! Listen, whoever you are, wherever you came from! The two of you, get out of here or you'll be sorry! You could get a little of the same yourselves. Or worse!"

Burnier stepped forward. The corporal looked from one to the other, confused. Which was which? "Corporal, do your superiors know that you are doing this to these poor women?"

"My superiors are very far away, commie."

"On my way home I have to pass through Cuiabà. Unless you stop what you're doing to these women, I guarantee you that I will bring your arbitrary actions to the attention of your superiors in the . . . ."

In a flash Feitosa lunged across Casaldàliga to Burnier and slapped him across the face. The priest reeled backward. Casaldàliga made to reach for him. "John-Bosco, let's go. It's no . . . ."

And in that instant Feitosa backhanded the priest across the right cheek with the barrel and butt of his pistol. In a flash the gun went off and everyone stood frozen. Burnier slumped limply to the ground, blood pumping from under his right ear.

For the flick of an eye, no one knew what had happened. Casaldàliga bent down, sure that Burnier was dead. He reached out his hand, not quite touching him. "John-Bosco?"

Then very faintly, drunkenly, "Yes?"

The corporal dry-laughed, loudly, "You see? It was only a shot to scare you!"

For a moment, the bishop felt like a man recovering from a stupor. He turned to Juraci and Messias. "Help me get him into the pickup."

Corporal Feitosa looked like a cornered animal. "It was an *accident!*"

The others ignored him. The two policemen helped the bishop get the bleeding body into the truck. Feitosa looked insanely about him. Then he ran.

The three men got Burnier onto the bed of the pickup. The soldiers stood wiping the gore from their hands on their sides, without realizing, mesmerized by the heap on the floor of the truck. Casaldàliga climbed up next to his friend. "Set those women free." He struck the cab, and the boy started the truck down the hill.

Sick with terror of what this stupidity might mean for them, the two soldiers ran into the jail, fumbled open the lock and ordered the two women out.

"What happened?" Margarida moaned. "We heard the shots. Are you going to kill us?"

But the two soldiers merely fled into the darkness, leaving the two women standing before the open door, numbed beyond pain or fear. Alone.

When the boy pulled the truck up outside the parish house, Dr. Luis and Sr. Beatrice, the nurse, were already out front, knowing before they could admit it where the shot had come from. When they saw, they were astonished who the victim was. They rushed Burnier into the little surgery off the kitchen of the parish house.

People began to gather in the yard, standing in the spill of light from the house. "I remember very well the presence in the little house of the mission where father was suffering," the bishop wrote later, "of many men from the town, deeply moved, friends, perhaps disposed to avenge this death." It was then that one of the men spoke from the darkness, "If it was one of the people of the town, that is something we're used to. It happens every day. But a priest! The police have gone too far."

When Dr. Luis had cleaned the coagulated blood away from the right side of John-Bosco's head, some brain substance was visible. He turned to the bishop and shook his head. He mouthed the word: "Slim."

"I remember the anguish of not having the means to take care of that poor wounded man the way he needed. The distances. The night besides. The terror that came and went in the faces of those standing around outside. An impression of being utterly alone at the dead center of an action of God in the midst of his people. And the poor young doctor, helplessly unable to do anything in that primitive little dispensary."

Bishop Casaldàliga gave John-Bosco the last rites and the Eucharist. The dying man kept whispering, "Jesus. Jesus." And then he smiled, his voice rasped, "Every imprudent word has its consequences."

Casaldàliga took his hand. "My friend, you said nothing imprudent. You were trying to stop the torture of two innocent women."

"Whatever suffering I have, I would like to offer to God that the Indian Commission could help these poor people. They are so . . . anonymous." For a moment he lapsed unconscious, then he opened his eyes a bit and smiled again softly. "I'm sorry I didn't take notes of that wonderful conversation the other night . . . with the Tapirapè. It would be nice . . . later . . . to remember."

His mouth kept filling with blood, and Dr. Luis kept telling him, "Spit it out!" But Burnier shook his head, "No, no. It will soil the floor."

Finally, he coughed and grasped Casaldàliga's hand. He murmured the words of St. Paul, "I've finished my course," and then the last words of Jesus: "*Consummatum est.*" He smiled at his friend, "Dom Pedro, we've come to the end of the job together."

And he lapsed into a coma. His mind was dead.

There was the remotest chance of the Neurological Institute at Goiânia. It was 200 miles away as the crow flies, but almost a day's trip over mountainous roads by car. And carrying a man with a wound from a dum-dum bullet splayed out through his brain? What if the police had set an ambush in the dark along the Barra road, to cover up the crime and all its witnesses? They'd done it before. Father Parèdes tried the radio but could make no contact.

Someone remembered that the Goias Air Taxi always parked for the night at one or other of the plantations rather than fly in the dark. So they bundled the comatose priest into Dr. Luis's station wagon and raced out to the São Felix road. For four hours they searched helplessly, one farm after the other, the priest shuddering and wheezing at every bump in the rough road. Finally, they found the plane, but there was no way the pilot was going to take off at night for a trip over the mountain passes in the darkness.

Before daybreak, the plane took off for Goiâna with John-Bosco, still unconscious, and the doctor, the bishop and Sr. Beatrice. When they arrived there was an ambulance waiting at the airfield, and they raced to the Neurological Institute. When the hospital team rushed Burnier to the operating room, the others could only wait.

At five in the afternoon, John-Bosco Burnier stopped breathing.

* * * * * * * *

Despite the fact that the funeral arrangements were somewhat hasty, because of the Jesuits' fear of reprisals, 2,000 people gathered at the Catholic University of Goiânia with Burnier's family for the Mass of the Resurrection. Over the altar was a banner: "Blessed are those who suffer for the sake of justice." Bishop Casaldàliga preached that this priest had offered his life for a new Brazil, rid of terror and oppression and fear, a land of free men.

Then the body was taken by plane to Diamantino, where Burnier was so much more at home. There was another Mass offered, and the coffin was carried not by priests but by ordinary people, and not to the Jesuit cemetery but to the burying ground of the ordinary people. And one by one the ordinary people came up and dropped three handfuls of earth apiece on his coffin. His grave in that plain field lay right next to a fence of barbed wire.

* * * * * * * *

On 13 February 1976, Corporal Ezy Feitosa was captured with his fellow fugitives 30 miles away from Ribeirão Bonito. They were held incommunicado in Cuiabà. The Commissioner of Military Police blamed the situation on the pitifully small salaries paid to policemen which don't allow for a rigorous selection of candidates. He also blamed the poor communications of Mato Grosso; headquarters in Cuiabà had heard the news only 36 hours after the death of the priest in that same city.

The Council for Human Rights asked for an intensive study of the factors which contributed to the possibility of such murders. The leader of the government party said there was no need.

The *Jornal do Brasil* (15 October 1976) reports that the Secretary for Mato Grosso claims his words the day before were taken out of context when he suggested that the priest had hit the soldier before being shot.

* * * * * * * *

18 October 1976,
7:30 p.m.

As is the custom at the death of someone who had been important to the whole village, the people of Ribeirão Bonito had gathered every evening for seven days since the death of John-Bosco Burnier to pray. On that last evening, in the center of the congregation at Mass was a large wooden cross, specially made—since it is also a custom to plant a cross where someone has met a violent and undeserved death, as Jesus had.

When the Mass was finished, Margarida Barbosa asked the people to say the rosary with her as they set out in procession behind the rough-hewn cross and two candles to plant the cross at the little jail of Ribeirão Bonito.

As they moved down the dirt highway, past the repair shop and the cantina and the whorehouses, they said the rosary, each carrying a small candle of his own.

When they saw the procession coming, the soldiers fled into the night.

The men began to dig, and in the candle-light the paradoxical symbol of liberation was planted in front of a jail.

Someone shouted, "Let's open up the jail!"

And they began, enraged, to pull at the barred door. Bricks began to shake loose. Suddenly the crowd went wild. In a frenzy of pent-up fury and frustration they tore with their heedlessly bloodied fingers at this symbol of injustice. They battered against the doors, and walls came crashing down.

Just as suddenly as they had started, they stopped and looked in the candle-lit silence at what they had done. Most of the walls were down. There were chains hanging limply from chinks in the broken walls. The plaster walls of the cell room were saturated with dried bloodstains from shoulder height to the floor.

Silently, the people turned and began moving back to their huts, leaving behind them the flowers and the still-burning candles and the cross, with the inscription burned into the wood:

On 11 Oct 76
in this place of Ribeirão Bonito, Mato Grosso,
was assassinated Father John-Bosco Penido Burnier
for defending the liberty of the poor.

He died, like Jesus Christ,
offering his life for our liberation.

As they walked away, one woman turned to another: "And what if they dig up the cross?"

And the other said, grimly, without turning, "We will plant another one."

* * * * * * * *

On 23 February 1977, Ash Wednesday, Bishop Geraldo Sigaud, in an interview with the press accused his fellow bishop Dom Pedro Casaldàliga of being a communist foreigner and asked that he be deported. When one of the illiterate *posseiros* heard the report, he responded, "If being a communist means being common, then there is no doubt about it: our bishop is very common and unpretentious. If that's a communist, he's a communist."

Casaldàliga's response was to ignore the charge. "Our church," he wrote, "is the people of God in the *sertão*. It is a poor church, oppressed, persecuted. But it is also a church free of vested interests. It seeks neither prestige nor privilege. It is full of hope in the midst of struggle. I would not change it for any other."

* * * * * * * *

Burnier's was a life and death filled with ironies. In trying to write this life, the author received not a single letter from a Brazilian Jesuit

—except for one saying to write elsewhere, to a man who turned out to have nothing he could send. Until his death—and after—Burnier carried the burden of having been a hold-the-fort provincial and master of novices, at a time when some of his peers and most younger men were trying to pull down the very barricades he was defending. Then, when he himself threw in his lot with the outcasts, trying—and finally succeeding!—to save two of them, at least a few still mutter, "Right! Now they're trying to canonize Burnier! I knew him. Inept. Brusque. And that bishop? Worse."

Poor little man. He tried so hard with what he had.

Ironically, there is also every likelihood that the wrong man was shot, that Burnier looked too much like a bishop and was not really the notorious intended victim at all. Even more pitifully, there is also every likelihood that the whole thing was an accident. A gun will often discharge unintentionally when used as a bludgeon. A nervous little petty tyrant, 25 years old, confused, cornered—torn between his own need to act superior and his fear of this little man's threat to take away the only job he could hold down—feels his gun go off by mistake and a priest dies. Perhaps he didn't intend to kill a priest. Or a bishop. Or anybody.

But that is hardly the point, is it? Martyrdom is judged not by the motive of the killer but by the offering of the victim. John-Bosco could have been back in Rio with his slippered feet on a hassock watching television. He even could have been on a dusty bus trundling back to the no-exit of Diamantino. But instead he stopped, for a little rite which many would sneer at as naive superstition, among nameless and hopeless people, out of friendship.

For all his numberless faults and blindnesses and shortcomings, he walked fearfully up to a little jail, with little hope of success, because he could not sit idly by while human beings were in torment. He was blind to many things, perhaps, but not to injustice.

Martyrdom cannot be improvised. Either a whole lifetime prepares one for it, or it will never occur. There are warnings for those who dare to love so vulnerably for a lifetime. But God alone knows who will be chosen. Or when.

Some men will die contentedly and peacefully with their slippers on. John-Bosco Burnier was not one of them.

* * * * * * * *

"Our freedom is bought with his blood, and life is born of death."

Fr. John-Bosco Burnier

The small jail-police station destroyed by people after the death of Fr. Burnier. The inscription on the cross is translated as follows: "Here on 11 October 1976, in defense of liberty, Father John B. was killed by a soldier."

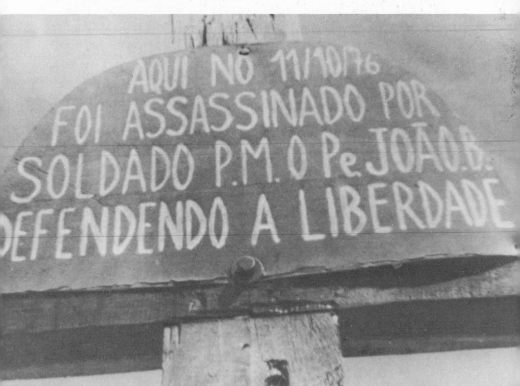

Be it known to you that we have made a league—all the Jesuits in the world, whose succession and multitude must overreach all the practices of England—cheerfully to carry the cross you shall lay on us, and never to despair your recovery, while we have a man left to enjoy your Tyburn, or to be racked with your torments or consumed with your prisons.

The expense is reckoned. The enterprise is begun. It is of God. It cannot be withstood.

—Edmund Campion, S.J.

About This Book . . . and the Author

Research has always reminded me of Madame Curie. She started with a mountain of pitchblende in order to distill from it one small vial of radium. When I set out to research this book, I felt very like the little friar in Thornton Wilder's *Bridge of San Luis Rey*, who set out to discover why God chose that precise moment to have these three particular people on this particular bridge when it suddenly broke and plunged them to their deaths. When he finished, he found that it had been the perfect moment for each of them. And so it was, I found, with these five men.

Journalists or historians who wish to study further the events of this book, may write to the publisher for the supporting bibliographic information.

W.J. O'M.

Father William J. O'Malley was ordained in 1963. He has spent the last 14 years at McQuaid Jesuit High School in Rochester, N.Y. where he teaches religion and is drama director. He has written dozens of articles and book reviews and four other books (including *Meeting the Living God* and *The Fifth Week*, available from Paulist Press). Father O'Malley has also written musicals, plays, songs and material for television. His acting credits include the part of Fr. Joe Dyer in the motion picture, *The Exorcist*.